PASSENGER TRANSPORTATION SERVICE IN THE CITY OF NEW YORK

Passenger Transportation Service in the City of New York

A REPORT TO THE MERCHANTS' ASSOCIATION OF NEW YORK BY ITS COMMITTEE ON ENGINEERING AND SANITATION

SEPTEMBER, 1903

THE MERCHANTS' ASSOCIATION OF NEW YORK.

PREFACE.

IN December, 1902, public indignation was aroused by the disregard of public rights, then evinced to an extraordinary degree, by the street and elevated railway companies of this city.

Extreme overcrowding had long been a notorious evil, unresisted by the public and practiced without scruple by the companies. About the time cited this abuse was greatly increased as to some lines of transit and certain hours of the day, by the deliberate policy of the companies. The Manhattan Elevated Railroad reduced its train service to a minimum during non-rush hours; the service of the Brooklyn Rapid Transit Elevated lines, at all times grossly defective, spasmodic and overtaxed, was likewise reduced; and in both cases facilities which the companies could readily have supplied were withheld for reasons of economy in order that a maximum of passengers might be crowded into a minimum of trains and cars.

The Metropolitan Company aggravated conditions already extremely bad by the abuse of the "car ahead" rule, whereby the passengers of two comfortably full cars were often compelled to crowd into a single car, to the intolerable discomfort and inconvenience of all. This company still further concentrated its traffic, and thereby increased overcrowding, by refusing transfers over certain lines.

As to sanitary rules, little or no effective effort to enforce them had at that time been made by the transportation companies, despite constant public protest against the filthy conditions usual in public vehicles.

These conditions culminated in formal protests by various associations of women against the public indecency of promiscuous overcrowding in public vehicles, and against the repulsive personal contact and frequent secret insult to which women passengers were subjected. Following this initiative, several civic organizations moved in the matter with a view to securing a reform of the existing abuses.

The Merchants' Association of New York called a public meeting and organized the following committees for investigation and action, with a view to relief:

1: By direct representations to the street railway companies.

2: By procuring such legislation as should be necessary to control and regulate the conditions.

Legal Committee for Reform of Street and Elevated Railway Service.

Philip B. Adams.
Addison Allen.
Isaac M. Aron.
Seldon Bacon.
Seward Baker.
Elliot S. Benedict.
Harold Binney.
William C. Breed.
George W. Bristol.
Harcourt Bull.
Francis X. Butler.
Frederick B. Campbell.
Charles R. Carruth.
Stewart Chaplin.
Charles W. Coleman.
Stephen W. Collins.
Aaron J. Colnon.
Rufus B. Cowing, Jr.
Crane & Baer.
Louis A. Cuvillier.
Maurice Deiches.
Joseph L. Delafield.
John Ross Delafield.
John S. Durand.
John A. Dutton.
Bela D. Eisler.
Mark H. Elison.
Edward R. Finch.
Dallas Flanagan.
William D. Gaillard.
William Henry Gardiner.
George H. Gilman.
Andrew H. Green.
Bert Hanson.
John M. Harrington.
Walter F. Hayward.
J. Aspinwall Hodge, Jr.
Wirt Howe.
Antonio Knauth.
Richard D. Knabe.
Edgar J. Lauer.
Leopold Leo.
Luke J. Le Rolle.
Frank E. Loughran.
James F. McNaboe.
David Ives Mackie.
Charles E. Manierre.
Seabury C. Mastick.
Joseph S. Menline.
John S. Montgomery.

George E. Morse.
Bernard Naumburg.
Roswell S. Nichols.
Emmet R. Olcott.
William A. Purrington.
Henry C. Quinby.
Theodore N. Ripsom.
Clarence De W. Rogers.
Livingston Rutherfurd.
Seward & Dungan.
Willam H. Shepard.
Ellis B. Southworth.
Eugene Spiegelberg.
Theron G. Strong.
Louis Sturcke.
Edward A. Sumner.
H. T. Terry.
Robert W. Thompson, Jr.
E. W. Tyler.
William D. Tyndall.
G. Willett Van Nest.
William Bell Wait, Jr.
Samuel S. Watson.
Herbert G. Whipple.
Henry Crofut White.
James E. Walsh.

Executive Committee of Legal Committee.

Theron G. Strong, Chairman.
Wm. H. Shepard, Vice-Chairman.
E. W. Tyler.
John Ross Delafield.
Bernard Naumburg.
Francis X. Butler, Secretary.
Edward R. Finch.
George H. Gilman.
Emmet R. Olcott.
George E. Morse.
Bert Hanson.
Harcourt Bull.

Engineering and Sanitation Committee.

H. Waller Brinckerhoff.
Foster Crowell.
Charles H. Myers.
George A. Soper.
Samuel Whinery.
C. M. Wicker.

At the request of The Merchants' Association, the State Railroad Commission held a public hearing in the Aldermanic Chamber, at which The Merchants' Association was directed by the Commissioners to present specific instances of its complaints, with proof. This The Merchants' Association refused to do, contending that it was the statutory duty of the State Railroad Commission to inform itself in detail of all conditions affecting the management of street railways, to maintain control and to compel effective service.

At no time in its history had the State Railroad Commission exercised or attempted to exercise such control. In fact, the Commission had practically ignored its duty so far as the regulation of the street railways of New York City was concerned.

The Legal Committee of The Merchants' Association, therefore, after obtaining an explicit admission from the Commission to the above effect, formally demanded that the State Railroad Commission should itself make a detailed investigation into the causes of the undisputed defects and abuses of this city's street-car service, and should thereafter move to compel efficient service so far as the physical conditions would permit.

The State Railroad Commission concurred in the contention of The Merchants' Association, entered upon an investigation of the conditions of fact, and thereafter issued orders to the companies as to increasing their facilities.

The report of the State Railroad Commission shows that no data of passenger and car movement sufficient to warrant its conclusions was obtained, and that its recommendations were based upon imperfect knowledge of the facts.

The orders issued by the Commission, were, in consequence, but partly adapted to the necessities of the case. Above all, those orders, although ostensibly complied with by the companies, have not, in reality, been given such effect as to afford any substantial relief, and have, in fact, been largely disregarded.

Moreover, the Railroad Commission has made no serious attempt to enforce the orders issued by it; and it has been shown by the Legal Committee of The Merchants' Association that the Commission lacks the legal powers necessary to enforce its orders.

Thus the first results of The Merchants' Association's work showed:

1st. That the State Railroad Commission had not sought to regulate the operation of street railroads.

2d. That its investigation into such operation was superficial and insufficient.

3d. That it could not enforce its orders.

It was likewise shown that a comprehensive knowledge of the conditions affecting local street railway operation required continuous observation and study and more expert service than the Commission could command under the present law.

The Legal Committee, therefore, drafted a bill for enlarging the State Railroad Commission from three to five members; for securing expert services by requiring two of the members to be engineers; for securing adequate local reform by requiring those engineers to be residents of the City of New York, and for giving the Commission plenary powers to enforce its orders subject to review by the courts. This bill, which follows, was offered in the Legislature, but failed of passage:

AN ACT

To amend sections one hundred and fifty, one hundred and fifty-one, one hundred and fifty-six, one hundred and fifty-seven, one hundred and sixty-one, one hundred and sixty-two, one hundred and sixty-three, one hundred and sixty-nine and one hundred and seventy of the railroad law, in relation to the powers, duties, obligations and liabilities of the railroad commissioners and to increase the number of the same.

The People of the State of New York, represented in Senate and Assembly, do enact as follows:

SECTION 1. Section one hundred and fifty of chapter five hundred and sixty-five of the laws of eighteen hundred and ninety, entitled "An act in relation to railroads, constituting chapter thirty-nine of the general laws," is hereby amended so as to read as follows:

SEC. 150. Appointment and term of office of railroad commissioners.—There shall be a board of railroad commissioners, consisting of [three] five competent persons, one of whom shall be experienced in railroad business and two of whom at all times shall be qualified, practical, civil engineers of at least ten years' practice, who shall have resided in the city of New York for at least two years immediately prior to their appointment, appointed by the governor, by and with the advice and consent of the senate, each of whom shall hold office for the term of five years from the date of his appointment, and until his successor shall have been appointed and shall have qualified. The governor shall within thirty days from the passage of this act appoint as the two additional members of said board two qualified practical, civil engineers having the qualifications above described. A commissioner shall in like manner be appointed upon the expiration of the term of any commissioner; and when any vacancy shall occur in the office of any commissioner, a commissioner shall in like manner be appointed for the residue of the term. If the senate shall not be in session

EXPLANATION.—Matter underscored ———— is new; matter in brackets [ ] is old law to be omitted.

when the vacancy occurs, the governor shall appoint a commissioner to fill the vacancy, subject to the approval of the senate when convened.

SEC. 2. Section one hundred and fifty-one of chapter five hundred and sixty-five of the laws of eighteen hundred and ninety, entitled "An act in relation to railroads, constituting chapter thirty-nine of the general laws," is hereby amended so as to read as follows:

SEC. 151. [Suspension from office.] Removal from office.—Any commissioner may be [suspended from office by the governor upon written charges preferred. The governor shall report such suspension and the reasons therefor to the senate at the beginning of the next ensuing session, and if a majority of the Senate shall approve the action of the governor, such commissioner shall be removed from office and his office become vacant.] removed from office by the governor within the time for which he shall have been appointed, after giving to such commissioner a copy of the charges against him and an opportunity of being heard in his defense.

SEC. 3. Section one hundred and fifty-six of chapter five hundred and sixty-five of the laws of eighteen hundred and ninety, entitled "An act in relation to railroads, constituting chapter thirty-nine of the general laws," as amended by chapter five hundred and thirty-four of the laws of eighteen hundred and ninety-two, is hereby amended so as to read as follows:

SEC. 156. Quorum of board.—[Two] Three of the commissioners shall constitute a quorum for the transaction of any business, or the performance of any duty of the board, and may hold meetings thereof at any time or place within the state. All examinations or investigations made by the board may be held and taken by and before any one of the commissioners or the secretary of the board, by order of the board, and the proceedings and decisions of such single commissioner shall be deemed to be the proceedings and decisions of the board, when approved and confirmed by it.

SEC. 4. Section one hundred and fifty-seven of chapter five hundred and sixty-five of the laws of eighteen hundred and ninety, entitled "An act in relation to railroads, constituting chapter thirty-nine of the general laws," is hereby amended so as to read as follows:

SEC. 157. General powers and duties of board.—The board shall have power to administer oaths in all matters relating to its duties, so far as necessary to enable it to discharge such duties, shall have general supervision of all railroads and shall examine the same and keep informed as to their condition, and the manner in which they are operated for the security and accommodation of the public and their compliance with the provisions of their charters and of law. The commissioners or either of them in the performance of their official duties may enter and remain during business hours in the cars, offices and depots, and upon the railroads of any railroad corporation within the state, or doing business therein; and may examine the books and affairs of any such corporation and compel the production of books and papers or copies thereof, and the board may cause to be subpœnaed witnesses, and if a person duly subpœnaed fails to obey such subpœna without reasonable cause, or shall without such cause refuse to be examined, or to answer a legal or pertinent question, or to produce a book or paper which he is directed by subpœna to bring, or to subscribe his deposition after it has been correctly reduced to writing, the board may take such proceedings as are authorized by the code of civil procedure upon the like failure or refusal of a witness subpœnaed to attend the trial of a civil action before a court of record, or a referee appointed by such court. The board shall also take testimony upon, and have a hearing for and against any proposed change of the law relating to any railroad, or of the general railroad law, if requested to do so by the legislature, or by the committee on railroads of the senate or the assembly, or by the governor, and may take such testimony and have such a hearing when requested to do so by any railroad corporation, or incorporated organization representing agricultural or commercial interests in the state, and shall report their conclusions in writing to the legislature, committee, governor, corporation or organization making such request; and shall recommend and draft such bills as will in its judgment protect the people's interest in and upon the railroads of this state. Upon the application of the mayor of a city or the president of a village or the supervisor or highway commissioners of a town within which any part of any railroad is located, alleging grounds of complaint, the board shall examine the condition and operation of such railroad. If upon the petition in writing of twenty or more legal voters in such city, village or town to the mayor, president, supervisor or highway commissioners to make such application, he or they refuse to do so, he or they shall endorse upon the petition the reason of such refusal and return it to the petitioners, who may within ten days thereafter present it to the board, and it may thereupon make such examinaion as if called upon by the mayor, president, supervisor or highway commissioners, first giving to the petitioners and to the corporation reasonable notice in writing of the time and place of making such an examination. If upon such examination it appears to the board that the complaint is well founded, it shall so adjudge, and shall embody its decision in a written order, which shall be served upon the railroad corporation and shall be enforced, subject to the right of the corporation to move to vacate the same at special term, as provided for in section one hundred and sixty-one of this act.

Sec. 5. Section one hundred and sixty-one of chapter five hundred and sixty-five of the laws of eighteen hundred and ninety, entitled "An act in relation to railroads, constituting chapter thirty-nine of the general laws," as amended by chapter three hundred and seventy-three of the laws of nineteen hundred and two, is hereby amended so as to read as follows:

Sec. 161. Recommendations of board, when repairs or other changes are necessary.—If in the judgment of the board, after a careful personal examination of the same, it shall appear that repairs are necessary upon any railroad in the state, or that any addition to the rolling stock, or any addition to or change of a station or station houses, or that additional terminal facilities shall be afforded, or that any change of the rates of fare for transporting freight or passengers or in the mode of operating the road or conducting its business, is reasonable and expedient in order to promote the security, convenience and accommodation of the public, the board shall give notice and information in writing to the corporation of the improvements and changes which they deem to be proper, and shall give such corporation an opportunity for a full hearing thereof, and if the corporation refuses or neglects to make such repairs, improvements and changes, within a reasonable time after such information and hearing, and fails to satisfy the board that no action is required to be taken by it, the board shall fix the time within which the same shall be made, which time it may extend. [It shall be the duty of the corporation, person or persons owning or operating the railroad to comply with such decisions and recommendations of the board as are just and reasonable. If it fails to do so, the board shall present the facts in the case to the attorney-general for his consideration and action, and shall also report them in its annual or in a special report to the legislature.] The final directions of the board, and the time for carrying out the same, shall be embodied in a formal order, a certified copy of which shall be served upon the corporation, in like manner as a mandamus in a special proceeding, and said order shall have the full force and legal effect of a mandamus lawfully issued by the supreme court. It shall thereupon be the duty of said corporation and of its officers to comply with the said order within the time therein specified, or within such time as may be fixed by said board, if such time be extended by its order. Obedience to said order may be enforced by proceedings in the nature of a criminal contempt against said corporation and its officers, in like manner as if the said corporation had refused or neglected to comply with a mandamus lawfully issued by the supreme court, which proceedings shall be taken by the attorney-general upon the request of said board, and shall be taken before a special term of the supreme court in the county where said railroad corporation has its principal office in the state. At any time within thirty days after the service on said corporation of the formal order of the board of railroad commissioners said corporation may move, on eight days' notice to the board and to the attorney-general, or by an order to show cause, on such notice as shall be prescribed by a justice of the supreme court, at a special term of the supreme court, to be held in the county where said railroad has its principal office in the state, for an order vacating or modifying such order of the board, and, upon the hearing, the court may vacate or modify such order, or may deny the motion. From the decision of the special term on such motion either party may appeal to the appellate division of the supreme court, which court shall have power to review, upon both the facts and the law, and the determination of the appellate division shall be final, unless it shall grant leave to go to the court of appeals as to one or more or all of the questions of law or facts raised by said appeal, or unless such leave shall be granted as to one or more or all of such questions by one of the judges of the court of appeals, in which event the court of appeals shall have jurisdiction to review such determination of the appellate division as to the questions so specified. No stay shall be granted in any appeal from the order at special term as of course, nor unless the court shall be satisfied that the public interest will not be prejudiced by such stay; and the court may impose as a condition of granting such stay, such terms as shall be just, including the giving of an undertaking or the performance by the railroad corporation of part of the order of the board of railroad commissioners or the order appealed from. Elevated railroads are included in the application of this [section] article.

SEC. 6. Section one hundred and sixty-two of chapter five hundred and sixty-five of the laws of eighteen hundred and ninety, entitled "An act in relation to railroads, constituting chapter thirty-nine of the general laws," as amended by chapter six hundred and seventy-six of the laws of eighteen hundred and ninety-two, is hereby amended so as to read as follows:

SEC. 162. Legal effect of recommendations and action of the board.—No examination, request or advice of the board, nor any investigation or report made by it, shall have the effect to impair in any manner or degree the legal rights, duties or obligations of any railroad corporation, or its legal liabilities for the consequence of its acts, or of the neglect or mismanagement of any of its agents or employees. [The supreme court at special term shall have power, in its discretion, in all cases of decisions and recommendations by the board which are just and reasonable to compel compliance therewith by mandamus, subject to appeal to the general term and the court of appeals, and upon such appeal, the general term and the court of appeals may review and reverse upon the facts as well as the law.]

SEC. 7. Section one hundred and sixty-three of chapter five hundred and sixty-five of the laws of eighteen hundred and ninety, entitled "An act in relation to railroads, constituting chapter thirty-nine of the general laws," is hereby amended so as to read as follows:

SEC. 163. Corporations must furnish necessary information.—Every railroad corporation shall, on request, furnish the board any necessary information required by them concerning the rates of fare for transporting freight and passengers upon its road and other roads with which its business is connected, and the condition, management and operation of its road, and shall, on request, furnish to the board copies of all contracts and agreements, leases or other engagements entered into by it with any person or corporation. The board may order any railroad corporation to keep books containing such statistical information as to the physical condition and the operation of the railroad as shall be required by the commissioners, to enable them more efficiently to perform their duties as railroad commissioners in the interest of the general public. Such order may be enforced and may be appealed from, as provided for in the case of recommendations of the board in section one hundred and sixty-one of this act. The commissioners shall not give publicity to such information, contracts, agreements, leases or other engagements, if, in their judgment, the public interests do not require it, or the welfare and prosperity of railroad corporations of the state might be thereby injuriously affected.

SEC. 8. Section one hundred and sixty-nine of chapter five hundred and sixty-five of the laws of eighteen hundred and ninety, entitled "An act in relation to railroads, constituting chapter thirty-nine of the general laws," as amended by chapter five hundred and thirty-four of the laws of eighteen hundred and ninety-two, is hereby amended so as to read as follows:

SEC. 169. Salaries and expenses of members and officers of the board.—The annual salary of each commissioner shall be eight thousand dollars; of the secretary, six thousand dollars; of the marshal, fifteen hundred dollars; of the accountant and of the inspector such sum as the board may fix, not exceeding three thousand dollars each; of the clerical force such sums respectively as the board may fix. In the discharge of their official duties, the commisioners, their officers, clerks and all experts and agents whose services are [deemed to be temporarily of importance] required shall be transported over the railroads in this state free of charge upon passes signed by the secretary of state, and the commissioners shall have reimbursed to them the necessary traveling expenses and disbursements of themselves, their officers, clerks and experts [not exceeding in the aggregate five hundred dollars per month]. All salaries and disbursements shall be audited and allowed by the comptroller, and paid monthly by the state treasurer on the order of the comptroller out of the funds provided therefor. The attorney-general shall act as legal adviser of the board, and shall prosecute and defend all court proceedings, actions and appeals for the board as its attorney, and shall to that end, from time to time, assign from among its assistants such counsel as shall be necessary for that purpose.

SEC. 9. Section one hundred and seventy of chapter five hundred and sixty-five of the laws of eighteen hundred and ninety, entitled "An act in relation to railroads, constituting chapter thirty-nine of the general laws," as amended by chapter five hundred and thirty-four of the laws of eighteen hundred and ninety-two and by chapter four hundred and fifty-six of the laws of eighteen hundred and ninety-six, is hereby amended so as to read as follows:

SEC. 170. Total annual expense to be borne by railroads.—The total annual expense of the board authorized by law, excepting only rent of offices and the cost of printing and binding the annual reports of the board, as provided by law, shall not exceed [sixty] one hundred and twenty thousand dollars; and shall be borne by the several corporations owning or operating railroads, according to their means. The comptroller, before July first of each year, shall assess upon each of such corporations its proportion of such expenses, one-half in proportion to its net income for the fiscal year next preceding that in which the assessment is made, and one-half in proportion to the length of its main road and branches, except that each corporation whose line of road lies partly within and partly without the state, shall in respect to its income be assessed on a part bearing the same proportion to its whole net income that the line of its road within the state bears to the whole length of road, and in respect to its main road and branches shall be assessed only on that part which lies within the state. Such assessment shall be collected in the manner provided by law for the collection of taxes upon corporations.

SEC. 10. This act shall take effect immediately.

The thanks of The Merchants' Association are due to both the Legal and the Engineering and Sanitation Committees for their arduous and long-extended labors in the effort to improve this city's transportation facilities. Their services were volunteered and without compensation and entailed upon them, especially the Engineering Committee, many months of almost continuous labor, which called for special professional knowledge.

The Report of the Engineering and Sanitation Committee, which follows, is the first adequate examination which has been made in this city into the transportation conditions. It embodies the only comprehensive and reliable data thus far gathered. Practically all official reports have rested upon data supplied by the railway companies, and therefore from an interested source, while discussions of this subject have hitherto been largely academic and have not rested upon ascertained and reliable data. The report which follows supplies the first intelligent basis for suitable legislation upon this subject, which affects every citizen of the metropolis.

WILLIAM F. KING, *Chairman,*

Committee on Franchises and Transportation.

New York, September 1, 1903.

TABLE OF CONTENTS.

ADDENDA.

INDEX.

D.

E.

L. PAGE.

M.

N.

O.

REPORT OF THE COMMITTEE ON ENGINEERING AND SANITATION.

NEW YORK, July 15, 1903.

To the Merchants' Association of New York.

GENTLEMEN:

THE Committee on Engineering and Sanitation presents herewith its final report.

When this Committee was appointed on January 10, 1903, there were referred to it certain propositions, seventeen in number, which had previously been made by your Association to the State Railroad Commission in a communication dated January 5, 1903, and we were asked to report to you upon these propositions. After as careful consideration as the time permitted, the Committee made a preliminary report, under date January 21, 1903, in which the propositions referred to were answered seriatim and provisional opinions expressed upon each. Subsequently the Committee was requested to continue and extend its investigations with the view of submitting a final report on the whole subject of the improvement of passenger transportation conditions in New York.

Mr. Cassius M. Wicker, member and first chairman of the Committee, having resigned soon after the presentation of the preliminary report, the final organization of the Committee was as follows:

SAMUEL WHINERY, C. E., M. Am. Soc. C. E., Chairman.
H. WALLER BRINCKERHOFF, C. E., M. Am. Soc. C. E.
FOSTER CROWELL, C. E., M. Am. Soc. C. E., M. Inst. C. E.
CHARLES H. MYERS, C. E., M. Am. Soc. C. E.
GEORGE A. SOPER, Ph. D., Assoc. M. Am. Soc. C. E.

Mr. F. F. Woodward, detailed by your Association, was appointed to act as Secretary of the Committee.

The Committee divided its work among eight sub-committees, to each of which were assigned certain specific subjects for investigation. These sub-committees were as follows:

On Street Observations,
MR. CROWELL,
MR. BRINCKERHOFF.

On Vehicular Traffic and Obstructions,
MR. CROWELL,
MR. WHINERY.

On Proposed Subway at 34th Street,
MR. MYERS.

On Cross-town and Horse-car Lines (Including the 86th Street Line),
MR. MYERS,
DR. SOPER.

On Unused Tracks,
MR. BRINCKERHOFF,
MR. WHINERY.

On Routes,
DR. SOPER,
MR. MYERS.

On Elevated Railroads,
MR. BRINCKERHOFF,
MR. MYERS.

On Sanitation,
DR. SOPER,
MR. MYERS.

In the absence of sufficient data to enable us to take up the subject intelligently, it was deemed best by the Committee to institute and conduct a series of observations upon car and vehicular travel over congested streets, upon the elevated railroad service, and upon the sanitary conditions relating to both, and your Association authorized the expenditure of such sums as might be found necessary for the purpose. Thereupon, a corps of observers was organized and put to work, an office room was secured, and the necessary office force, including draughtsmen, was employed.

Although the problems attending passenger transportation in New York City are local, and in many respects far more difficult of solution than elsewhere, it was thought that the experience gained in some other cities, where passenger transportation has received great attention, might prove of value, and accordingly a sub-committee was sent to Philadelphia and Boston, spending a number of days at each place in personal examination and study of special features of street railroad operation and in conference with municipal and transportation officers, from whom valuable information was obtained. The Committee avails itself of this opportunity to acknowledge its obligation and to express its sincere thanks to the following gentlemen in these cities for information given and courtesies extended:

HON. A. B. WEAVER, Mayor of Philadelphia.

MR. ROBERT GRIER, Private Secretary to the Mayor.

MR. C. F. WEAVER, Special Agent Philadelphia Rapid Transit Company.

MR. C. O. KRUGER, General Manager Philadelphia Rapid Transit Company.

HON. DAVID J. SMYTH, Director of Public Safety.

HON. ALEXANDER COLVILLE, Assistant Director of Public Safety.

MR. HARRY M. QUIRK, Superintendent of Police.

COL. J. LEWIS GOOD, Chief, Bureau of Health, Department of Public Safety.

MR. E. H. SANBORN.

HON. PATRICK A. COLLINS, Mayor of Boston.

HON. GEO. B. CROCKER, Chairman Boston Transit Commission.

Hon. Horace G. Allen, Member Boston Transit Commission.

Hon. B. Leighton Beal, Member Boston Transit Commission.

Prof. Geo. F. Swain, M. Am. Soc. C. E., Member Boston Transit Commission.

Mr. Howard A. Carson, M. Am. Soc. C. E., Chief Engineer Boston Transit Commission.

Mr. W. A. Crafts, Clerk Massachusetts State Board of Railroad Commissioners.

Mr. C. S. Sergeant, Vice-President Boston Elevated Railroad.

Mr. Paul Windsor, Assistant to the Vice-President Boston Elevated Railroad.

Dr. Samuel H. Durgin, Chairman Board of Health.

The Committee expresses its obligation also to those in New York who have aided in its work, including the officers of your Association. Special thanks are due to the following gentlemen:

The Members of Your Legal Committee.

Hon. A. R. Piper (Capt. U. S. Army, ret'd), Deputy Police Commissioner.

Hon. John McG. Woodbury, Commissioner of Street Cleaning.

Mr. John A. Bensel, M. Am. Soc. C. E., Engineer in Chief, Department of Docks and Ferries.

Mr. Nelson P. Lewis, M. Am. Soc. C. E., Chief Engineer to the Board of Estimate and Apportionment.

Mr. William Barclay Parsons, M. Am. Soc. C. E., Chief Engineer Rapid Transit Commission.

Mr. H. H. Vreeland, President Interurban Street Railway Company.

Mr. Oren Root, Jr., General Manager Interurban Street Railway Company.

Mr. Milton G. Starrett, M. Am. Soc. C. E., Chief Engineer Interurban Street Railway Company.

Mr. George H. Pegram, M. Am. Soc. C. E., Chief Engineer Interborough Rapid Transit Company.

Particular value is attached by the Committee to the facts collected in Boston regarding street-car movement, for it is a subject which has there received unusual attention and careful study, with the very striking result, after several years of assiduous effort, that the maximum number of cars now being run per hour in one direction on a single street surface track in Boston as a daily performance exceeds by 40 per cent. the highest number reached in New York. The practical aspect of this will be discussed later on.

As the work of collecting data progressed, it was found desirable to extend and enlarge it in unforeseen directions, and this preparatory work occupied a much longer time than was originally contemplated.

The data gathered was compiled, tabulated and platted upon numerous diagrams, which in turn are condensed and formulated in forty-two sheets of drawings, which were turned over to your Association with this report. A list of these diagrams and tables is submitted herewith, marked Addendum A.

In its investigations, and in this report, the Committee has not adhered strictly to the specific matters embraced in its preliminary report, but has rather taken up the broad and general subject of the conditions of the passenger transportation problems in New York and the methods and means by which the capacity and efficiency of the service can be increased. We have followed the lines of inquiry which, from our observations, seemed to promise opportunity for the improvement of the present conditions, and have framed this report accordingly.

While we have devoted a great deal of time and study to the technical features and to the details of the various subdivisions of the subject referred to, in order that we might feel reasonably sure of the conclusions we have arrived at, we have endeavored to keep the report as free from technical treatment as possible, at the same time giving the reasons upon which our conclusions are based in such detail that the reader may be able to judge of their substantial weight and accuracy. We have thought this particularly desirable in reference to the operation of surface cars, since some of our conclusions do not accord with the views generally held by the public.

CONCLUSIONS AND RECOMMENDATIONS.

WE think it well to state at the outset of our report the conclusions we have reached, and our recommendations for the improvement of the passenger transportation service in the city of New York. Following each paragraph will be found reference to the pages of the report where the subject referred to is considered more at length. They are as follows:

1. That more cars be put in service at once during the rush hours. The Committee believes that the number of cars now operated during the rush hours can be considerably increased even on the most congested lines.

(See pages 19, 20; 40, 44.)

2. That during other than rush hours the number of cars be so increased that the travel shall be comfortably accommodated. There can be no doubt that it is entirely practicable to do so.

(See pages 41, 42.)

3. That immediate measures be taken to reduce to a minimum the obstructions to the movement of cars caused by vehicular travel and standing vehicles, as well as by building operations, and other preventable obstructions. The Committee thinks that when this is done it will be possible to increase the present number of cars operated more than twenty per cent. even during the rush hours.

(See pages 45, 46.)

4. That measures be taken to substitute, at the earliest possible date on all the congested lines, cars having a seating capacity of fifty-two passengers each. The present average seating capacity of the closed cars on Broadway being about thirty passengers, the substitution of an equal number of the larger cars would increase the seating and carrying capacity of the line more than seventy per cent.

(See pages 27-31.)

5. We recommend that a fair trial be given to double-deck cars, though we are not prepared to advise their immediate adoption.

(See pages 29-31; 89, et seq.)

6. That all cars carry distinct and properly placed signs showing the route and destination by day and night.

7. That at the principal transfer stations the cars be stopped in sets of two or more instead of singly as at present.

(See pages 22, 23.)

8. That immediate steps be taken to equip all cars used on congested lines with effective power brakes, to be followed, as early as practicable, by their general adoption.

(See pages 39, 40.)

9. That upon the congested lines, on all cars having a length of car body of twenty-eight feet and over, two men in addition to the motorman should be employed, at least during the rush hours. The respective duties of each man should be properly defined, so that one man will be constantly upon the rear platform. The Committee believes that the movement of cars will be expedited, the danger of accidents materially lessened, the convenience of the traveling public enhanced, and that, in the end, the interests of the operating company will be promoted by the adoption of this expedient.

(See pages 23-25; 27.)

10. That upon the congested lines cars be stopped to take on and let off passengers at alternate cross streets only, the stopping places to be properly designated. The Committee believes that this would sufficiently expedite the movement of cars, to outweigh the very slight inconvenience to the public.

(See page 25.)

11. That the provisions for the regulation of vehicular travel upon overcrowded streets, embraced in the code of rules submitted with this report, be enforced. The Com-

mittee is convinced that such enforcement would materially lessen the vehicular congestion on these streets and thus permit the more rapid and regular movement of cars.

(See pages 48-54.)

12. The Committee believes that if the above recommendations are carried out the result will be an increase in the carrying capacity of the Broadway and other congested lines of about 85 per cent., and urges their immediate adoption.

(See pages 30, 34, 54.)

13. That mechanical appliances to expedite the loading and unloading of freight on the congested streets should be adopted wherever practicable.

(See page 51.)

14. That, under the conditions now existing upon the congested car lines, it would be impracticable to attempt to prevent passengers from standing in any class of cars. The Committee believes that the deplorable state of affairs that now prevails in this respect can only be remedied by providing adequate transportation facilities, so that overcrowding will be unnecessary.

(See pages 57-58.)

15. That on the less congested streets there are no physical or engineering difficulties to prevent a satisfactory increase of service. It is a question merely of power and equipment, and it is within the ability of the operating company to provide ample accommodations. Such accommodations should be required of the Interurban Company.

(See page 56.)

16. That the transfer *system* now in use in New York is, upon the whole, quite satisfactory, and no radical changes are recommended. The Committee believes, however, that the extension of transfer privileges may sometimes be detrimental, rather than beneficial, to the interests of the public if allowed to increase the overcrowding on lines already congested.

(See pages 58-59; 60.)

17. It is not advisable to concentrate the work of snow removal upon the street car lines to the neglect of other commercial interests, but the public may expect in the future better service in the rapid removal of snow from all important streets through improved methods to be adopted by the Street Cleaning Department.

(See page 61.)

18. The construction of a surface car subway in Broadway under 34th street is not recommended. It is at present unnecessary, and its great cost, the physical difficulties that would be encountered, and the fact that the space will be required for the Rapid Transit Subway make its construction impracticable.

(See page 62.)

19. The equipment of many of the crosstown surface lines, especially the horse-car lines, is very poor, and the service inadequate and unsatisfactory. The fact that some of them are soon to be changed to electric power is not a sufficient excuse for their present neglect. This branch of the transportation service should be materially improved at once.

(See pages 62-64.)

20. After careful consideration the Committee concludes that the extension of the 86th street line from Central Park West to Amsterdam avenue and the conversion to an electric line of the present tracks thence to Riverside Drive, thus completing an electric line from river to river, is a public necessity and recommends that this be done as soon as possible.

(See pages 64-65.)

21. Several new surface car routes are believed to be practicable and desirable, and some changes in present routes are recommended.

(See pages 67-70.)

22. The prompt removal of all unused car tracks is strongly recommended.

(See page 66.)

23. The schedules for service on the elevated roads approved by the State Railroad Commission on January last are being substantially complied with, and the result has been a great improvement in the service, but the schedules do not provide adequate and satisfactory service during a part of the non-rush hours. The roads could do better during these hours, and the schedules should be so amended as to provide the additional trains and cars required.

(See pages 71-72.)

24. The connection between the east side and the west side elevated roads at South Ferry should be utilized for running through trains from one side to the other, and the South Ferry station should be improved so as to make this practicable.

(See page 72.)

25. Third tracks for express service should be provided on the Second Avenue line from Chatham Square to the Harlem River; on the Third Avenue line from Ninth street to the Harlem River, and on the Ninth Avenue line from Rector street to 155th street.

(See page 72.)

26. Many of the elevated road stations are inadequate for the present service. They should be enlarged and improved. Wider and more direct stairs are urgently needed. Provision should be made for separating the entering and the departing passengers.

(See pages 73-76.)

27. The elevated station at 127th street on the Second Avenue line should be abandoned and a new and commodious station should be built at 125th street.

(See page 74.)

28. The more general use of elevators or escalators at the elevated railroad stations is recommended.

(See page 74.)

29. Sanitary conditions on all the transportation lines should be generally improved. Better arrangements for cleaning, warming and ventilating the cars on both the elevated and surface lines are greatly needed.

(See pages 76-77.)

30. Cleaning, warming and ventilating elevated road stations, keeping waiting-rooms and toilets in order and plumbing in repair, should be given stricter attention.

(See pages 77-81.)

31. The discontinuance of the use of sand in lieu of spittoons at elevated railroad stations and the providing of large spittoons in sufficient number are recommended.

(See pages 76, 78.)

32. Roofing all elevated platforms for their full length is recommended.

(See pages 76, 77.)

33. All spaces and places in cars and stations wherein dust and dirt may collect should be open and readily accessible for cleaning and should be kept clean.

(See pages 63-80.)

34. Removable non-absorbent floor covering for use in all cars on all lines, both surface and elevated, is recommended.

(See pages 79-81.)

35. Cleaner and better lighted cars, kept in good repair, should be required for lines upon which horses continue to be used for traction.

(See pages 63, 79, 80.)

36. It is recommended that the companies adopt a rule against putting feet upon car seats, which rule, as well as the existing one against carrying burning tobacco into closed cars, should be rigidly enforced.

(See pages 77-80.)

37. It is recommended that suitable shelter be provided at exposed transfer points and termini of the surface roads, and that islands of safety be provided where necessary.

(See page 81.)

38. The strict enforcement of the ordinance against spitting and of all other sanitary ordinances and regulations appertaining to the transportation service in the city is strongly urged.

(See pages 76-81.)

IMPROVING THE SURFACE CAR SERVICE.

THE problem of improving the car service on congested surface lines seems to be the most important matter that has been brought to our attention. This is intimately connected with the problem of regulating vehicular travel upon these streets, and we shall, therefore, take these subjects up first. The Committee has concentrated its investigations upon thoroughfares like Broadway and West Broadway, believing that the conditions thereon are in general typical of those on all the more congested streets, and that remedies which would be effective on these streets will generally be effective on the others.

The passenger carrying capacity of any line of cars is measured, first, by the number of cars that pass a fixed point in a given time, and second, by the size or capacity of the individual cars. While high speed economizes time and thus adds to the convenience of passengers, it does not of itself increase the hourly number of cars that can be operated, provided the cars are not run more closely together than safety will permit. In fact, the passenger capacity of the line may be less at a high than a low speed, as will be shown later on.

NUMBER OF CARS THAT CAN BE OPERATED.

THE number of cars that can be moved past a given point in a given time is limited by the time interval or headway that must be maintained between them, and this in turn depends upon the speed of the cars, the number and length of stops made and the extent to which the movement of the cars is delayed by obstructions.

SPEED OF CARS.

THE average speed at which a car can be safely operated upon a double-track road is limited by certain physical conditions which may be briefly discussed. It is a matter of common observation that when power is applied to a car at rest it will be started and propelled at a gradually increasing velocity until the desired speed is reached. When the power equals the resistance the car will proceed at a uniform rate. When it is desired to bring the car to a stop the power is cut off and the brake applied, by which the speed is gradually reduced until the car comes to rest. The operation of stopping and starting consumes a certain amount of time which varies with the speed of the car, the power or effectiveness of the brakes and the ability of the motorman. The *distance* within which a car can be stopped varies nearly as the square of the speed. In other words, it requires about four times the distance to stop a car moving at ten miles per hour as to stop one moving at five miles per hour, and the same law holds goods in attaining a given speed. On the other hand, the *time* consumed in stopping or starting varies directly as the speed. While it is not intended to enter into a technical discussion of this matter, it is necessary to mention it, for the reason that the time lost in stopping and starting the car is an important element in determining the capacity of any line, and the percentage of time thus lost becomes greater as the speed is increased. Furthermore, if the stops are near together the car may not be able to attain its highest allowable speed before it becomes necessary to shut off the power and apply the brakes in order to stop at the point desired, and the speed attainable may be limited by that cause. In Manhattan the cross streets are unusually near together, and if a stop be made at each one of them, or the car held in control in readiness for a stop, it is physically impossible to attain a high average speed, even if no causes of obstruction or interruption occur.

To maintain a given average speed, including stops, it is necessary, of course, that a car shall run between stops at a higher speed than the average. Over crowded streets a speed

TABLE NO. 1.

AVERAGE SPEED IN MILES PER HOUR OF A NUMBER OF CARS ON BROADWAY.

From Observations on January 19th and 20th and February 11th, 13th and 14th, 1903.

HOUR.	Number of Trips Averaged.	Speed in Miles per Hour Between							Average Running Time Between Battery Place and 59th Street in Minutes.
		Battery Place and Canal St. 1.1945 Miles.	Canal Street and 14th Street. 1.2714 Miles.	14th Street and 23d Street. 0.4697 Miles.	23d Street and 34th Street. 0.5701 Miles.	34th Street and 42d Street. 0.4148 Miles.	42d Street and 59th Street. 0.8522 Miles.	Battery Place and 59th St. 4.7727 Miles.	
A. M.									
7 to 8	10	9.24	8.69	8.30	8.72	8.30	9.46	8.75	32.7
9 to 12	21	5.35	6.43	6.02	6.73	7.38	8.01	6.25	45.8
P. M.									
1 to 3	15	5.75	6.77	6.10	6.25	6.60	7.56	6.36	45.0
3 to 5	13	5.21	6.20	5.17	6.09	6.12	7.25	5.80	49.3
5 to 6:30	9	6.37	5.87	5.85	6.28	6.65	7.27	6.12	46.8
8 to 9	2	10.02	10.21	7.60	7.61	7.45	8.40	8.84	32.4
Average of all trips	70	6.23	6.82	6.23	6.76	7.03	7.90	6.62	44.2
Maximum, any trip	...	10.61	10.48	9.65	9.77	11.75	11.25	9.64	56.0
Minimum, any trip	...	3.79	4.18	3.63	4.63	4.74	4.99	5.07	29.7

NOTE—The trips referred to above include about an equal number of trips northward and trips southward.

of about twelve miles per hour cannot be exceeded with safety. At this rate a car moves about eighteen feet in one second, and from this speed a loaded car of the kind used on Broadway cannot probably be brought to an emergency stop with the hand brakes now in use in a distance much less than sixty feet. In ordinary service the average distance covered after application of the brakes before the car comes to a standstill from a speed of twelve miles per hour is probably about eighty feet and the time occupied is probably about nine seconds. The time occupied in regaining a speed of twelve miles per hour from the starting of the car is probably about seven seconds. These figures are reached by the Committee, after a study of the existing data upon the subject, which is rather meagre, supplemented by some observations made by its own observers. From them, and making the necessary allowance for stopping and for reduced speed at street crossings where the car does not stop, it may be computed that the average speed of a Broadway car, restricted to a maximum speed of twelve miles per hour, could not much exceed eight miles per hour, or two-thirds of the maximum speed, even if no obstructions to free movement existed. In fact, our observations show that during the early morning hours, and after 8 P. M., when the cars are least obstructed by vehicular travel, and when few stops are made, the actual average speed of Broadway cars between Battery Place and 59th street is about $8\frac{3}{4}$ miles per hour, and the quickest trip observed averaged only $9\frac{5}{8}$ miles per hour.

With a proper regulation of vehicular travel upon the street and the removal, so far as practicable, of other causes of delay, the Committee believes that a near approach to an average speed of eight miles per hour could be maintained at all times throughout the day.

The Committee has had its observers time the passage of a large number of cars on Broadway between Battery Place and 59th street at different hours throughout the day, noting the time at which the car passed each intermediate street in order to ascertain the actual speed now made by the cars on that line. The observations have been condensed and tabulated and are shown in Table No. 1.

TABLE NO. 2.

SHOWING NUMBER OF CARS PASSING A GIVEN POINT IN ONE HOUR AT DIFFERENT SPEEDS.

		Average speed = ⅔ of maximum speed. Brake retardation = 1¾ miles per hour, per second. Length of car = 36 feet, over all = (*a*). Minimum clearance allowable at stop = 15 feet = (*b*). Time allowance for delay in applying brake = 1 second.					
Speed in Miles Per Hour.		Feet Traveled in One Second at Max. Speed. (*c*)	Time and Distance Required to Stop after Application of Brake.		Distance from Front to Front of Cars ($a+b+c+d$).	Number of Cars per Hour and Headway.	
Max.	Average.		Time. Sec.	Distance Feet (*d*)	Feet.	No. per Hour.	H'dwy Seconds.
6	4	8.8	3.43	15.1	75	281	12⅘
8	5⅓	11.7	4.57	26.7	89	316	11⅖
10	6⅔	14.7	5.71	42.0	108	325	11 1/16
12	8	17.6	6.86	60.4	129	327	11
15	10	22.0	8.57	94.3	167	316	11⅖
18	12	26.4	10.28	135.7	213	297	12

It will be observed that we have grouped the trips into separate periods of the day and the whole distance into sections which are thought to represent typical conditions on the route. A study of this table is very interesting, particularly in connection with the subject of obstruction and delay caused by vehicular travel, of which we shall speak later in this report. It will be noted that the average speed over the whole route between 7 and 8 A. M. is 8.75 miles per hour, and between 8 and 9 P. M. an average speed of 8.84 miles per hour was attained. The average speed during the period of greatest congestion from 5 P. M. to 6.30 P. M. was but 6.12 miles per hour, and the average throughout the day from 7 A. M. to 9 P. M. was 6.62 miles per hour. If an average speed of eight miles per hour could be maintained at all times it would obviously result in a great saving of time to passengers, though, as we have said, the increased speed alone would not necessarily increase the carrying capacity of the line for the following reasons:

To insure safety in operation a certain distance must be maintained between cars operated in the same direction upon the same track. This distance depends mainly upon the maximum speed of the car and varies about as the square of that speed. In other words, cars operated at twelve miles per hour must be kept about four times as far apart as cars operated at six miles per hour. This fact that the safe distance between cars increases so much more rapidly than the speed of the cars explains why increasing the speed above a certain limit may decrease rather than increase the number of cars that can be moved past a given point in a given time. Knowing the maximum speed at which the cars are moved, the rate at which the speed can be reduced by the brake, the length of the car and the proper allowance for delay in applying the brake and for a safe margin of space at the stopping point, it is possible to compute the distance that must be maintained between cars when running at full speed.

Table No. 2 has been computed on assumptions applicable to the crowded streets of New York, and it demonstrates the statements made above.

It will be noted in Table No. 2 that, under the conditions assumed, the greatest number of cars per hour can be moved when the maximum speed is ten or twelve miles per hour and the average speed is about seven or eight miles per hour, and that with speeds higher or lower than these the number of cars that can be operated grows less. It is of interest to note further that the number of cars that can be operated at an average speed of twelve miles per hour is but slightly greater than the number that can be operated at an average speed of four miles per hour.

The table shows that at a maximum speed of twelve miles per hour, equivalent to an average speed of about eight miles per hour, the space between cars cannot safely be less, theoretically, than 129 feet. The average speed of the car being eight miles per hour the number of cars 36 feet long, spaced 129 feet apart that will pass a given point in one hour is 327. In practice, under usual conditions of service on congested streets, the number of cars moved per hour past any given point would be materially less. Even if the tracks were kept reasonably clear of slow-moving vehicles and other preventable obstructions, the interference caused by the vehicles that cross the tracks at cross streets would delay the car movement very seriously, and as we shall next point out, the time lost at stops will still further reduce the number of cars that can be operated.

EFFECT OF STOPS.

THE influence of stops, for whatever purpose they are made, in limiting the number of cars that can be operated over a track, must next be considered.

The theoretical time consumed by the operation of stopping and starting the car may be closely computed when the speed, the efficiency of the brakes and the power of the motor are known. This time increases directly as the speed.

In the case of the cars on Broadway, the time lost in coming to a stop and regaining full speed is about three and one-half seconds at a speed of six miles per hour and about seven seconds at a maximum speed of twelve miles per hour, at each stop. These periods do not include the time the car remains at a standstill for taking on or letting off passengers or for other causes, which time must be added in each case. Our observations show that the average stop for taking on and letting off passengers, excluding the longer stops at some of the transfer points, is about five seconds. The total time lost at each stop for passengers is therefore about eight and one-half seconds at six miles per hour and about twelve seconds at twelve miles per hour.

In order that the cars may not interfere with each other at these stops a certain spacing between the cars, both in time and distance, is necessary. When a car stops, the following car approaches it rapidly, and, if the stop exceeds a certain time, may approach too closely for safety, unless its speed be reduced, thus adding to the time lost by it. In operation the cars should be kept under such control that they may be prevented from approaching nearer to each other at stopping places than, say, fifteen feet. Without entering upon a technical discussion of the subject it may be stated that to insure this condition the time interval between cars of usual length operated at ordinary speed is approximately nine seconds, plus the number of seconds the cars actually remain at rest. Thus, to allow a stop of five seconds the time interval between cars must be fourteen seconds, and for every second longer that the car remains standing the time interval between the cars must be increased one second. It is probable that in practical operation, at an average speed of eight miles per hour, requiring a maximum speed of twelve miles per hour, an average time interval of sixteen seconds between cars on crowded streets is as small as safety would permit. *If this conclusion is correct, it appears that the time consumed by stops is a limiting element in the car capacity of a line, regardless of other considerations.*

With a time interval of sixteen seconds the number of cars that may be moved past a given point per hour is 225. The Committee does not believe that on congested streets like Broadway a service of more than 220 cars per hour passing a given point in one direction could be reasonably expected under the most favorable circumstances likely to occur, but we believe that this number per hour is a reasonable estimate of what should be done. We are confirmed in this belief by our own observations of what is being done at this time in Boston, and a large number of headway observations on Broadway at Cham-

TABLE NO. 3.

MAXIMUM NUMBER OF CARS PER HOUR IN ONE DIRECTION, PASSING VARIOUS POINTS OF OBSERVATION ON BROADWAY, MANHATTAN.

POINT OF OBSERVATION.	Date. 1903.	Hour.	Direction.	Number of Cars.
Fulton street	March 10	9 to 10 A. M.	Southbound	190
Waverly place	May 25	5 to 6 P. M.	Northbound	175
Eighth street	March 6	5 to 6 P. M.	"	176
22d street	April 21	5:30 to 6:30 P. M.	"	181
34th street...........	Feb. 10	6 to 7 P. M.	"	123*

* Above 22d street the Lexington avenue cars diverge, thus reducing the number at 34th street.

TABLE NO. 4.

OBSERVATIONS OF LENGTH OF TRANSFER STOPS.

TRANSFER STATION.	No. of Cars Passed.	No. of Cars Stopped at Transfer Point.	Average Time per Stop.	Average Time for all Cars.
			Seconds.	Seconds.
Broadway and Astor Place.............. (Longest Stop, 47.5 seconds. Shortest Stop, 2 seconds.)	92	69	16.	10.
34th Street and Broadway.............. (Longest Stop, 29 seconds. Shortest Stop, 2 seconds.)	62	62	10.1	10.1
34th Street and Sixth Avenue.......... (Longest Stop, 20 seconds. Shortest Stop, 5 seconds.)	22	22	9.8	9.8
Total..............................	176	153	12.6	10.

bers and at Houston streets appear to practically confirm the above conditions. These observations are shown graphically in the diagrams Nos. 21, 22 and 23 submitted herewith. They show that during the early morning and late evening hours, when the average speed of cars, as checked at the two points of observation, exceeded eight miles per hour, their headways, although they varied greatly, scarcely ever were less than sixteen seconds, their averages being much longer; during the rush hours shorter headways were sometimes observed, but they occurred only when the average speed was greatly reduced, and even the average headway of groups of cars exceeded sixteen seconds. Our observations taken at a number of points show that in the present service the number of 220 cars per hour is never reached in this city.

The maximum number of cars passing per hour in one direction on one track at various points of observation upon Broadway is given in Table No. 3.

If we assume that a movement of 220 cars per hour is practicable under favorable conditions, the average time interval between them will be about sixteen and one-half seconds, and this would admit of a stop for passengers of from seven to eight seconds. In practice this length of stop is rarely exceeded except at some of the more important transfer points. If stops longer than this occur the movement of the cars following will be delayed.

To ascertain if possible the average duration of stops made for the purpose of transferring passengers on the Broadway lines the Committee caused a large number of observations to be taken at Astor Place and at 34th street. The results are given in Table No. 4.

As was to be expected, the table shows these stops to vary greatly in length. At Astor Place it was observed that not all of the cars enumerated in the table stopped at the usual transfer point; the remainder transferred their passengers further down the street when blocked by cars ahead, an extra transfer agent being at times employed. These facts explain why the time of the average transfer stop per car, as given in the table, is less than the average length of the stops, it being apparent that the stops at the main transfer point must overlap the others. This shows very clearly that there is a saving of time in stopping simultaneously two or more cars at a transfer station and points significantly to the conclusion that if it should prove practicable to extend the length of the transfer station so as to accommodate several cars at once the loss of time per car could be greatly reduced. Applying the rule for computing headway which we have given above to the Astor Place car movement and assuming that the average stop for each car is about eleven seconds, the average headway would be about twenty seconds and the number of cars passing would be 180 per hour; the two highest observations gave, respectively, 176 and 181 northbound cars per hour past this point.

Operating detached cars at stopping points in groups instead of singly simulates a train movement. In crowded streets, and especially where cars are run at such short headway as to make it unnecessary and undesirable to stop every car at every street, this mode of operating is not feasible, but at certain points where nearly every car must stop in turn, as at transfer stations, it is employed with marked success. Your Committee has carefully investigated its application in Boston. There the trolley cars leaving Park Street Station in the subway are loaded and despatched in sets of five, and, after emerging from the subway at the Public Gardens, they proceed on the surface tracks along Boylston street to Huntington avenue, making regular stops in sets of threes in separate "berths," as they are called, the latter being simply designated portions of the same track, each berth being a little longer than a car length and marked by a numbered post erected in the sidewalk. By this means a set of five cars can be loaded and despatched from the Park Street Station in a little over one minute, under the most favorable circumstances, and, as a daily performance during the rush hours, from 240 to 250 cars per hour are thus started. It is instructive to note that this same number of cars per hour must be moved on Boylston street in order to maintain the movement in the subway, and this is accomplished at a speed as low as the average rush-hour speed in New York. The operation is so striking in comparison with the best results in Manhattan, so far as the number of cars per hour is concerned, that it is believed by the Committee to be worthy of a fair trial at Astor Place and at 34th street on Broadway and at Columbus Circle and other congested transfer stations. It should be stated here that its introduction would require the consent of the city authorities and the cooperation of the police in reference to the use of additional portions of the streets for the purpose. In the opinion of the Committee this question should be treated as a provision for public safety and convenience, rather than as an investure of the railroad company with greater street rights than it has at present. The Committee recommends that the subject be taken up by the Interurban Company and the city officials in order that the best results can be worked out.

Since, as we have shown, the length of stops is the controlling factor in determining the number of cars that can be operated over a line, it is obviously important that every possible means should be employed to keep the time consumed by stops at the lowest limit. As one expedient for limiting stops to the shortest time and for other reasons herein stated, the Committee renews the recommendation made in its preliminary report that on congested lines upon each closed car, having a length of car body exceeding twenty-eight feet, two men, in addition to the motorman, should be employed. We believe that such an arrangement will not only tend to reduce the length of stops, but will also conduce to the safety and convenience of passengers.

The chief objections that have been raised to the employment of a second man upon these cars are:

First. That there will be conflict of duties and division of responsibility between the two men. The Committee does not think this objection is worthy of serious consideration. No sufficient reason appears why the duties and responsibilities of the two men cannot be so clearly defined that no confusion can result. The division of duty, authority and responsibility among a great number of employees is common in all large industrial establishments and upon all railroads of every kind. A familiar example is found in the operation of every steam railroad train, and more particularly in those cases where one employee, the conductor, has control of the movement of the train, while another is charged with the collection of tickets and fares. The Committee cannot believe that it is impossible for able executives like those in charge of the operation of the Interurban Railroad to so define and separate the duties of the two men suggested, and to so enforce necessary discipline, that all confusion of duty and responsibility will be avoided.

Second. It is objected that the employment of two men would entail a burdensome expense upon the operating company. This is an objection that should be given all proper weight, and the public should not demand expenditures by the company that are either unreasonable, or that the good of the service and the rights of the public do not make clearly necessary. But if it is practically certain that the additional expenditure will add to the efficiency of the service and will materially contribute to the safety, or even to the convenience of the traveling public, it may be reasonably required. It is a matter of common observation that one conductor, when collecting fares within a crowded large closed car, can seldom see the rear platform clearly, and cannot, therefore, know when to signal the motorman to start. The familiar question, "All right there?" addressed by the conductor to no one in particular, and answered by any one who chooses to take the responsibility, is sufficient evidence of the truth of the above statement, if any were required. It is obvious without any argument that such methods of operating crowded cars must greatly increase the liability of accident to passengers. It is well known that a majority of accidents on street railroads occur to passengers when getting on or off the car, and it might, therefore, be reasonably expected that the saving in accident litigation and damages would alone go far toward paying the expenses of the extra employee, to say nothing of the inconvenience and suffering that would be thereby prevented. Furthermore, it is reasonable to believe that the greater certainty of collecting fare from every passenger would in itself make profitable the employment of a second man, who would devote his whole attention to that duty. It is the common experience and observation of passengers that, in the overcrowded cars, many fares are missed by the conductor, whose time and attention must be divided between operating the car and collecting fares. The Committee, therefore, is forced to conclude that these objections are not well founded.

The advantages that would seem certain to result from the employment of the extra man have already been partly referred to. From the point of view of the public, it might be confidently expected that, if one man were stationed constantly upon the rear platform of the car, whose duties were to give starting signals and have control of the letting off and taking on of passengers at the end of the car, no unnecessary time would be lost at stops, and at the same time no start would be made until passengers were safely on or off the steps. His presence on the rear platform would expedite the loading and unloading. The other employee would always remain inside the car collecting fares and issuing transfers and beyond giving signals to stop, as passengers may indicate their wish to get off, would have no control over the movement of the car. It might be sufficient if the extra man were used during the rush hours only.

The substitution of larger cars, which the Committee recommends, would make the employment of the second man still more desirable, and the larger number of passengers that could be carried in each car would go far to meet the increased expense of providing the second man. The committee very strongly recommends that the company be urged to make a practical trial of this plan by putting a second man on a number of the larger sized closed cars for a week or more during the rush hours of the day. Such a trial would give both the company and the public an opportunity to judge of the practicability and the value of the plan.

If every second cross street only were designated as a stopping place, the reduction in the number of stops would enable the cars to make better time, though the necessity for keeping the car under control at the intermediate crossings would, to some extent, reduce the advantage gained by the fewer stops. In the opinion of your Committee the adoption of a rule to stop cars for passengers at every second street only might be expected to aid materially in bringing the average speed of cars up to eight miles an hour, provided the tracks were kept reasonably free from obstruction. If the stopping places were properly designated and plainly marked they would soon become familiar to those using the cars, and the inconvenience of sometimes having to walk an additional block would be so slight that it ought not to be objected to.

CAPACITY OR SIZE OF CARS.

THE second element to which we have referred as affecting the carrying capacity of a surface line is the size of the individual cars. At the present time the best size for cars for use in city service is largely a matter of opinion. In practical use there is doubtless a certain size of car, which, all things considered, is suited to give the most satisfactory results upon the streets of a large city.

The street railroad owner or manager naturally considers the question from the point of view of net financial returns, and may ignore the feature of maximum service to the public. Where the capacity of the line is adequate to the needs of the public this view is justifiable. But in Manhattan, in the present condition of affairs, the public has a right to demand increased carrying capacity on the congested lines, even if the best financial results are not thereby fully realized. The Committee has, therefore, given careful consideration to the matter of the size of car best suited to give maximum carrying capacity on crowded lines like Broadway. If the cars are too small, not only is the capacity for service to the public diminished, but the earning capacity to the operating company is also reduced without any corresponding benefits to either party. If they are excessively large the aggregate capacity of the line may be decreased rather than increased, because, as we have seen, the length of stop made for taking on and letting off passengers is practically the controlling element in determining the number of cars that can be operated, and it is a well-demonstrated fact that more time is consumed in letting off passengers from very large cars, particularly when crowded with passengers, than from smaller cars.

The Interurban Company now runs upon the crowded lines two sizes of closed cars, the smaller having a seating capacity of twenty-eight and the larger a seating capacity of thirty-six. Our observations on Broadway indicate that when closed cars alone are operated they are run during the rush hours in the ratio of about seven of the smaller to two of the larger. If all the cars run were of the larger size the aggregate carrying capacity of the Broadway line would be increased over 20 per cent.—a very material addition to the service.

While the largest size of closed cars now in use on Broadway and other lines, which have a body about twenty-eight feet long and a seating capacity of about thirty-six passengers, may be most economical for operation on the most crowded streets, the Committee is inclined to believe that still larger cars, seating about fifty-two passengers each, would be practicable and would increase the present carrying capacity of the lines nearly 75 per cent. Cars even larger than those we here suggest are already in common use on suburban lines, and the Committee learns that the general tendency at the present time is toward larger cars for urban use also. The objection that, in city service where stops are frequent, the difficulty of collecting fares in large cars is increased, would not apply, if, as we recommend, two men besides the motorman, were employed on each car.

Attention is called to the fact that in his recent "Report Upon the Engineering and Operating Features of the Chicago Transportation Problem," Mr. B. J. Arnold, a recognized authority upon the subject, recommends the exclusive use of cars having a seating capacity of fifty-two passengers upon the crowded lines of that city.

LARGER CARS FOR MANHATTAN.

IN investigating the question of the feasibility of using cars of greater capacity than are now run in Manhattan, the Committee has considered four different types of closed cars, which are, respectively, as follows:

(A) A single-deck, cross-seated, closed combined summer and winter car with center aisle, seating fifty-two passengers.

(B) A double-deck closed car of about the same length as the present larger closed car used by the Interurban Company, with longitudinal seats below for thirty-six passengers and cross seats with center aisle for forty-four passengers on the upper deck or eighty seats in all. The lower deck is like the present closed car, except that above the large windows are smaller transom windows for ventilation; the upper deck has a roof and closed sides, with removable windows. The height from rail to roof is 15 feet 9 inches.

(C) A double-deck closed car of the "knife-board" pattern, with the lower deck as in type (B), and with two longitudinal, back to back, or "knife-board" seats along the center of the upper deck, facing outward. This type seats thirty-six passengers on each deck, or seventy-two in all. The upper deck has a roof and closed sides with removable windows similar to type B. The height from rail to roof is 13 feet 6 inches.

(D) A single-deck, longitudinal-seated closed car, seating twenty-six passengers on each side, or fifty-two in all, with a length of car body of 39 feet 6 inches and length over all of 47 feet 6 inches. In its details this car closely resembles the present standard longer closed car of the Interurban.

Type A is the one recommended by Mr. B. J. Arnold for Chicago. The Committee has considered the feasibility of adopting it in Manhattan, but finds that the space between car tracks here is on many streets too narrow to permit of its safe operation, owing to the greater width of car body required for this arrangement of seats.

Types B and C represent two of the most modern forms of double-deck cars. This class of car has received our earnest attention and close study, in which we have been greatly aided by Mr. John P. Fox, who, for the express purpose of investigating the latest developments in the construction and operation of double-deck cars, has recently visited a number of European cities, where they are in successful and growing use. His report to us in regard thereto appears in full herewith as Addendum (B), and will be found to contain valuable matter well worthy of perusal and study, including the leading historical and statistical facts concerning their introduction and use, together with statements and references regarding their merits and demerits.

The Committee, while recognizing the many advantages which the double-deck car affords and feeling well satisfied that in many localities it would provide the solution of the most serious of the various problems affecting street passenger transportation, is yet compelled, but not without great reluctance, to withhold an unqualified recommendation for its introduction in Manhattan for the following reasons, which will be briefly stated: In the first place, we find that double-deck cars could not be used universally, or even generally, in Manhattan, because of insufficient headroom beneath the elevated railroad structures at a number of places; while it is true that at all points where the Broadway lines are crossed by the elevated roads it would be feasible, by making slight alterations in the structure, to secure the necessary headroom for double-deck cars of the type B, so that they could be run on Broadway, on Seventh avenue and on Lexington avenue, for example, yet on Second, Third, Fourth (Park), Sixth and Columbus avenues it would not be practicable to secure headroom even for Type C without very extensive and costly changes not only of the elevated structures, but in street grades and surface tracks as well. In the second place, it cannot be foretold whether the public would favor the double-deck car in Manhattan; that could only be ascertained by actual trial. Experience gained in other cities, where climatic conditions and the habits of the people are different from ours, cannot be taken as an absolute guide.

The prospective advantages, however, both to the public and to the company, appear to be so great, especially in view of the abundant and increasing foreign experience, that we would urge the great importance of putting a sufficient number of Type C cars in service to give the matter a fair trial, which could be done on the Broadway line without any alteration of the elevated railroad structure being necessary. But, whatever the outcome of this trial of double-deck cars might be, a conclusion could not be speedily reached, and, therefore, the Committee recommends the immediate adoption of the Type D of car in sufficient numbers to relieve the present congested conditions. If, as we believe, the number of cars now operated can ultimately be increased to 220 per hour, and if the capacity of the individual cars can be increased from the present average seating capacity of about thirty to a seating capacity of fifty-two, the seating capacity of the lines, so far as closed cars are concerned, would be more than doubled.

Double-deck cars, even if they prove successful, cannot, as has been stated above, be generally used throughout Manhattan because of the low points on the elevated road and the limited height of the Fourth (Park) avenue tunnel section, while the long, single-deck car, Type D, can be used everywhere. It is probable that cars of this size could not be operated around some sharp curves that now exist on the lines where they should be used without coming unduly close to one another when passing on the curves, and that some changes in the track alignment at such places would, therefore, be necessary. If so, the required changes should be made even if it is found necessary in some few cases to alter the routes at such points for a few blocks. Such changes would, doubtless, involve the expenditure of considerable sums of money, but if the adoption of the longer cars would result in the benefit, both to the public and to the operating company, that may reasonably be anticipated the cost of the changes would be relatively unimportant. On Broadway, fortunately, no radical changes in the track alignment would be necessary, and it would be entirely in the power of the operating company to at once make the few necessary alterations to permit of the running of the Type D.

Type C could be run anywhere on Broadway without interference with the elevated structures, and by suitable choice of routes could go nearly the entire length of Manhattan Island and to most places in its width. Its advantages, as compared with Type D, are as follows: It seats twenty more passengers and is 11 feet shorter; it, therefore, accommodates nearly 40 per cent. more passengers than the D type and takes up 20 per cent. less room in the street, or, in other words, while the D type accommodates only 1.7 passengers per lineal foot, the C type accommodates two passengers per lineal foot, or nearly 75 per cent. more, and is no longer or wider than the large cars now in use, and hence will require no change in the tracks.

The objection made to cars of large capacity, that they cause delay by more frequent and longer stops, may be neutralized in the double-deck cars by requiring upper-deck passengers to be on the platform before the car is stopped for them, and Mr. Fox reports that where this regulation is enforced the double-deck cars make even shorter stops than the ordinary ones. The reversed stairway recently adopted and brought into almost universal use on the later English double-deck cars makes it possible for passengers to ascend and descend the stairs with perfect safety, even while the car is in rapid motion. The one objection to the double-deck cars is the uncertainty of that most uncertain thing—popular favor for a new article—and for that reason we have hesitated to positively recommend their adoption, but the probable advantages, both to the public and to the companies, seems so great, especially in view of abundant and increasing foreign experience, that we would urge the great importance of putting a sufficient number of these cars in use to give the matter a fair trial.

CAR SIGNS.

BEFORE leaving the subject of cars the Committee desires to call attention to the general inadequacy of the signs which they carry. A car sign should always show the route and destination, but in many cases, notably on Broadway, the signs indicate the principal street on the route only, and the destination signs, if any, are battered sheet-iron affairs, often hardly legible, and hung on the dashboard, where they are often hidden by passing vehicles or pedestrians. In arranging these signs the convenience of shifting the cars to different routes seems to have been more considered than the convenience of the prospective passenger. In Philadelphia transparent glass signs are displayed over the front of the hood, so arranged that the daylight shines either on them or through them, and even at night the light from the monitor top makes them quite distinct. These signs give the destination and route in each direction, and the proper one is exposed by turning a flap. Something of this kind would be a great improvement on anything seen in Manhattan, and, doubtless, even a better arrangement could be devised with a little painstaking ingenuity. Certainly the public should not lack the great convenience of readily knowing just where and how each car is going. To assist in securing this end a system of colored signs by day and of corresponding

TABLE NO. 5.

NUMBER OF NORTHBOUND CARS AND PASSENGERS PASSING ON BROADWAY AT WAVERLY PLACE AND AT 21ST STREET DURING PERIODS OF TIME STATED.

DESCRIPTION OF CARS.	WAVERLY PLACE.						21ST STREET.					
	May 25, 1903. 5 to 6 P. M.			May 26, 1903. 5 to 6 P. M.			May 28, 1903. 5 to 6 P. M.			May 28, 1903. 5:30 to 6:30 P. M.		
	No. of Cars.	Total No. of Passengers.	Passengers per Car.	No. of Cars.	Total No. of Passengers.	Passengers per Car.	No. of Cars.	Total No. of Passengers.	Passengers per Car.	No. of Cars.	Total No. of Passengers.	Passengers per Car.
Closed, long...	14	509	36	9	350	39	13	453	35	7	320	46
Closed, short.	84	2277	27	74	2313	31	82	2541	31	79	2918	37
Open, long.....	27	1453	54	31	1510	49	25	1410	56	29	1825	63
Open, short...	50	2377	48	47	2087	44	46	2175	47	49	2710	55
Totals and averages..	175	6616	38	161	6260	39	166	6579	40	164	7773	47
Maximum No. of passengers in any car............			75		....	65		....	70		....	70
Minimum No. of passengers in any car...........			2		....	1		....	2		....	15

lights by night would be very effective. It has long been used in parts of this and other cities and is now doing good service on the elevated roads and could readily be adapted to the surface cars.

CAR AND LINE CAPACITY REQUIRED.

IN estimating the carrying capacity required to accommodate the business of any surface car line, the character, as well as the quantity of travel, must be considered. On lines where a large number of the passengers ride for short distances only it is difficult to determine the average number of passengers occupying the cars at any given time, or to compute therefrom the number of passengers that should be provided for on a given route. The number of fares registered during a trip of any car furnishes no reliable indication of the number of passengers occupying that car at any one time. Observations taken at a given point will usually show that while many cars may be overcrowded others following them closely may have a number of vacant seats, while at some point further on these conditions may be reversed with reference to these particular cars, showing that, in order to avoid overcrowding, accommodation must be provided in excess of the actual number of passengers to be carried.

In a report made by Mr. F. H. Shepard to the State Board of Railroad Commissioners, dated January 21, 1903, the statement is made that the Broadway line, including the Lexington avenue cars, carried in December, 1902, in one hour in one direction 21,000 passengers. This, doubtless, means that that number of fares were registered during the time, but it cannot be inferred that the cars were at any time loaded with the number of passengers that the figures would indicate.

In order to determine, approximately, the average load carried by the northbound Broadway cars during the evening rush hours the Committee had some observations made on different days at two different points where the cars are heavily loaded. The points chosen were at Waverley place, the last cross street before reaching the transfer station at Astor Place, and at 21st street, the most convenient point near the divergence of the Lexington avenue cars. The results are given in Table No. 5, which requires little explanation.

It will be observed that the number of cars passing per hour agrees very closely with the number shown by Diagram 27,* which gives the results of observations on other dates. The average number of passengers per car varied from 38 to 40 in the hour from 5 to 6 P. M. and from 47 to 50 in the hour from 5.30 to 6.30 P. M. The records show, however, that the heaviest loading occurring in any one half hour was from 6 to 6.30 P. M., when the average load was about fifty passengers. They also show that the maximum load on any car observed was seventy-five passengers, while the minimum load was one passenger. It is worth noting that of all the cars observed seventy-nine of them carried over sixty passengers each and twenty-one of them carried less than ten passengers each. The figures given in the above table, as the result of our own observations, are substantially corroborated by figures and diagrams published in the "Street Railway Journal" of January 31, 1903, presumably with the sanction and upon the authority of the Metropolitan Railway Company.

Owing to the fact that a large number of the passengers carried ride only a short distance, and that, when these get off their places are taken by others, and so on, the actual capacity of a car is not a true measure of the total number of passengers carried per trip and, conversely, the actual car capacity of a line need not equal the total number of passengers who ride, since the same seat or space may be occupied on each trip by several passengers in turn.

If all those who ride were through passengers the present seating capacity of 180 thirty-seat cars per hour would be only 5,400, and, with an average of forty-five passengers, the total carrying capacity would be but 8,100 per hour. Mr. Shepard's figures, however, indicate that 21,000, or more than two and one-half times that number of passengers per hour, actually use these cars for longer or shorter distances. Assuming the same ratio of seating capacity to total number of passengers to be maintained, the substitution of fifty-two-seat cars for those now in use, which average thirty seats, would provide accommodation for a total of over 36,000 passengers per hour, of which 24,000 would have seats. This last figure is 3,000 per hour more than all the passengers that are said by Mr. Shepard

*See Addendum A.

to ride on the Broadway line during one rush hour, and, if passengers would wait a short time for the arrival of uncrowded cars, it is probable, for some time to come, that few would have to stand.

While it is true that the total number of passengers carried per hour is greater on the Broadway lines than on any other line observed by us, the degree of crowding is greatly exceeded elsewhere. Table 6 gives a comparison of observations of northbound rush-hour travel on Lexington avenue at 59th street, on Madison avenue at 59th street and on Broadway at 21st street; it shows that whereas the average number of passengers standing on the Broadway cars was 19 per cent. of the whole number, the average on Lexington avenue was 31 per cent. and on Madison avenue it was 16 per cent., which comparatively low figure was in part due to the fact, which the table shows, that no short cars were being run on that line. The total number of Lexington avenue standing passengers, according to the table, was 1,599; to provide that number of additional seats would require twenty-nine cars of the long, open type, making the total number of cars per hour in that case 120, instead of 91 as actually observed. On Madison avenue 18 additional cars would be required, making the total number 134 per hour, as against 116 observed. With 120 cars per hour the headway would be 30 seconds, and with 134 cars the headway would be 27 seconds, permitting of the higher speeds that cars are run in the upper portions of these lines. It might not be found desirable to run additional complements of cars on either Madison or Lexington avenues from below 23d street, but to turn them back, say at 24th street.

The conditions shown in Tables 5 and 6 are believed to be fairly typical of the usual rush-hour conditions at the points indicated, but probably do not show the extreme degree of crowding sometimes to be found. If the same number of the larger cars we recommend, seating fifty-two passengers each, had been substituted for those actually used, as shown in Table 6, the percentage of standing passengers on the Lexington avenue line would have been reduced from 31 per cent. to 10 per cent., and on the Madison avenue line from 16 per cent. to 2½ per cent., while on the Broadway line there would have been ample seating capacity for all.

TABLE NO. 6.

NUMBER OF NORTH-BOUND CARS AND PASSENGERS PASSING ON LEXINGTON AVENUE, MADISON AVENUE AND BROADWAY, RESPECTIVELY, DURING PERIODS OF TIME STATED.

DESCRIPTION OF CARS.	LEXINGTON AVE. AND 59TH STREET.						MADISON AVE. AND 59TH STREET.						BROADWAY AND 21ST STREET.					
	June 10, 1903.						June 11, 1903.						May 28, 1903.					
	5:30 to 6:30 P. M.						5:30 to 6:30 P. M.						5:30 to 6:30 P. M.					
	Number of Cars.	Total Number of Passengers.	Average No. Passengers per Car.	Number of Seats.	Number of Passengers Standing.	Per Ct. of Passengers Standing.	Number of Cars.	Total Number of Passengers.	Average No. Passengers per Car.	Number of Seats.	Number of Passengers Standing.	Per Ct. of Passengers Standing.	Number of Cars.	Total Number of Passengers.	Average No. Passengers per Car.	Number of Seats.	Number of Passengers Standing.	Per Ct. of Passengers Standing.
Closed: Long............	21	1180	56	756	424	35	45	2205	49	1622	583	26	7	320	46	252	68	20
Closed: Short	20	1070	53	560	510	48	None.		......	....	......	......	79	2918	37	2212	706	24
Open: Long..............	None.		......	....	....	......	47	2765	59	2585	180	6	29	1825	63	1595	230	13
Open: Short.............	50	2915	58	2250	665	23	None.		......	....	......	......	49	2710	55	2205	505	19
Combination..............	None.		......	....	....	......	24	1210	54	1008	202	17	None.		......	....	....	......
Totals and averages	91	5165	57	3566	1599	31	116	6180	53	5215	965	16	164	7773	47	6264	1509	19

OPEN CARS.

IN what has heretofore been said the Committee has had reference chiefly to closed cars. The condition in regard to the open cars is somewhat different, and some of the statements made cannot be fully applied to them. The open cars in use on Broadway vary in seating capacity from forty-five to fifty-five passengers, but standing in these cars is accompanied with much greater discomfort both to those seated and those standing than in the closed cars. It is popularly supposed that because of the opportunities for loading and unloading along the sides of these open cars these operations are conducted more expeditiously than is possible with closed cars. Our observations do not confirm this conclusion. The cross seats, holding five passengers each, and being placed as near together as practicable, make both the entering and leaving of passengers slow and difficult. This is true in an aggregated degree where standing passengers are admitted between the seats or upon the running board, and the time and difficulty of entering or leaving these cars is, usually, as great or even greater than on the closed cars.

On account of greater liability of accident to passengers on open cars with side entrance and also in order to save the expense of maintaining duplicate equipment, the efforts of street railroad managers have long been directed toward perfecting a combined summer and winter car, readily adaptable to sudden changes in the weather. In the New York *Sun* of May 28, 1903, appeared a statement attributed to the president of the Brooklyn Rapid Transit Company, to the effect that the abandonment of the present type of open car was under consideration by his company on account of the extra expense resulting from damage suits.

A type of combined summer and winter car, seating fifty-two passengers, has been recommended by Mr. Arnold for Chicago. It has crosswise seats for two passengers each on either side of a central aisle and the windows are removable. The Committee has considered the feasibility of adopting this type of car in Manhattan, but has found that the space between the car tracks is not sufficient to permit of it, except by making the car so narrow as to leave only sufficient width for three seats instead of four, besides the aisle, and, consequently, we do not recommend it.

OPERATING SURFACE CARS IN TRAINS.

THE operation of surface cars in trains of two or more has been suggested, and the Committee has given the matter consideration. Trains of two cars have been operated in a number of cities, but in most cases the rear car has been a "trailer"—that is, it has been drawn by the forward car and has not been equipped with power of its own. The results have not been satisfactory, and the tendency at this time is to discard the practice and to operate each car independently.

Some of the objections to the operation of cars in trains are the following: As both cars must be stopped whenever even one passenger is to be taken on or let off, the aggregate number of stops and the time lost by stops per car is materially increased; the frequency of the cars is decreased; experience has shown that the danger of accidents is increased; one of the cars must stop at a considerable distance from the street crossings, and passengers must get on or off among the teams and other travel on a part of the street which should be kept as clear as possible for vehicles. As the cars are stopped by independent brakes and not coupled together with sufficient firmness they are subject to sudden shocks which are very unpleasant to the passengers.

The last-named objection might be largely overcome by equipping each car with motors and with power brakes, all under control of one motorman, and couplings might be devised that would hold the cars more firmly together, so that there would be no slack, but all the other objections would remain and become more pronounced as the individual cars are made longer. With cars of the size and capacity we have recommended their operation in trains would not only be disadvantageous, but positively objectionable. The shorter cars now in use in New York might be operated in trains of two cars if they were properly coupled and equipped with power brakes and electrical connections, so as to be controlled as a unit by the motorman, but the necessary changes would be somewhat expensive, and it would be very much better to procure at once a sufficient number of the large cars we have recommended to supply the congested lines. The small cars thus relieved could be very well employed upon lines of comparatively light travel, as these are rebuilt for electrical equipment.

POWER BRAKES.

IN order to operate the maximum number of cars on a line, a high degree of precision and expedition is requisite, both in accelerating and retarding the movement of the individual cars. In Manhattan the motors and current are usually adequate to secure any reasonable rate of acceleration, although it may be said that the controller apparatus does not usually afford the degree of smoothness in starting that is desirable. Hand brakes are still in general use throughout the city. As it has already been noted that the length of time consumed in stops is the controlling factor in limiting the number of cars that can be safely operated, and hence limits the capacity of the line, it becomes of the utmost importance to determine all the causes affecting this loss of time. Among these is the length of time consumed in bringing the car to rest, and this obviously depends upon the efficiency of the brake employed. It should be noted, also, that, in the rapid retardation required by high speeds and short headways, the comfort of the passengers is seriously affected. It follows, therefore, that while the brakes must be capable of stopping the car very promptly, it must not be so sudden in its action as to discommode the passengers. If too slow, it wastes time; if too quick, it shakes people up. The discomfort to passengers is measured mainly by the maximum resistance of the brake, while efficiency depends mainly on such promptness of application as will permit the car to be brought to rest by a uniform resistance, which is also the condition of least discomfort to passengers. This points plainly to the power brake as alone fulfilling this requirement. With the hand brake, in order to secure the necessary power from a man's unaided strength, the brake handle must travel a long distance in setting the brake, which consumes much valuable time, and, to make up for this loss of time, the brake must be made to act much more powerfully at the end, with corresponding discomfort to the passengers, to say nothing of the wear and strain on the mechanism. The effect on the motorman should also be considered. It is not merely a severe tax on his physical strength, but on his nerves as well, for knowing that the brake will not act promptly, he will often apply it at the least sign of danger, while at another time his fatigue may lead him to neglect its application when really required. Any one who has observed the ease with which a touch on the power brake handle controls a heavy car, and the severe effort required to accomplish the same result by the hand brake, will need no further argument. The capacity of the line, the safety and comfort of the passengers and the well-being of the motorman would all be enhanced by the substitution of the power-brake.

The use of power brakes on surface cars is constantly increasing, and their necessity on all important lines is now generally acknowledged. It will be admitted that in no other city are conditions such as to make their employment more necessary than on the congested streets of Manhattan. We therefore recommend that all cars now in use on the crowded lines be equipped with power brakes as soon as possible, to be followed by their general adoption on all the lines within a reasonable time.

OBSTRUCTIONS TO CAR MOVEMENT.

THE management of the Interurban Railway Company has repeatedly declared that it is impossible either to move more cars or to attain a higher rate of speed on the congested streets in their present condition than it is now doing through the rush hours. The Committee is not prepared to deny this statement unreservedly, recognizing, as it does, that nothing short of actual trial under favorable auspices can determine the matter. We recognize, and have tried not to underestimate the difficulties under which cars are moved on the crowded streets, but it is our opinion, based upon our observations in New York and other cities, that a considerable increase of service during these rush hours is both possible and practicable. We have heretofore stated that 220 cars per hour could, in our opinion, be operated on streets like

Broadway under the very best conditions attainable as regards freedom from interruption. Under existing conditions that number cannot be run, but we believe that it is possible to run 200 cars per hour. Assuming, as our observations indicate, that the present service on Broadway below 23d street does not average during the rush hours more than 180 cars past a given point per hour, an increase to 200 cars per hour would be equivalent to increasing the service 11 per cent. This is not a large increase, but in the present overcrowded conditions, it would be of considerable importance.

But whether our opinion that such an increase is practicable during the rush hours is well founded or not, it is evident that it is entirely possible and practicable to maintain throughout the whole day the volume of the service now rendered during these rush hours, or so much of that volume as may be found necessary to relieve the present crowded conditions during the non-rush hours.

We call attention to Diagrams Nos. 10, 11, 14 and 15, submitted with this report, showing the car movement on Broadway at Canal street, at 18th street and at 34th street. While these diagrams do not cover long periods of observation, there is every reason to regard them as typical of the average car movement on Broadway, throughout the business day. The diagrams are very interesting, and merit careful study. While common experience proves conclusively that the cars on the congested lines are overcrowded during most of the hours of the day, these diagrams demonstrate that the number of cars operated during the non-rush hours is largely decreased, apparently with the object of securing the maximum earning capacity of each car without due regard for the comfort of the traveling public. They conclusively disprove the assertion that all the cars it is possible to operate are kept in service during the whole day.

Taking the diagram of Broadway car movement at 34th street, it will be observed that the number of southbound cars passing that point is rapidly increased from 6 A. M. to the southbound rush period between 8 and 10 A. M., when it reaches the morning maximum of nearly eighty cars per hour. From 10 A. M. until about noon, the numbers of southbound and of northbound cars are each about seventy-five per hour. About noon and for an hour thereafter, additional cars are put into the southbound service, presumably to meet the shopping and matinée travel, these additional cars appearing in the northbound service from 1 to 2 P. M. For the next two hours the service is again about equal, being about 80 cars per hour in each direction. About half-past three and for an hour thereafter, a large number of additional cars are put into service southbound to provide for northbound rush-hour travel of the evening. These begin to return and to increase the northbound service between 4 and 5 P. M., and the northbound service reaches its maximum between 6 and 7 P. M., when an average of nearly 120 northbound cars per hour pass the point of observation. After 7 P. M. the number of cars in both directions rapidly decreases until about 10 P. M., when additional cars are fed into the southbound service to accommodate, on their return, the theater crowds. Study of the diagram of travel at the other points on Broadway will confirm these facts and deductions. The observations at 18th street show a maximum of 176 cars northbound between 5 and 6 P. M., and those at Canal street show a maximum of 155 cars northbound between the same hours. The Lexington avenue cars are on the line at both these points, which accounts for the greater number observed. The largest number of cars observed per hour—176 at 18th street, moving at a speed of six miles per hour—allows an average time interval between cars of more than 20 seconds, which, at that speed, can safely be reduced.

The average number of cars per hour passing north on Broadway at 34th street during the hour of greatest congestion—6 to 7 P. M.—was about 120, or two per minute. The committee was informed by the present general manager of the Interurban Company that the crossings at Broadway and 34th street are so overcrowded with cars as to be a controlling factor in the number that can be operated past this point. At the same time he informed us that 975 cars had been operated over these crossings in one hour, and that three-fourths of this number, or 731 cars per hour, would be a reasonable estimate of their ordinary capacity. During several days' observations the highest number of cars that passed this intersection in all directions in one hour was 525, and the conditions observed indicated that a much larger number could have been operated over these crossings. The Committee therefore concludes that these crossings are not a serious obstacle to the increase of the service on these streets. This conclusion is confirmed by the fact, shown by our observations, that a considerably larger number of cars are daily operated over the crossing at Fourth avenue and 23d street than over the 34th street crossings.

A further examination of the records shows that at 23d street and Fourth avenue, where there are two north and south tracks crossed by two east and west tracks, the maximum number of cars per hour was 558 on four tracks, giving an average of 139 on each track; the maximum number on any one track was 199 per hour; the maximum number of successive occupations of a single-track crossing by the cars on the two intersecting tracks was 314, being at the rate of one occupation in about 11½ seconds. At 34th street and Broadway and Sixth avenue, where there are four north and south tracks crossed by two east and west tracks, the maximum number of cars per hour was 525 on six tracks, giving an average of 88 cars on each track, the maximum number of successive occupations of a single track crossing by the cars of two intersecting tracks was 212, or at the rate of one occupation in about 17 seconds.

A comparison of these results shows that if the 23d street rate of occupation were reached at 34th street, the hourly car number would thereby be increased to 871, which agrees very nearly with the statement of the railroad company's general manager as to what has been done at this triple crossing. It has been urged that the long skew crossing of Broadway by the Sixth avenue tracks diminishes the capacity, because a longer time of occupation is required. This is undoubtedly true, but a careful study of the situation convinces us that the controlling factor is the length of time required for the transfer stops at 34th street. This is proved by the fact that sometimes for short periods, when cars are not held so long at the transfer point, they have been observed to pass the crossing at the rate of 835 per hour.

A study has been made by the Committee of the practicable increase in the hourly number of cars at the 34th street crossing by the adoption, with local modifications, of the Boston system of stopping them in sets, which has been hereinbefore described, and we are of the opinion that a total of twelve cars per minute on the six tracks could be run, divided among the three lines in about the present ratios, and that at the same time a much longer transfer stop would be possible for each car. Twelve cars per minute is equivalent to 720 cars per hour, agreeing very closely with the estimate of the reasonable capacity of the crossings by the representative of the operating company. If, as we have stated, the maximum capacity of the Broadway tracks below 23d street, under the most favorable conditions that are likely to be brought about, be 220 cars per hour in each direction, the divergence of the Lexington avenue cars will leave the number remaining on the Broadway line at 34th street well within the capacity of that crossing.

OBSTACLES TO CAR MOVEMENT.

THE problem of increasing the service, during the afternoon rush particularly, is one to which the committee has given very great attention. The Interurban Company asserts that it is giving the best service possible during those hours; that the congestion of the vehicular travel and the lack of any systematic regulation of this travel, together with other obstructions, make it physically impossible to run a larger number of cars or to attain a higher rate of speed in the movement of cars than at present. It must be admitted that this claim, even if not altogether well founded, is very plausible and is difficult to disprove, whatever our opinions, based on careful observation and reasoning, may be. There can be no question that the present conditions of vehicular travel upon the congested streets of New York make it impossible to secure the maximum service which the street car lines would otherwise be capable of rendering. The contention of the Metropolitan Company has such a foundation of fact that the city authorities cannot well press a demand for very much better service from the railroad company until they themselves shall first have done all that is within their power to remove the obstacles complained of. Viewed in this light, the question of regulating vehicular travel on the congested streets becomes one of great importance. The Committee has, therefore, given a great deal of attention to the matter. It has investigated the conditions that now prevail and has endeavored to devise remedies for the abuses which exist. The conditions at present on streets occupied by surface roads are found to be as follows:

1. Broadway and most of the other congested streets occupied by double-track surface railroads are generally of such restricted width between curbs that two vehicles cannot stand or pass abreast between the curb and the cars without obstructing the passage of the latter.

2. Vehicles in large numbers stand along the curb for various purposes, or for no other reason than to wait, and every moving vehicle on the same side of the street must, in order to pass these standing vehicles, turn out and go around them, thus obstructing the cars. The Committee finds that this practice of permitting vehicles to stand along the curb is a crying abuse and a positive nuisance, which should be vigorously opposed and speedily abated. Were it not so common and so long tolerated it would undoubtedly meet with general protest and opposition. In the downtown district, particularly, trucks and other vehicles seem to be constantly in the habit of standing along the curb when they have nothing else to do. Even when there for a legitimate purpose, such as loading and unloading goods, they occupy far more time than is necessary. It is not unusual to find trucks standing before business houses for from fifteen minutes to half an hour, and even longer, waiting an opportunity to load or unload goods, when the actual operation, after it is begun, may require but five minutes, or even less time.

Cabs deliver passengers and deliberately stand along the curb awaiting their return. In the uptown shopping district long strings of carriages wait before the store, often for half an hour and longer, while the owners are shopping inside. In the meantime every moving vehicle must pass around these standing carriages, and in doing so must encroach upon and obstruct the car tracks. These conditions are not sporadic or occasional. They may be seen on Broadway and other shopping streets at almost any hour during the day and on almost every block. On other business streets a similar abuse exists in still more aggravated forms. On West Broadway, for instance, may be seen great numbers of trucks backed against the curb at right angles to the street, so that not only is there no room for other vehicles to pass on the same side, but they actually extend to and obstruct the cars. Our observation disclosed in some cases as many as eighteen such vehicles backed against the curb on one side in a single block—a number greater than could stand longitudinally along the curb within the block.

The Committee has systematically counted the number of such vehicles standing along the curb line on Broadway and on West Broadway, and the results are shown by diagrams Nos. 26 and 27, which give the number of vehicles found standing along the curbs on each block and at different hours during the day. These diagrams will be readily understood. An inspection of the Broadway diagrams for different periods during the day shows between what streets and at what time this nuisance assumes its greatest proportions. Some idea of its magnitude may be gathered from the fact that the total numbers of vehicles standing along the Broadway curbs on both sides between Battery Place and 34th street, counted from cars on March 4, 1903, were as follows:

Car	leaving	Battery Place	at	9.51	A. M.,	232	vehicles
"	"	34th street	"	10.48	"	273	"
"	"	Battery Place	"	11.32	"	271	"
"	"	"	"	1.33	P. M.,	251	"
"	"	"	"	3.28	"	281	"
"	"	34th street	"	4.19	"	265	"
"	"	Battery Place	"	5.28	"	186	"

The distance from Battery Place to 34th street is about 18,500 feet, from which must be deducted the width of sixty-seven cross streets, so that on one of the trips designated above one vehicle was found standing along the curb for about each fifty feet of the whole curb distance on both sides.

The conditions found on Broadway are intensified on West Broadway, and the Sixth and Eighth avenue cars, which occupy that street, are found to be much more obstructed even than those on Broadway. A glance at the graphic representation of relations of car speeds to traffic congestion shown on Diagram 28 will be found interesting in comparison with the corresponding Broadway diagrams. It will be at once noted how much more densely packed together are the standing vehicles on West Broadway, and how the car speeds are still further reduced. It will be seen by reference to Table No. 1 of our car-speed observations that during the hours when the vehicles are most numerous, say from 12 noon to 5.30 P. M., the average speed of the Sixth and Eighth avenue cars from Battery Place to Canal street is only 4.34 miles per hour, which is literally a footpace, and that the average speed from Canal street to Fourth street is but little better, being but 5.41 miles per hour, the corresponding speeds on Broadway during the same hours, bad as the conditions are there, being 5.5 miles per hour and 5.9 miles per hour, respectively. On this account the running time from Battery Place to 34th street, where the two routes intersect, is about eight minutes longer on the Sixth avenue line than on the Broadway line, although the difference in their lengths is only about 475 feet, representing about one minute at the Broadway speed.

Aggravating still further the West Broadway condition is the very crowded and difficult intersection with Canal street, where the Sixth avenue, Eight avenue and Canal street tracks cross and connect, and where the resulting arrangement of electrical conductors leaves so-called "dead points" or broken contacts which are liable to stall the cars, and frequently do so. The vehicular traffic here is also very great, sometimes amounting to 1,360 vehicles per hour, or 23 per minute, being heavier than at almost any other point covered by our observations. The problem of satisfactorily regulating the vehicular travel, difficult as it must be under the most favorable conditions, is greatly complicated by this nuisance of standing vehicles. This reprehensible practice can only be defended upon the assumption, which seems to be general, that the streets and sidewalks may be occupied as places to carry on other affairs than traveling and transportation—an assumption that has no foundation in justice, nor, we are informed, in law, whenever such occupation interferes with the rights of others.

3. The habit of driving trucks along and upon the rails of street car tracks, when not necessary to avoid vehicles standing along the curb or other obstacles, is very prevalent, and drivers often refuse for long distances to leave the tracks to allow cars to pass.

4. The practice of opening street pavements to construct or repair underground structures during the daytime and leaving the excavations open with barricades around them, sometimes for days, offers a very serious obstruction to travel, compelling vehicles to resort to the car tracks to get around them.

5. The ordinances of the city now allow building material to be unloaded and stored upon the street in front of buildings under construction, and these ordinances are often taken advantage of to very seriously obstruct the street for long periods of time.

6. The enormous travel upon many of the crosstown streets is allowed to engorge the intersections and thus very greatly delay the passage of vehicles and street cars on the main lines of travel.

REMEDIES.

IN attempting to find some means to relieve these causes of obstruction the Committee recognizes the difficulties to be dealt with under the abnormal conditions prevailing on many of the streets of Manhattan. Some of these difficulties are the results directly, and others indirectly, of the enormous concentration of business in the part of the city below 42d street. Any policy or any measures that would impair or seriously interfere with this business, as a whole, are, of course, not to be thought of, but in every city and in every walk of life some concession must be made by individuals for the good of the whole. In Manhattan we have reached a stage of congestion on our principal streets where it becomes absolutely necessary to readjust to some extent the conditions that have prevailed in the past, and the public welfare demands that such readjustment shall be made without delay. The true policy is that which best subserves the welfare of the whole community and avoids, as far as possible, injury to the individual. In the important matter of intercommunication and transportation Manhattan has almost reached a crisis. The difficulties and dangers which citizens encounter in going to and from their daily business need not be described here, and any measures that will help to improve this condition of affairs should meet with the approval of all.

The most serious cause of obstruction and delay—the standing of vehicles along the curbs of congested streets—should be abated by the enforcement of existing ordinances, which seem to be ample for the purpose. If it is found, however, that these ordinances do not fully meet the requirements further legislation should be secured. We are informed through the Legal Committee of your Association that the municipality has ample power to enact and enforce such ordinances. We beg to submit herewith two communications from your Legal Committee relating to this matter, marked Addenda C and D, which are of great interest as outlining the legal status of vehicles, street cars and pedestrians on the streets of the city. If, as the Committee believes, the proper regulation of vehicular travel would permit an increase of over 20 per cent. in the street car service on the crowded streets, such regulation becomes a matter of so much importance to the public as to justify the immediate and stringent enforcement of the ordinances necessary to bring about such result.

After a careful study of the subject in the light of the data collected we have formulated a brief code of rules for the regulation of vehicular travel upon the streets, a copy of which is attached hereto marked Addendum E. These rules were adopted after the Committee had had a number of conferences with Capt. A. R. Piper, Deputy Commissioner of Police, who was at the time engaged upon a similar study of the regulation of street travel, and we are glad to be able to say that these conferences resulted in a substantial agreement of views in reference to the matter contained in these rules. We have not undertaken, it will be observed, to formulate a complete code of "Rules of the Road," our object being to embrace only those features which affect the street car movement on the congested streets.

In the light of the legal opinions we have referred to, it would appear that these rules require very little that is not already covered in the existing laws and ordinances of the city. Through long neglect to enforce them, they appear to have been lost sight of, and it is certain that they are generally disregarded and violated. It would seem that the Police Department has now ample power to enforce compliance with the rules we have presented, without any additional legislation.

The most important provisions of the rules submitted by us are designed to prevent the unnecessary standing of vehicles in the streets, thus obstructing other travel, and to prevent slow-moving vehicles from occupying the street railway tracks, and thus delaying the movement of cars. The requirement that vehicles shall not be allowed to stand upon the congested streets when not actually engaged in loading or unloading freight or passengers is so reasonable that no serious objection should be raised against it. In nearly every part of the city there are numerous cross and side streets that are comparatively uncrowded, and these can and should be made use of by the vehicles that now stop and wait on the congested streets. At the entrance of most of the hotels, theaters and large retail stores employees are stationed who could readily call the carriage of patrons when they are wanted, so that little inconvenience need result.

The most serious and difficult problem is the proper regulation of trucks and delivery wagons that stop to load and unload in front of business houses. The great majority of business houses are so located that they have no entrance except from the front, and to prohibit loading and unloading at their front entrances would be practically to force the occupants out of business. While it is not, therefore, possible to prohibit vehicles from standing on the crowded streets to load and unload, there can be no doubt that the privilege is now very greatly abused and that the resulting obstruction can be greatly diminished. It is certainly fair and reasonable that vehicles should not be allowed to stand upon these streets for any longer than is absolutely necessary to take on or discharge their loads, nor is it unreasonable to require that both teamsters and business houses should adopt means to expedite the operation as much as possible. Observation will convince any one that little effort is now made to do so. On the contrary, many owners and occupants of buildings seem to consider that they practically own the street in front of their premises, and may occupy it for any time or to any extent that suits their pleasure. They should be made to realize that the whole of the street, including the sidewalk, belongs to the public at large, that streets are primarily for the purposes of travel and transportation, and are not places in which to transact other business. Legally, a street cannot be appropriated by any one person for any purpose other than actual travel if such use becomes a nuisance to other individuals or to the public at large. If this rule were kept in mind by business men, and enforced by the municipality, a vast improvement in present conditions would result, without seriously interfering with the proper transaction of business. There are numerous places in the city where a single business house practically monopolizes one-half of the street in front of it. The time is sure to come in Manhattan when it will be necessary to enforce the rights of the public in such cases, and to compel the offending business houses to provide space for loading and unloading their merchandise elsewhere than on the streets.

It is remarkable that while great advances have been made by business men in almost every other direction, the handling of merchandise from street to storehouse is still done as it was centuries ago. Little or no attempt has been made to expedite or economize the process by mechanical appliances. There can be no reasonable doubt of the possibility of employing such appliances for rapidly and cheaply handling parcels, both large and small, between the truck and the store entrance, as well as distributing them throughout the building where required, as is now done in many large manufacturing establishments. For the purpose of loading and unloading the trucks some of the numerous forms of crane, or overhead tramway, can be utilized, and the power to operate them may be either steam, hydraulic, compressed air or electricity, as may be most convenient in each case. It is almost certain that the use of such appliances would result not only in a material saving of time, but in such greater economy of handling as would soon repay the cost of the apparatus. The Committee calls particular attention to this matter in the hope that it may be the means of helping to abate the nuisance of standing vehicles on the streets, without in any way adding to the inconvenience or expense of conducting business.

The occupation of the car tracks, or the driving so near them as to obstruct the free movement of cars, by vehicles moving at a speed lower than that of the cars, should be strictly prohibited, except where the vehicles are forced upon the track by other standing or slower-moving vehicles or by other obstructions. Vehicles on or so near the track as to delay the movement of cars should move out of the way as soon as possible after the driver is signaled to do so by the motorman.

The rules for controlling travel should be strictly enforced by the police, and offenders should be fined or otherwise punished for each offense. Much of the delay to the movement of cars at the present time is due to disregard of these rules, and their enforcement would result in a very considerable improvement in the car service without detriment to the vehicular travel as a whole.

Wherever it is at all possible, the work of cleaning manholes and of constructing or repairing underground works should, on all congested streets, be done during the night. While the cost of the work might be thus sometimes increased, the benefit resulting to the traveling public would fully warrant its requirement.

The ordinances relating to the erection of buildings and the occupation of the street with building material should be so amended as to prohibit the obstruction of congested streets, except under circumstances where it is impossible to avoid it. In the great majority of cases, all building material can be stored in or upon the site of the new building, or on platforms over the sidewalk, without serious expense or inconvenience to the builders. At present, materials to be used in the construction, as well as waste material to be hauled away, are often allowed to remain for several days, and sometimes for weeks, in such positions as to practically cut off the use of nearly one-half the street, to the very serious inconvenience and loss of time to street travel and street cars. Such misuse of the crowded streets should be prohibited.

Broken-down vehicles that are not promptly removed from the streets are often a cause of serious obstruction. Some system should be devised and enforced that will insure their removal as quickly as possible. If a fine were imposed upon owners who allowed broken-down vehicles to remain on the street longer than one hour it would have a salutary effect.

The delays caused by interfering currents of travel at street crossings cannot be wholly avoided, but a proper regulation of vehicles at these street intersections would considerably decrease the present inconvenience and loss of time occasioned thereby. The Police Department has recently taken this matter in hand, and the careful study of conditions, and the vigorous application of systematic regulation which the Deputy Commissioner is applying to this and other needed reforms, promise very material improvement. The matter may safely be left in the hands of the Police Department.

The use of heavy, slow-moving trucks on the present overcrowded streets having car lines upon them should be discouraged, and, as far as practicable, prevented. It many cases the nearby parallel streets could be used by these trucks without inconvenience or loss of time. To encourage the use of such side streets they should be well paved, and, as far as possible, cleared of obstructions to vehicular travel. The unused car tracks on a number of these streets are serious obstructions to vehicular travel, and they should be removed as soon as possible. More will be said upon this point under the head of "Unused Car Tracks."

The congestion now so common at certain street intersections could be reduced, and the movement of both vehicles and cars greatly expedited, if teamsters would avoid these particular intersections, as they might often do, not only without any serious inconvenience, but with positive advantage and actual saving of time, since the delays at these places often extend over several minutes. The intersection of Fulton street with Greenwich street, where the congestion is often very great, resulting in frequent delays both to trucks and cars, is a notable example.

When the city, by the enforcement of the necessary regulations, shall have made possible the reasonably free and unobstructed movement of surface cars upon the congested streets it may then, with entire propriety, demand that the street car service shall closely approach, in efficiency and capacity, the maximum which we have shown to be theoretically possible. It should be practicable under such conditions to move each way on Broadway not less than 220 cars per hour past a given point at an average speed of eight miles per hour during the rush hours, and such part of that number during other hours as will amply accommodate the volume of travel. If cars, having a seating capacity of fifty-two passengers each, were used exclusively, the hourly through capacity of 220 cars would be nearly 11,500 seated passengers, and if, in addition, each car carried an average of twenty standing passengers, over 15,000 through passengers could be carried hourly, without serious overcrowding. This is about double the number considered as through passengers now carried on that line during the rush hours. It must not be expected, however, that this additional capacity would be adequate to the demand for any considerable period in the future. In fact, it may be questioned whether it would be more than sufficient at the present time, since it is probable that a very much larger number of people would even now use the crowded car lines if their capacity permitted.

Some idea of the magnitude and importance of the transportation problem in Manhattan, and the expansion of it that may be reasonably expected in the future, may be gained from a brief review of past experience, and the deductions that seem to logically result therefrom. It is stated on what seems to be good authority that at the present time about one billion passengers are carried yearly by the surface and elevated lines of Greater New York,* and that this is about one-fifth of the total street railroad transportation of the whole United States. This enormous passenger travel is not due merely, or even mainly, to the increase of population alone, but in a large degree to what may, for lack of a better term, be called "the trolley habit." How this has increased may be realized when it is stated that, whereas in 1853 each inhabitant of the City of New York used the public conveyances, on the average, thirteen times a year, each inhabitant of Manhattan Island now uses the elevated and surface roads an average of 415 times a year, or thirty-two times as often. It is the increase of population multiplied by this increase

*See Addendum G, compiled from "Report of the Board of Railroad Commissioners of the State of New York, in the Matter of the Transportation Problem in Greater New York," June 30, 1903.

of the "trolley habit" that gives the enormous figure mentioned above. The significant fact seems to be that this vast increase is mainly the result of increased facilities and better service, and the inference is justified that as we increase the facilities and improve the service the number who will ride will be increased in a far greater ratio. Paradoxical as it may seem, it appears that to a certain extent the more effective are the remedies provided for congestion the more aggravated does the malady become. It is, therefore, difficult to say what amount of remedial measures will be effective. Beyond the more or less temporary remedies we herein recommend, the only permanent relief must be looked for in augmenting the capacity of the present lines, or the construction of new lines, on a scale that has not up to the present time been even seriously suggested. The Committee has not undertaken to deal with these problems, except as they relate to the present and the immediate future.

As a rule, in Manhattan, surface lines should be depended upon to take care of local and short-distance travel only, and long-distance travel must be provided for largely by the construction of additional elevated or underground roads. The proper provision for the short distance travel alone already demands a very great enlargement of the surface car facilities, particularly in a north and south direction, and the requirements will be more imperative in the future. These requirements must be met, not only by diverting travel to some of the present lines that are now less crowded, but by the construction of additional north and south lines upon every available route not now occupied. We believe that something may be done at once toward drawing off from Broadway a part of the travel that now insists upon using the Broadway cars. This is, however, a problem that requires a greater knowledge of the origin and destination of the Broadway travel than we have been able to obtain. There is, we think, reason to believe that if a part of the cars from some of the less crowded lines were carried to terminals on the cross streets at various points along Broadway they would attract a considerable number of passengers, and to that extent relieve the Broadway line. Thus, if a number of the Seventh, Eighth and Ninth avenue cars could be run to terminals abutting on Broadway at Park place or at Vesey street, and at Worth street, they should be well patronized, provided, of course, that passengers could reach their destinations quickly and comfortably. It would seem to be a wise general policy to withdraw the travel from the present congested lines in every practicable way.

DELAYS CAUSED BY THE SUBWAY.

THE delays to travel of all kinds on many of the city streets, caused by the construction of the subway, have been and continue to be very great. To a large extent these are unavoidable, but the Committee believes they could be materially reduced by the enforcement of proper restrictions and remedies by the Rapid Transit Commission. The subway is rapidly approaching completion, however, and this source of trouble and delay will soon disappear. In any future work of this character that may be undertaken better provision should be insisted upon for keeping important streets free for vehicular and street car travel.

CAR SERVICE ON THE LESS CONGESTED STREETS.

IN what has been said we have dealt with the improvement of the service upon the streets and lines of congested travel only. Wherever the service is inadequate or unsatisfactory upon the less crowded lines the remedy is simply to increase the number of cars in service until the needs of the traveling public shall be fully provided for. Since a much higher rate of speed can be safely maintained in such streets, the service can be made satisfactory with a relatively smaller number of cars than are necessary on the more congested streets of the city. This applies particularly to the lines in the Bronx, and if, as alleged, their present capacity is in some cases insufficient, there is no apparent reason why it should be so. The remedy lies wholly within the power of the railroad companies, and involves no engineering or other technical questions. A more or less well-defined line of demarcation separates the suburban from the urban conditions of operation. The former conditions usually permit of fewer stops, higher speeds and larger cars. They involve some additional provisions for the comfort of passengers which will be referred to in the chapter on "Sanitation."

STANDING PASSENGERS IN CARS.

IT has been urged that the practice of allowing passengers to stand in the cars, particularly the open cars, should be prohibited, and that no car should be allowed to take on more passengers than can be seated. It was stated in our preliminary report that "While your Committee recognizes that the standing of passengers between the seats of open cars not only occasions great discomfort, but leads to grave injury to health and morals, we are of the opinion that the practice can only be stopped by prohibitory laws rigidly enforced, and we believe that the enforcement of such laws would be very difficult until such time as the transportation facilities of the city are greatly increased." We see no reason to change this opinion. The question has continued to receive our careful study. In both Philadelphia and Boston we found that standing between the seats of open cars is not permitted, excepting in cases of emergency due to sudden showers, baseball games, etc. Public sentiment disapproves of the practice, and the concentration of travel not having reached the acute stage under usual conditions, it is entirely practicable to prevent it without causing undue hardship and delay. But in the present transportation conditions of Manhattan it is otherwise. Here each rush hour creates an emergency, and public sentiment does not disapprove the practice of standing between the seats when the alternative is standing on the pavement indefinitely. This applies to closed as well as to open cars.

When it is considered that, even under the best conditions that can be hoped for in the near future, the crowded lines cannot possibly supply seating capacity during the rush hours for all the people who must use them at that time, and that, if not allowed to ride standing, a large number must wait, sometimes for hours, in order to get seats in the cars, it will be realized not only how difficult it would be to enforce such a regulation, but also what an unbearable hardship it would impose on a great mass of the people—a hardship compared with which the inconvenience and suffering caused by standing passengers would be insignificant. People do not often overcrowd and stand in the cars from choice, but usually from pressing necessity. Most of them are compelled to reach their destinations at a stated time and could not wait indefinitely, even if by so doing they could avoid the fatigue and discomfort of standing.

If an increased number of cars be provided, before and after the present rush hours, as the Committee recommends, it would be within the ability of the public to reduce the acute degree of overcrowding by avoiding, so far as possible, those hours. This would have the effect of extending the rush hours, but at reduced tension, for it is probable that, though a great number of rush-hour passengers are compelled to travel at the height of the rush, there may be many who could time themselves to avoid it, and who would do so if they were reasonably sure of having seats by going earlier or later.

Whether anything can be done toward preventing the excessive overcrowding by standing passengers, so common now, is an open question. Even if conductors were forbidden to permit passengers to board cars after seats and aisles were as full as reasonable comfort would allow, there would be practical difficulties in the way of enforcement which the Committee believes would prove almost insuperable.

If the recommendations made herein for increasing the carrying capacity of the lines shall be carried out, the necessity for drastic measures in this respect will, we believe, largely disappear.

TRANSFERS.

THE Committee approaches the subject of transfers with some hesitation. It is a subject of much complexity and difficulty in every large city and is the cause of more petty annoyance and of more constant friction between the public and the transportation companies than almost any other single matter. It seems very difficult to organize and administer a transfer system that shall be satisfactory to every one, and at the same time be fair and just to the transportation companies. We believe that, by those best acquainted with the transfer systems in large cities, that in use in New York is considered a very satisfactory one. This view is confirmed by the fact that there is very little criticism by the public of the system as a whole, complaints being generally confined to the details of its administration.

Beyond a statement of the following general principles that should govern in framing and operating a transfer system for the City of New York, the Committee does not feel justified in going at this time. The fact that the question involves the interpretation of existing laws, and legal complications arising therefrom, which are now before the courts, confirms the Committee in this conclusion.

1. A fair and reasonable transfer system in New York may be stated in general terms to be one that will enable a passenger to go for a single fare, and as directly as practicable, from the point where he boards the car to his destination, provided that such destination can be reached by proceeding in the same general direction over lines under one management. This principle should hold good whether a single transfer or one or more re-transfers are necessary.

2. In the application of the principle last stated, the transportation company may fairly claim the right, where two or more routes are nearly equally direct, to designate which shall be used, and to decide whether a choice of transfers shall be given over more than one of the available routes. This implies the right of the transportation company to route transfer passengers over lines which in its judgment will best serve the interests of the public at large, and to refuse transfer privileges over routes that are already overcrowded, provided other direct routes are available.

3. Granting that the transportation company may exercise such option, passengers wishing transfers would need only to state their destination and the operating company would then issue the proper transfers. But the practice of asking transfers over stated lines, rather than to a stated destination, has become so fixed in the minds of the New York public that it would probably be difficult to bring about a change, and there seems to be no necessity for altering the present practice, although the Committee believes that, owing to the peculiar shape of Manhattan Island, it could be simpli-

fied materially. This is, however, a matter in which the transportation companies are more interested than the public.

4. A transfer system should be as simple and as free from complications as it is possible to make it, consistent with practical application. Much of the present trouble and friction relative to transfers is caused by ignorance or misunderstanding of what are the rights of the public, and what the operating company offers. Placards should be placed in the cars, stating plainly and concisely the lines to which transfers will be given and the conditions under which they may be used, and the transfer tickets should have plainly and conspicuously printed upon them the conditions of their use.

5. The employment of two men besides the motorman on each large closed car would, as a rule, allow all transfer tickets to be issued on the car, and thus avoid the expense of transfer agents on the street, as well as save the time of transferred passengers, and contribute to their convenience.

6. It is entirely reasonable that the operating company should have the right to enforce conditions that will prevent the improper or fraudulent use of transfer tickets, even though such conditions occasionally result in some inconvenience to the traveling public.

7. Demands for the excessive extension of transfer privileges may, if complied with, prove a detriment rather than a benefit to the service as a whole. It does not, for instance, seem to be advantageous to throw additional travel upon lines that are already overcrowded in order to extend the transfer privilege to a comparatively few individuals, to the inconvenience of the whole public.

8. The practice, which is very common, of demanding transfers to avoid walking one or two blocks, should be discouraged and prohibited if possible. Such prohibition would result in little inconvenience to the mass of the traveling public, and would afford some relief to the overcrowded lines and save some time in making stops that would not be otherwise required.

SNOW REMOVAL.

THE Committee has investigated the subject of snow removal with a view to the possible improvement of street car movement in winter.

It has been suggested that better progress could be made in clearing the snow from the streets if the tracks and electric power of the street railroad company could be utilized in place of horses and carts to move snow cars.

After conference with the Commissioner of Street Cleaning and with other city officials, it does not seem that much can be expected at present in that direction, because of the practical difficulties of extending the street car tracks to water-side snow dumps. This branch of the subject has received the joint attention of the Department of Street Cleaning, the Department of Docks and Ferries and the Interurban Railway Company without meeting with a practical solution. It seems that it would be necessary for the city to construct tracks and other facilities to make such a system useful, and it is questionable whether even then the investment would prove to be economical.

In removing the snow first from special streets or districts there are vital matters to be considered besides the convenience of street car service, important as that is, which must take precedence in order that the public may not suffer from interruption to its daily food supplies, to its commerce or to its out-of-town ferry and rail communication. The best policy to follow would seem to be to try to secure some relief over the entire business district as soon as possible after each snowstorm, rather than to concentrate the effort on particular lines of street travel, excepting so far as the latter action may facilitate the former. This is the present policy of the Street Cleaning Department, and it is believed by the Committee that with the improved methods of handling the snow problem recently adopted considerably greater expedition in snow removal may be looked for hereafter.

SURFACE CAR SUBWAY AT 34TH STREET.

THE construction of a subway for the Broadway surface cars under 34th street has been proposed and recommended by the State Railroad Commission and by some city officials. The result of our investigations seems to prove that such a subway is unnecessary, since our observations and the representations of the operating company demonstrate that it is possible to operate over the surface crossing a considerably greater number of cars than now pass there, and that the crossing will accommodate all the cars per hour that can be operated on Broadway at other points, as we have previously shown. We are informed that the space this subway would occupy is required for the construction of the Rapid Transit Subway, which it is planned to build under Broadway at this point, and beneath this will be constructed the crosstown Pennsylvania tunnel. The subway is structurally feasible, but, even if it were shown that it would afford material relief, its great cost, the room occupied by its surface entrances and the necessity for openings and stairways near the intersection to accommodate transfer passengers, which openings would occupy surface space that cannot well be spared at this crowded intersection, would, in our opinion, make the construction of such a subway inadvisable.

CROSSTOWN AND HORSE CAR LINES, INCLUDING 86TH STREET EXTENSION.

IN Manhattan there are some thirty crosstown and horse car lines, of which twenty-four are distinctively crosstown lines —that is to say, lines that run mainly across the Island of Manhattan from one side to the other, nine being electric and fifteen horse car lines.

A state of affairs is found on crosstown lines differing from that prevailing on the important longitudinal electric lines, in that on a number of lines there are no apparent rush hours, while on others a period of heavy travel occurs in the middle and not at the close of the day. There are also some lines that do have the usual rush-hour patronage, which continues but for a short time. This appears on downtown lines connecting with ferries.

The electric are improved lines similar in character to the main longitudinal lines, except that some dilapidated and unclean cars are in use, more particularly on the 42d street lines. All do a good business, and, to some extent, answer the demands of travel made upon them, a noticeable improvement having taken place since the agitation for better service was begun. The service is not, however, always adequate. The horse car lines in nearly every case are in bad order, especially as to equipment, and such of them as are not to be changed at once to electric lines should be put into improved condition. The Interurban Company has signified its intention to alter a certain number to electric lines during the present year, and work has already been begun upon some, but such as are to be continued as horse car lines demand immediate attention.

One of the lines not to be changed at present is that through Fulton street, which gains importance from the circumstance that it runs between the Fulton Ferry and the west side ferries at Barclay and Cortlandt streets. The Liberty Street Ferry adjoins the Cortlandt Street Ferry. The patronage seems nearly uniform throughout the day on this line, and it should be maintained in good order. A peculiarly bad feature observed in the cars is the presence of a base-board extending six inches above the floor under the seats, admitting refuse of various kinds and at the same time preventing free access for the proper cleaning of the space. Other objectionable conditions are those referred to for all horse car lines generally under the head of "Sanitation."

It has been suggested that detentions to the running of the cars on Fulton street might be lessened and also the freer use of the street by vehicles be permitted if one track were taken out of Fulton and located on John and Dey streets, but the two streets last mentioned, not being quite in line with each other, a diagonal crossing at Broadway would be necessitated if the suggestion were carried out. Instead of John and Dey streets Ann and Vesey streets have been suggested for one track, to be taken from Fulton street, partly because there are now some tracks in those streets, but Ann street is narrow and runs only three blocks east of Broadway, while Vesey street is crowded and in some parts narrow, so that conditions as to these streets are rather worse for the proposed diversion than John and Dey streets.

For illustrations of the condition of travel on crosstown lines reference is made to the tables and diagrams accompanying this report. The following lines are scheduled for conversion to electric lines:

HORSE CAR LINES TO BE CHANGED FOR ELECTRIC TRACTION DURING THE PRESENT YEAR, AS STATED BY THE INTERURBAN COMPANY IN A COMMUNICATION DATED MARCH 9TH, 1903.

FIRST avenue line. Second avenue line from Tenth street to Grand street; work in progress. Grand and Desbrosses Street Ferry line from Desbrosses Street Ferry, North River, to Grand Street Ferry, East River. Fourteenth street line, from West 14th Street Ferry to Grand Street Ferry via Avenue A; work in progress. Thirty-fourth street crosstown line, now operated by storage battery; work in progress. Eighty-sixth street crosstown line, from 86th street and Eighth avenue to Astoria Ferry, East River; work in progress.

EIGHTY-SIXTH STREET CROSSTOWN LINE.

THIS line is now being changed to an electric one, while a part continues to be operated with horses from Madison avenue through 86th street and First avenue to the Astoria Ferry. The portion discontinued at present is across Central Park through the transverse road, which reaches Eighth avenue at 86th street and Fifth avenue at 85th street, and the remainder of the route from Fifth avenue through 85th street and Madison avenue to 86th street.

As the change will be completed without delay, the line will become an improved electric line as far as it extends. The line is now well patronized. In order that it may be as useful to the public as it should be, an extension ought to be built from its present terminus at Central Park West, or Eighth avenue, to a connection with the existing branch line of the 42d street, St. Nicholas avenue and Manhattanville railroad in 86th street between Amsterdam avenue and Riverside Drive, and that branch should also be altered and operated by electricity, thus making a continuous crosstown line.

The Committee feels the greatest regret that this recommendation involves disturbance of the beauty and repose of the two residential blocks of 86th street between Central Park West and Amsterdam avenue, and appreciates the property-owners' reasons for opposing the extension of the railroad, but can see no other way to give the entire public the convenience and service that a continuous line would afford. It must not be overlooked that the streets of the city are primarily for the use of the public at large, and the interests of local property owners must be made subordinate thereto.

The Committee is of the opinion that the establishment of a continuous crosstown electric line in 86th street, besides being an urgent local necessity, would tend to relieve the congestion on the 59th street lines, and 86th street being 100 feet wide, and, moreover, in direct connection with a transverse or traffic road across Central Park, is the proper location for a crosstown railroad. No other street in its vicinity is as suitable for the purpose.

A tunnel line beneath 86th street has been suggested, but the Committee, after examination, considers that the unusual physical difficulties which would be encountered in crossing the line of the Rapid Transit Subway and the great consequent expense, render the plan impracticable. It has been suggested that the extension of the 86th street crosstown railroad westward from Central Park might be rendered unnecessary and the public be as well served by the establishment of a line running across the Park in the transverse road at 97th street to extend eastwardly and westwardly, upon the supposition that less injury to property would be occasioned thereby and less opposition be met with from property owners, but your Committee does not take that view altogether, because it believes it is necessary to have crosstown lines at both places. We are, therefore, strongly of the opinion that the connection of the existing lines of railroad in West 86th street should be made.

UNUSED CAR TRACKS.

THERE are nearly twenty miles of streets in Manhattan alone that are cumbered with either single or double car tracks that are not now, and in all probability never will be, used. In nearly every case they are retained by the transportation companies owning them, solely for the purpose of preserving the franchises under which they were built. They have absolutely no value as lines of transportation, as they are of antiquated construction, and would have to be entirely rebuilt before they could be utilized for electrical cars. At the same time the material in them is worth a large sum of money as old metal, and the companies owning them would doubtless be glad to remove them and sell this material if their franchises would not be endangered thereby. In addition to their great obstruction to travel tracks are always injurious to street pavements from their tendency to produce ruts by the tracking of vehicle wheels along the rails, and these ruts and the projection of the rails above the surface are the cause of many accidents and breakdowns. The unused car tracks on Amsterdam avenue from 72d street to Manhattan street, a distance of nearly three miles, are in many places conspicuous examples of the evils of unused tracks, and the Committee knows of no reason why they should longer be tolerated. We recommend, therefore, that immediate measures be taken to secure the removal of all these unused tracks and the thorough repair of the pavement where they are taken out. In consideration of the removal of these unused tracks the city should safeguard any franchise rights of the owners which may now depend upon the retention of the tracks in the streets. A list of unused car tracks in Manhattan is attached hereto marked Addendum F, and a map showing their location is submitted with this report.* The fact that some of these tracks occupy parts of routes that may be utilized in the

*Not printed.

future affords no reason why they should not now be removed, since they must eventually be taken up as a necessary preparation for modern construction.

PROPOSED NEW ROUTES.

AMONG the propositions originally referred to our Committee was that of "The practicability of hereafter turning northbound Broadway cars into Sixth avenue at 34th street, and northbound Sixth avenue cars into Broadway at 34th street, thus abolishing the congestion at that point." In our preliminary report we stated that we did not regard such a change as necessary at the present time. We see no reason to alter that conclusion, but the study of the question has led the Committee to consider the general subject of routes, and the possible advantages of changes in present routes, and the establishment of such new routes as seem to be practicable and desirable. The subject is surrounded with difficulties and its intelligent consideration requires an intimate knowledge of the requirements of the public, the trend of travel and the physical conditions that must be met.

Public opinion cannot always be followed, for it is often capricious and after a change of route has been asked and preparations made therefor, it may itself change, and demand material alterations. New routes, in which the initiative is taken by the operating companies generally meet with strong opposition, often from the public at large, but more frequently from interested property owners who refuse to give the necessary consents. For this reason these companies may be more influenced in establishing a route by the desire to secure prompt action and to avoid excessive cost than by considerations of most efficient service to the public. Just now the Rapid Transit Subway is approaching completion, and a number of new subway routes are under discussion, and likely to be built. The new bridges over the East River and means for connecting them with one another are under consideration. It is not now possible to know in what manner and to what extent these new channels of transportation may effect the routes of the surface lines. For these reasons what the Committee has to say upon the subject of routes, particularly those running north and south, should be regarded as suggestions rather than as positive recommendations. The routes named seem, in the light of the information attainable by us, to be both practicable and desirable.

We have already called attention to the desirability of relieving the lower Broadway line by diverting a portion of the travel at convenient side streets. With this in view, it is recommended that a double track line be constructed, starting from Broadway at Park Place, an unusually wide street, running through Park Place and West Broadway to and through Canal street, Varick street, Carmine street, Sixth avenue, Greenwich avenue, Seventh avenue and Broadway to Manhattanville, and beyond, if practicable, to Kingsbridge Road, where it could join with the line already in Kingsbridge Road. The Committee believes that with proper regulation of vehicular travel there would be room on the present West Broadway tracks for the proposed new line. The existing inadequate horse-car line running from Sixth avenue and Fourth street to Desbrosses Street Ferry could then be superseded by an electric branch from this new line. Portions of this route are already electrically equipped, and where not, the railway companies own or control, except north of Manhattanville, so that only privileges for connections and change of motive power will have to be obtained with exception mentioned and unless consents for a double track may be required on Park Place between Church street and West Broadway, where there has heretofore been only a single track.

The Committee considers that New Elm street should be kept free of railroad tracks and reserved for the exclusive use of vehicular travel, and thus help to relieve the pressure upon Broadway.

Much needed relief for Broadway and 23d street, also, would be obtained if the Lexington avenue road should be extended southwardly along Lexington avenue and around Gramercy Park to and through Irving Place, a continuation of Lexington avenue, to and through Fourteenth street, Third avenue and the Bowery to Great Jones street, and through the latter, to Broadway. The present connection of the Lexington avenue cars with Broadway should be retained, to be used to whatever extent may be found necessary. Great Jones is a wide street with moderate travel, and seems to be the most desirable one for bringing the Lexington avenue cars to Broadway. Fourteenth street and Astor Place are already greatly congested and all the other cross streets from 23d street down to Broome street are too narrow for double tracks. If desirable to avoid 14th street, single-track connections between Irving Place and Third avenue through 15th and 16th streets could be substituted.

When the new street between Broome and Spring streets from the Bowery to Elm street is cut through, as an extension of Delancey street, the latter to be widened as an approach to the new Williamsburg Bridge, the car line at present in Spring street could be removed into the new street and its westbound track only be left in narrow Spring street. The eastbound track should turn from West Broadway into Broome street, crossing Broadway and continuing to Marion street, and through the latter to a connection with the double track. This change would give relief to both the railroad and Spring street. By an extension of this route through Broome and Spring streets to a northbound connection on Hudson street an important new route between the upper west side of the city and the new Williamsburg Bridge would be secured.

Park Row should, for many important reasons, be widened from the Bridge Plaza to Chatham Square. If this were done room would be afforded for one or more additional surface lines on that street, and one of the additional lines could follow the route to East Broadway, which is quite wide, and by making use of Market, Division and Allen streets, if widened, reach First avenue; then continuing through First avenue to the bridge over the Harlem River, a long, direct, comparatively straight line would be formed from the Brooklyn Bridge to a connection with the Borough of the Bronx.

From 42d street of 59th street there is at present no crosstown line. One is very greatly needed and the Committee would recommend 50th street for its eastbound track and 51st street for its westbound track. It cannot be built until the streets named are bridged across the tracks of the N. Y. and Harlem Railroad at Park avenue on practicable grades.

North of 59th street, the Central Park interposes an obstacle to crosstown-car communication, there being at the present time only one line traversing it about midway. That is the line known as the 86th street crosstown, now being altered from horse to electric power.

A double-track railroad should be built in the traffic road crossing the Park on the line of 97th street, and this should extend eastwardly through 97th street to Madison avenue; through Madison avenue over existing tracks to 96th street, and through 96th street to the East River. The railroad should also extend westwardly through 97th street to Columbus avenue; then over existing tracks to 96th street and through 96th street to the Hudson River. By connecting the proposed road with the existing line in First avenue and constructing spurs to reach the ferries at 92d and 99th streets additional much-needed means of communication with the Borough of Queens would be provided. As 96th street is one hundred feet wide, and seems destined to become a business street for the greater part of its length, both on the east and west sides, a railroad in it will be an important one on that account, and it would be at once a great public convenience. At the easterly end of the street the large car barn of the First and Second avenue lines is located and near it a large power house. At the westerly end is the only group of wharves on the Hudson River from 79th to 129th streets. Coal depots and yards for receiving building materials are also located there. Ninety-sixth street is the only one giving direct access to the Hudson River between the streets mentioned above.

The rapid commercial development in the vicinity of the foot of 130th street will soon require additional crosstown transportation facilities in that part of the city. An extension of the 135th street railroad westwardly to the Hudson River is therefore advisable. This could be by way of Eighth avenue, 127th, Lawrence, Manhattan and 129th streets.

A crosstown line will be desirable in the future in 145th street from the Harlem River, where a bridge is in course of construction, to the Hudson River.

A direct through Broadway line from South Ferry to Kingsbridge can be established by connecting the tracks of the Broadway lines with those of the 42d street, Saint Nicholas avenue and Manhattanville railroad at the intersection of Broadway and 45th street and extending north of Manhattan street to and through Kingsbridge road.

Extensions of the elevated railroad system being a matter within the purview of the Rapid Transit Commission, this Committee has not thought it proper to introduce the subject in this report, although some excellent additional elevated routes were considered.

SERVICE ON ELEVATED ROADS.

RESULTING from the agitation last winter for improvement in the transportation of passengers in this city, better service than formerly is now given by the elevated railroads, but a still larger measure of efficiency can be reached with the means at command.

Schedules for running trains offered by the Manhattan Railroad Company were finally accepted by the State Railroad Commission, after the investigation it made last winter, and these schedules were put in operation. Under our direction careful observations were made for the purpose of comparing the actual operation of the roads with the schedules, and it was found that with some minor variations the service nearly agrees with that called for by the schedules.

We believe the company can do better and the public has the right to demand that it should. It appears that, during rush hours, trains are operated under as close headway as is consistent with safety, but at other times too great a reduction is made in the length and frequency of trains. It is the right of the public to be provided with seats at all times, when the roads are not taxed beyond their capacity to furnish that accommodation, and also not to be obliged to lose time in long waiting for trains. It is not a good plea that, except in rush hours, trains are crowded for a portion only of their runs, and that, as the trains approach the termini, the emptying of cars, proceeding faster than the filling, finally affords seats for all passengers and therefore justifies a reduction of service. Franchises for city railroads are granted for the accommodation of the citizens and not merely that the companies may profit by them. They are in the nature of a contract. The public convenience is part of the consideration upon which the companies obtain their rights and the contract ought to be enforced. It is not to be admitted that the companies have any right to run only enough trains to be profitable at all times, and trains should run upon the elevated roads with more frequency beyond rush hours. Trains at frequent intervals tend to prevent the accumulation of passengers at stations and give better service than longer trains at long intervals.

During rush hours, on the Sixth avenue line, especially the uptown rush, the running of 58th street trains should be subordinated, more than is now done, to the through or Harlem trains, the travel on the 58th street branch being in small proportion to that on the through line.

A material improvement in the elevated service could be effected by making use of the existing connection between the east and west side lines, near South Ferry, whereby downtown trains from the west side might be run uptown over the east side roads and back again to South Ferry and up on the west side roads and vice versa. In that case additional station accommodations would be required at this point.

Additional trackage for through express service should be provided as follows: The Second avenue line should have a complete third track from Chatham Square to the Harlem River and the Third avenue line from Ninth street to Harlem River for the use of express trains. The Ninth avenue line should have a complete third track from Rector street to 155th street. This will necessarily require the remodeling of the island stations at 116th and 125th streets.

It is not recommended that a third track be built on the Sixth avenue line, because to do so would require the entire remodeling of the structure, and, as the Sixth avenue road joins the Ninth at 53d street, there could be no great gain over the express service the Ninth avenue line could be made to give.

The storage of empty cars on the center tracks adds to the disfigurement and interferes with the use of the streets, taking away light and free circulation of air. It is an imposition on the people and should be prevented. The company should purchase property for this purpose.

STATIONS ON ELEVATED ROADS.

A GREAT many of the stations on the elevated railroads have become inadequate for the proper accommodation of the patrons of the roads, and they should be enlarged, and, in a number of cases, rebuilt. This will in some cases make necessary the acquirement of additional property, but the necessity for greater accommodation justifies the very considerable expense that would be incurred.

Special examples of stations that are entirely inadequate are those at Rector, Cortlandt, Barclay and Warren streets on the Ninth avenue line; at Hanover Square, City Hall, Houston street, Ninth street and 99th street on the Third avenue line, and at 80th and 92d streets on the Second avenue line. The station at the City Hall terminus of the Third avenue line is altogether unequal to the demands upon it. The Committee has not worked out plans for what should be done to improve the station, under existing circumstances, but a slight amelioration may be gained by adding an outside platform for discharging passengers from the trains on the west side of the tracks, as has been done on the east side, and removing the newsstands that block the contracted passageway. The conditions at Hanover Square approximate those at the City Hall station. An outside egress platform on the west side with a stairway at the north end, directly to the sidewalk, should here be provided. If this be done it would be desirable to widen the sidewalk at Hanover Square, for which there is ample room.

Whether or not the connection suggested is made between the east and west side lines, the South Ferry station should be enlarged and improved. At the west side of 58th street on the Sixth avenue line the station now built should either be opened for use or else be removed. If used, an overhead bridge should connect the two stations. All narrow platforms should be widened and all lengthened to suit the increased length of trains. Wherever not fully roofed over, they should be.

The station at 129th street and Third avenue should be so altered and improved as to facilitate the movement of passengers when changing trains. Signs directing the way to the different trains should be put up and employees should be stationed there to give information.

The station at 92d street on second avenue is a temporary structure and is inadequate. It should be replaced by a new and commodious one. The station at 127th street on Second avenue should be removed and a new one built at 125th street. This change is desirable because 127th street is too near the end of the line, and 125th street being a wide and important street, containing an important crosstown surface line, is the proper place for a station to that vicinity. There is room for great improvement in the manner in which the elevated stations are cared for. This will be referred to more at length under "Sanitation."

The stairways leading to and from most of the stations are of entirely too limited capacity, and in many cases are very tortuous and unsatisfactory in other respects. They should, wherever possible, be enlarged and straightened. In the present conditions of overcrowding the stairs for ingress and egress should be separated. The interference of up and down travel on the same stairs is responsible for much of the present discomfort and confusion. The recent experiments of confining upgoing travel to one stairway and downgoing travel to another during the rush hours seem to promise a great improvement. While somewhat confusing until the public becomes familiar with the arrangement, the permanent adoption of the plan at all the crowded stations would result in considerable relief of the stair congestion without any serious inconvenience to the public.

The substitution for stairways of elevators or escalators, particularly at the high stations, would be a very important improvement. Criticism of the few elevators now in use is confined to their inadequacy and unsatisfactory management. If commodious and properly handled, they would be as great an improvement over stairways as they are in buildings. The escalator may be said to be past the experimental stage and its use for ascending travel should prove highly satisfactory.

The following improvements are recommended and the Interborough Rapid Transit Company should be urged to carry them out as promptly as possible:

ELEVATED RAILROAD IMPROVEMENTS RECOMMENDED.

1. The replacement of all old and dilapidated cars by an increased number of new cars, and the complete substitution of electric power for steam should be hastened.

2. Adopt some method to protect the third or contact rail from snow and ice and to prevent accidents to persons.

3. Increase the non-rush-hour service so as to provide adequate accommodation throughout the day.

4. Complete the third tracks on the Second, Third and Ninth avenue lines and provide express service as follows: On Second avenue from Chatham Square to Harlem River, on Third avenue from Ninth street to Harlem River and on Ninth avenue from Rector street to 155th street.

5. Utilize the connection between the east and west side lines at South Ferry to operate trains from one side to the other reciprocally. This may be done by simply opening the Battery loop and extending the stations.

6. Provide additional storage yards so as to avoid the use of middle tracks for storage purposes.

7. Provide adequate and comfortable stations and waiting-rooms at all points where the existing accommodations are inadequate, acquiring sufficient additional property if necessary. Construct additional discharging platforms and stairways at City Hall and Hanover Square stations and additional and more commodious stairways wherever needed.

8. Improve the arrangement at 129th street and Third avenue, so as to facilitate the movement of passengers in changing trains.

9. Remove the present station at 92d street on Second avenue and build a new station at that point. Remove the station at 127th street on Second avenue and build a new station at 125th street.

10. Restore to use or else remove the station on the west side of Sixth avenue at 58th street. If retained, provide an overhead bridge communication to the station on the east side.

11. Separate the upgoing and downgoing stairways at all crowded stations. The substitution of elevators or escalators at all the high stations is recommended. Improve and regulate the elevator service at the 116th street station on Eighth avenue. The entrances and the platform leading from the elevators to the stairs beneath should be widened pending some more permanent improvement.

12. Roof over all platforms for their full length.

SANITATION.

THE investigations made by the Committee in reference to the need of better sanitary conditions on passenger transportation lines in the city show that there is much room for improvement, both in the arrangements of surface and elevated cars and elevated railroad stations, and in the methods of caring for them. It is the opinion of the Committee that part of the duty of initiating the improvements rests upon the transportation companies, part upon the city government and part upon the public. The companies should provide better facilities for warming, ventilation and cleaning and give closer attention to regulating these matters. The officials of the city should see that the sanitary ordinances are enforced. It is the right of the public to insist upon proper conditions and its duty to observe the regulations relating thereto.

Up to the present time the Department of Health appears not to have received the amount of assistance from the Department of Police which the sanitary needs of the city require. There should be a larger detail of police for sanitary duty, who should be thoroughly instructed in their duties. Among the unsanitary conditions prevalent in the city one, which may serve as an example, is the sand pile used in lieu of spittoons on the elevated railroads. It is impossible to conceive of a greater menace to the public health. The sand which is thrown upon the platforms invites and receives infectious material from the lungs and throats of sick persons to an extent which is as dangerous to health as it is disgusting to sight. The expectorated material becomes dried in the sand and is distributed by winds and by travel of passengers through the cars and stations and through the atmosphere of the street below. The sand pile nuisance is the most unsanitary condition which calls for attention in connection with the transportation problem in New York City.

Using car seats as foot-rests and allowing children to stand upon seats with soiled or dirty shoes is very objectionable and should be prohibited by a rule or regulation of the transportation companies. Carrying burning tobacco on the cars is forbidden, but the rule is seldom enforced.

The question of allowing passengers to stand between the seats of open cars has been given very careful thought. In the interest of health, comfort, decency and morality it should not be permitted. The Committee does not, however, believe it practicable to prevent it under present conditions of congestion, as has been explained at length in another part of this report. The overcrowding of cars besides causing great inconvenience and discomfort is exceedingly unsanitary.

SANITARY RECOMMENDATIONS.

FOR dealing with the dangerous conditions above described the Committee makes the following recommendations, which are based upon a mass of facts collected and observations made under its direction.

The rearrangement or reconstruction of a number of the elevated railroad stations is desirable in order that some unsanitary features which now exist may be eliminated. An example of the better type of station now in service in the city is the 18th street station on the Sixth avenue line, and this type of station is especially perferred, as being more easily cleaned, warmed and ventilated.

It is desirable that the platforms be roofed over for their whole length.

Proper attention to the ventilation of the stations is needed. Better ventilation may be secured by the careful regulation of transoms, windows and ventilating devices, whereby the air may be continually refreshed and unpleasant odors avoided.

At present the toilet-rooms of the stations are not always clean. In many cases the plumbing is out of order, the closets overflowing and the waste pipes stopped. It is unnecessary to point out the objectionable nature of these unsanitary conditions.

The stations should be warmed in winter to a temperature between 55 and 65 degrees Fahrenheit.

Better care of the stations is needed. At present proper attention is lacking in this respect, and the waiting-rooms, closets and platforms are not uniformly maintained in a cleanly or orderly condition. Dirty pails should not be left standing in the waiting-rooms or passageways; dust and dirt from the platforms and stairs should not be swept into the streets. It should be a rule that no dust is to be raised in cleaning. The methods of cleaning which are suitable for the stations, including platforms and stairways, require the use of mops, soft hand brooms and cloths. Stiff brooms should not be used. Sand should never be used anywhere on the station floors, platforms or stairways unless to guard against slipperiness.

A provision of the Sanitary Code requires that the elevated railroad company should provide cuspidors for use on the elevated platforms. The number is now insufficient, and those which are in use are too small. It is desirable that cuspidors of ample size and decent appearance should be provided. Observation shows that where these conveniences are properly supplied they are generally used by the public.

It is desirable that the cars of the elevated railroad should be improved with respect to ventilation and warming. An advantageous way for improving the air of the cars without drafts is to provide for the introduction of air at a greater number of points. The ventilation is more satisfactory on the elevated roads than on the surface cars, but it is by no means all that could be desired. More air should be admitted and a part of the air should be carried over the heaters, for the double purpose of warming the fresh air and reducing the intensity and concentration of the heat now given off under the seats. There are various means of accomplishing this end. The experiments of the Pennsylvania Railroad Company and a popular device now being employed on the windows of large office buildings furnish sufficient illustrations of the practicability of this method.

The temperature of the cars should be more carefully regulated and placed under the control of the conductor of the train, who is best able to judge of the need of adjusting the warming and ventilating apparatus, and he should be properly instructed and held responsible. Under the present circumstances the cars are allowed to become sometimes too warm and frequently too cold. The temperature should not be permitted to fall below 55 degrees nor in cold weather to rise above 65 degrees Fahrenheit.

The use of cocoa mats on the floors of cars has frequently been condemned. They serve as collecting and propagating places for bacteria, and it is impossible to clean them. Attempts to disinfect such articles, except in large and expensive sterilizers, are useless.

Other objectionable floor coverings include slats or strips of wood permanently fixed to the floor and which cannot be cleaned without the raising of dust, which is objectionable. The floors of the cars should be covered with a smooth, non-porous material, or a grating of non-absorbent material which may be easily removed for cleaning.

As far as practicable, all corners and moldings which can collect dust should be eliminated in the construction of new cars. The parts of the cars which are not exposed, such as the spaces in the bottom and backs of seats, should be readily accessible for cleaning. Careful observations of the dust pockets to which this recommendation refers have shown that they not only collect dirt and waste from the floor, but are gathering places for germs of disease.

It is recommended that the cars be cleaned more thoroughly. More attention should be given to systematizing this matter, so as to avoid such objectionable practices as the morning running of cars which have been used all night.

The catch-pans, which are located under the tracks to catch drippings, should be regularly and systematically inspected and kept clean. Under the present circumstances, the catch-pans serve not only to collect drippings, but also as reservoirs of filth.

If the spitting ordinance cannot be construed so as to prevent passengers and elevated train men from expectorating into the streets and onto the tracks, it would be desirable to so modify it that this objectionable practice may be forbidden.

The transportation companies should adopt and enforce a rule to prohibit the placing of feet upon the car seats. The rule against carrying burning tobacco into closed cars, waiting-rooms, etc., should be rigidly enforced.

In order to improve the ventilation of the cars of the surface roads, the same recommendation is made which was offered in connection with the cars of the elevated road. The air should be introduced at a greater number of points, and some of it should be permitted to pass over the electric heaters under the seats. Under the present conditions there is not enough fresh air in the cars; there is no systematic ventilation; the employees of the road do not appear to be instructed to follow any rules with respect to ventilation; the temperature is not maintained within proper limits. The Committee believes that while there are difficulties in the way of securing satisfactory ventilation, and that perfect results cannot be secured when cars are overcrowded, a very considerable improvement could be secured by systematizing the ventilation and warming. As an aid to ventilation, it is recommended that the transoms in the monitor tops be protected on the outside by guards to prevent the entrance of sudden gusts of wind. The transoms should also be connected and operated by a lever placed at the ends of the car and controlled by the conductor.

The floors should be covered with non-absorbent material or removable gratings, as recommended for elevated railroad cars.

The spaces under the seats of horse cars, where now closed, should be opened, so that the dirt and refuse often thrown into the window casings behind the seats may be seen and promptly removed.

For the convenience of readers it is desirable that, on electric cars, lights be placed on the sides of the cars.

The rods and straps which run the length of the cars and are used for registering fares and signaling, should be placed nearer the center. In their present position the rods and straps oblige the conductor, in reaching for them, to come into closer contact with the passengers than is either agreeable or conducive to health.

Many horse cars are insufficiently lighted, and should be provided with additional lamps kept in good order.

The floors and seat coverings of cars should be kept clean. Many of the surface cars at present have fixed slats on the floors and some have cocoa mats.

The 34th street crosstown line has been a public nuisance ever since storage batteries were first used upon it, and experience has shown that no method of disposing of the noxious gases given off by the batteries has been effective. We are, therefore, gratified to observe that it is now being converted into an underground trolley line.

Wherever the public is subjected to exposure while waiting to take cars at termini or when transferring from one car line to another on the surface roads, suitable shelter should be provided. If physical conditions at those points are such that shelter cannot be provided in close proximity to the tracks, it should be provided in nearby buildings. Islands of safety should be provided where necessary.

CONCLUSION.

IN concluding this report and making the above recommendations, your Committee do not feel that they have by any means exhausted the subject. Indeed, they have only been able to touch upon the salient features of a most intricate and comparatively unstudied branch of engineering. It is not considered that the action of winds and currents has been fully mastered, although they have received careful scientific study for centuries. The study of the tides of humanity, their ebb and flow under urban conditions, and with enormous and complicated transportation facilities, has only just begun to be possible, and their modes of action have not yet been crystallized into formulæ whereby results can be readily foretold. We have especially recognized this in attempting to deal with the street railway service, whose shortcomings have been cited not in a spirit of harsh criticism, but with object of pointing out the surrounding difficulties and the desire to aid in the great task of ameliorating them. To accomplish real and lasting benefit will call for the intelligent and hearty cooperation of the City and State authorities, the railroad companies and the public. If through our investigation we have contributed in any material measure to the solution of these complex and difficult problems of human dynamics, and have shed any light upon the needs and possible relief of the traveling public in this imperial city, we shall feel that the result has fully justified all the labor that has been bestowed upon it.

Trusting that our report will meet your expectations and assist you in your tireless efforts for the betterment of commercial conditions in this great metropolis, it is herewith respectfully submitted.

S. Whinery, Chairman;
H. W. Brinckerhoff,
Foster Crowell,
C. H. Myers,
George A. Soper,
F. F. Woodward, Secretary.

New York, July 15th, 1903.

ADDENDA.

ADDENDA.

A: Diagrams and Tables of Observations on Street Transportation.

B: Double-Deck Cars in European Cities.

C: As to Street Obstructions.

D: As to Laws Governing Use of Streets.

E: Rules for the Regulation of Vehicular and Surface-Car Travel Upon the Streets of New York, and to Prevent Obstructions to Such Travel.

F: List of Unused Surface Track in Manhattan.

G: Tabular Statement of Urban Railway Transportation in Greater New York.

ADDENDUM A.

DIAGRAMS AND TABLES OF OBSERVATIONS ON STREET TRANSPORTATION.

MADE UNDER DIRECTION OF THE COMMITTEE ON ENGINEERING AND SANITATION OF THE MERCHANTS' ASSOCIATION OF NEW YORK, 1903.

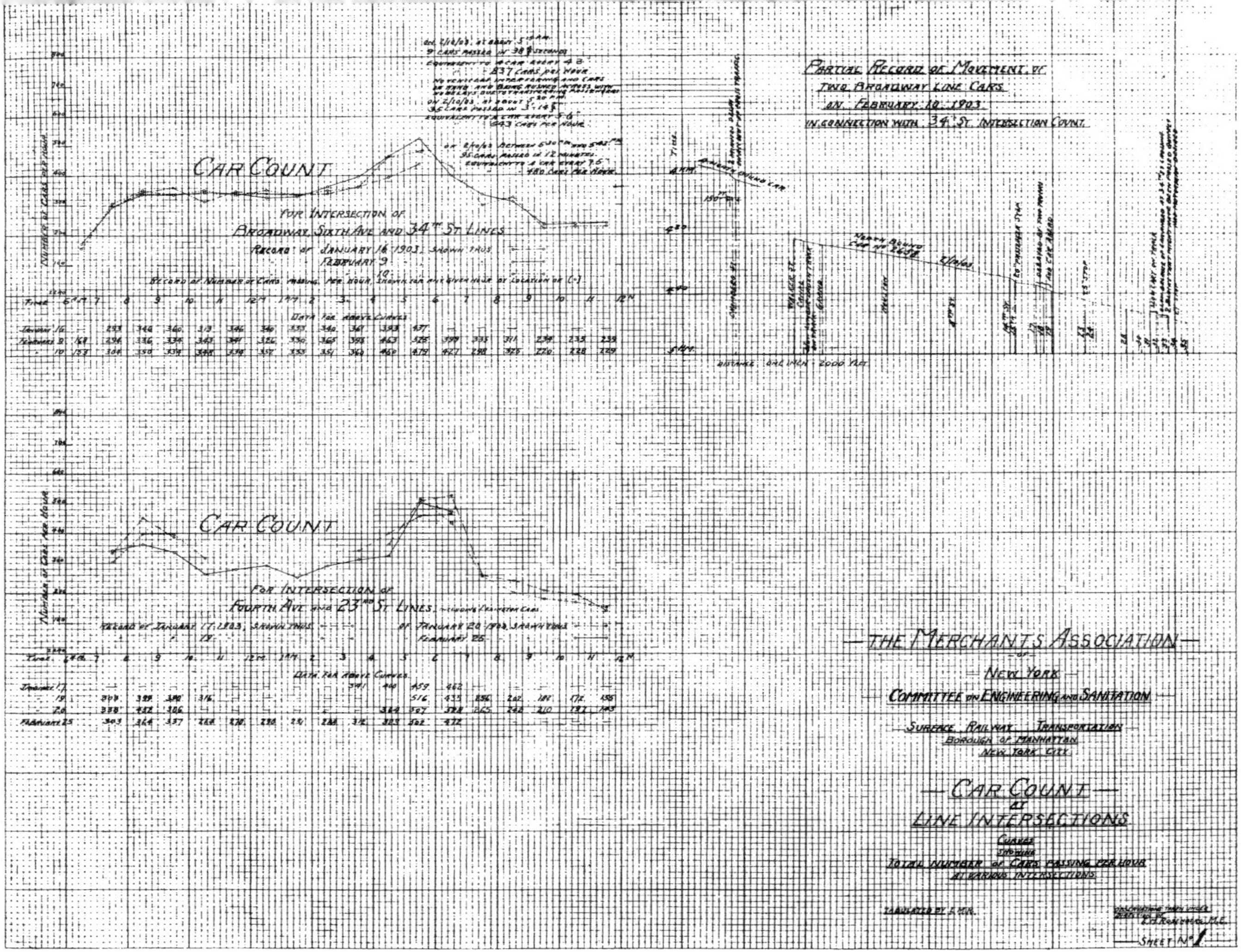

CAR COUNT

FOR INTERSECTION OF BROADWAY, SIXTH AVE AND 34TH ST. LINES

RECORD OF JANUARY 16, 1903, SHOWN THUS
FEBRUARY 9
10

On 2/10/03, at about 5 P.M.
9 cars passed in 38 seconds
Equivalent to a car every 4.3"
837 cars per hour

On 2/10/03, at about 5 P.M.
35 cars passed in 3' 14"
Equivalent to a car every 5.6"
643 cars per hour

On 2/10/03 between 5 P.M. and 5 P.M.
95 cars passed in 12 minutes.
Equivalent to a car every 7.6"
480 cars per hour

RECORD OF NUMBER OF CARS PASSING PER HOUR, SHOWN FOR ANY GIVEN HOUR AT LOCATION OF (•)

DATA FOR ABOVE CURVES

Time	6 A.M.–7	7–8	8–9	9–10	10–11	11–12 M.	12 M.–1 P.M.	1–2	2–3	3–4	4–5	5–6	6–7	7–8	8–9	9–10	10–11	11–12 M.
January 16	—	293	346	360	313	346	340	333	340	361	393	437	—	—	—	—	—	—
February 9	168	296	336	334	343	341	326	330	365	393	463	525	399	333	311	239	235	239
" 10	153	304	350	334	348	334	357	333	351	360	460	479	427	288	325	270	228	229

CAR COUNT

FOR INTERSECTION OF FOURTH AVE AND 23RD ST. LINES

RECORD OF JANUARY 17, 1903, SHOWN THUS
19
OF JANUARY 20, 1903, SHOWN THUS
FEBRUARY 25

DATA FOR ABOVE CURVES

Time	6 A.M.–7	7–8	8–9	9–10	10–11	11–12 M.	12 M.–1 P.M.	1–2	2–3	3–4	4–5	5–6	6–7	7–8	8–9	9–10	10–11	11–12 M.
January 17										341	440	459	462					
" 19		307	399	380	316							516	433	256	202	187	172	155
" 20		338	452	306							364	507	378	265	242	210	191	143
February 25		303	364	337	268	270	290	251	288	312	383	502	472					

PARTIAL RECORD OF MOVEMENT OF TWO BROADWAY LINE CARS ON FEBRUARY 10, 1903 IN CONNECTION WITH 34TH ST. INTERSECTION COUNT.

TIME.

North bound car

North bound car No. 2658

DISTANCE: ONE INCH = 2000 FEET

— THE MERCHANTS' ASSOCIATION —
OF
NEW YORK
COMMITTEE ON ENGINEERING AND SANITATION
SURFACE RAILWAY TRANSPORTATION
BOROUGH OF MANHATTAN
NEW YORK CITY

— CAR COUNT —
AT
LINE INTERSECTIONS

CURVES
SHOWING
TOTAL NUMBER OF CARS PASSING PER HOUR
AT VARIOUS INTERSECTIONS

SHEET No. 1

DIAGRAM 1.

North Bound Cars on Broadway Line at 34th St. Intersection
South Bound Cars on Broadway Line at 34th St. Intersection
North Bound Cars on Sixth Ave. at 34th St. Intersection
South Bound Cars on Sixth Ave. at 34th St. Intersection
The Merchants Association of New York
Committee on Engineering and Sanitation
Surface Railway Transportation
Borough of Manhattan
New York City
Car Count at Line Intersections
Sheet No. 2

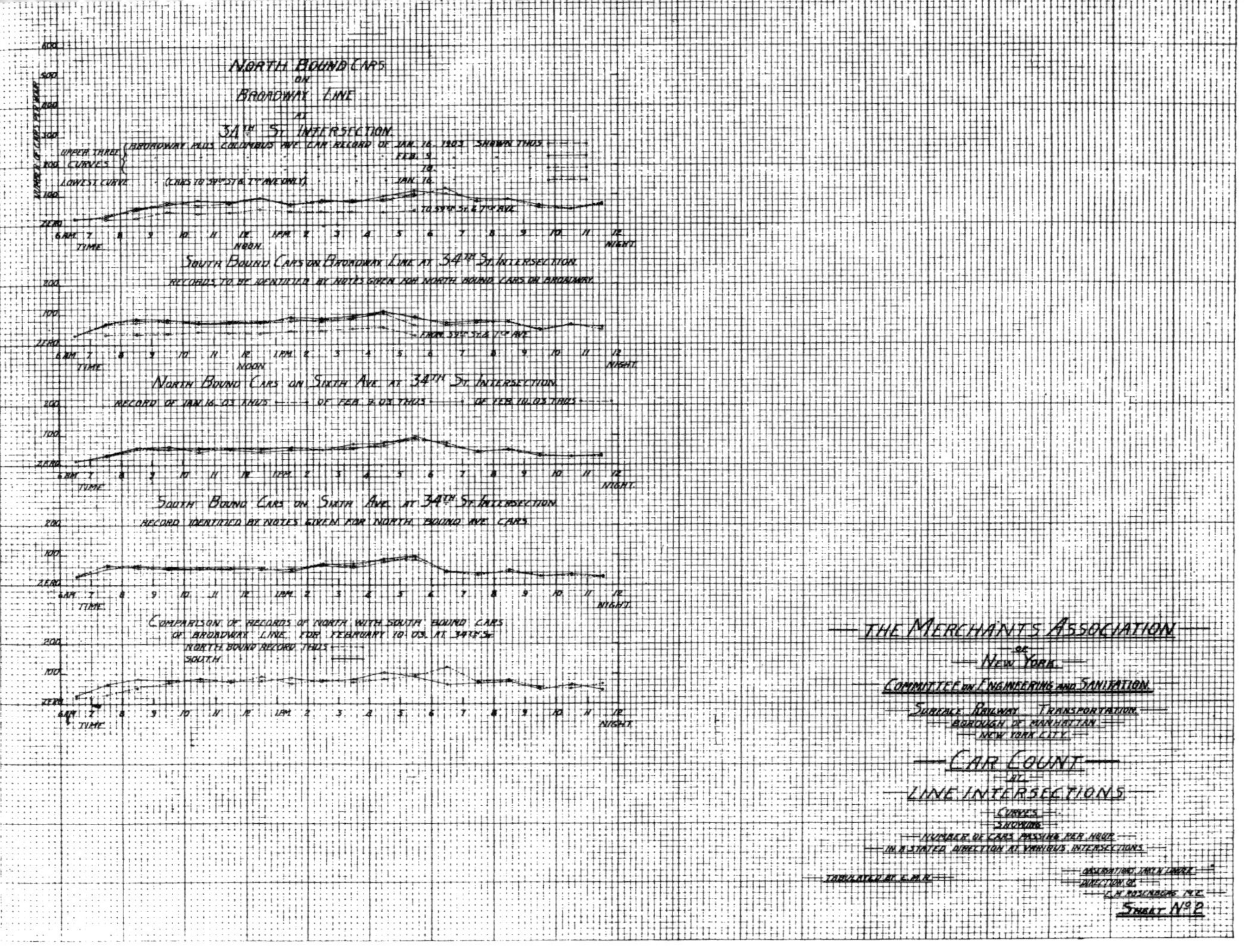

DIAGRAM 2.

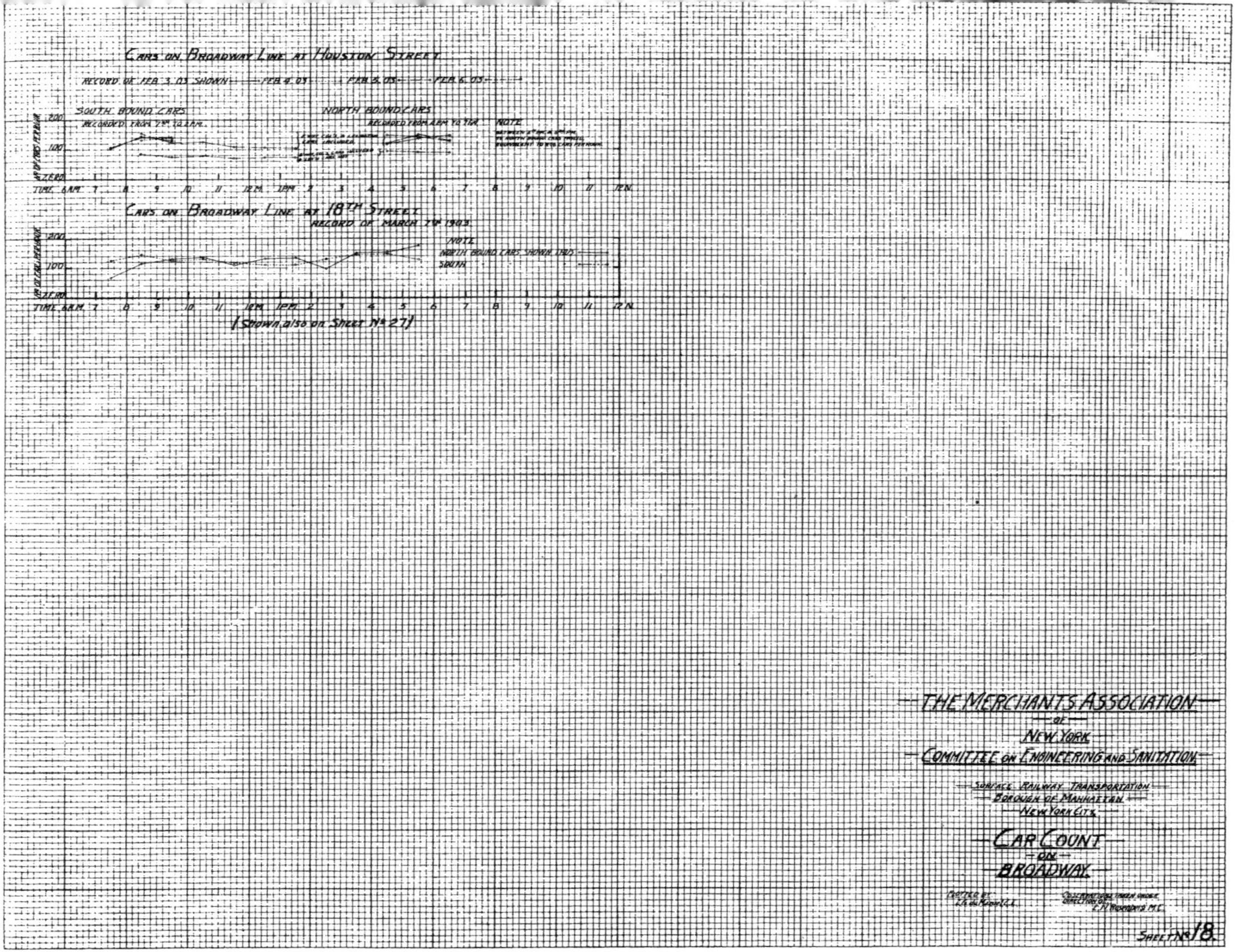

CARS ON BROADWAY LINE AT HOUSTON STREET

RECORD OF FEB. 3. 03 SHOWN —— FEB. 4. 03 —— FEB. 5. 03 —— FEB. 6. 03 ——

SOUTH BOUND CARS — RECORDED FROM 7 A.M. TO 12 A.M.

NORTH BOUND CARS — RECORDED FROM 1 P.M. TO 7 P.M.

NOTE

TIME 6 A.M. 7 8 9 10 11 12 M. 1 P.M. 2 3 4 5 6 7 8 9 10 11 12 N.

CARS ON BROADWAY LINE AT 18TH STREET

RECORD OF MARCH 7th 1903.

NOTE

NORTH BOUND CARS SHOWN THUS ——

SOUTH " " " " ——

TIME 6 A.M. 7 8 9 10 11 12 M. 1 P.M. 2 3 4 5 6 7 8 9 10 11 12 N.

(Shown also on Sheet No. 27)

THE MERCHANTS ASSOCIATION

OF

NEW YORK

COMMITTEE ON ENGINEERING AND SANITATION

SURFACE RAILWAY TRANSPORTATION

BOROUGH OF MANHATTAN

NEW YORK CITY

CAR COUNT

ON

BROADWAY

SHEET No. 18

DIAGRAM 3.

COMPARISON OF AVERAGES OF RECORDS OF NORTH BOUND CARS WITH AVERAGES OF RECORDS OF SOUTH BOUND CARS OF BROADWAY LINE AT 34TH ST.

NORTH BOUND CARS SHOWN THUS
SOUTH BOUND CARS SHOWN THUS

RECORDS INCLUDED

COMPARISON OF RECORD OF NORTH BOUND CARS WITH RECORD OF SOUTH BOUND CARS ON BROADWAY AT 18TH STREET

MARCH 7TH 1903

NORTH BOUND THUS
SOUTH BOUND THUS

COMPARISON OF RECORD OF NORTH BOUND CARS WITH RECORD OF SOUTH BOUND CARS ON BROADWAY LINE AT FULTON ST.

MARCH 10TH 1903

NOTE: BROADWAY, COLUMBUS AND LEXINGTON CARS INCLUDED

NORTH BOUND THUS
SOUTH BOUND THUS

ON BROADWAY AT CHAMBERS

MARCH 6TH 1903

NORTH BOUND THUS
SOUTH BOUND THUS

ON BROADWAY AT CANAL

MARCH 13TH 1903

NORTH BOUND THUS
SOUTH BOUND THUS

NUMBER OF CARS PER HOUR

TIME 6 A.M. 7 8 9 10 11 12 M. 1 P.M. 2 3 4 5 6 7 8 9 10 11 12 N.

THE MERCHANTS ASSOCIATION OF NEW YORK

COMMITTEE ON ENGINEERING AND SANITATION

SUITABLE RAILWAY TRANSPORTATION
BOROUGH OF MANHATTAN
NEW YORK CITY

COMPARISON OF CAR COUNTS

SHEET NO. 27

DIAGRAM 4.

SPEED IN MILES PER HOUR OF CERTAIN CARS ON BROADWAY.

Date 1903	Car Number	North Bound from Battery Pl. at: Hr.	Min.	Sec.	South Bound from 59th St. at: Hr.	Min.	Sec.	Between Battery Place and Canal St. 1.1945 miles: Time in seconds	Miles per hour	Between Canal St. and 14th St. 1.2714 miles: Time in seconds	Miles per hour	Between 14th St. and 23rd St. 0.4697 miles: Time in seconds	Miles per hour	Between 23rd St. and 34th St. 0.5701 miles: Time in seconds	Miles per hour	Between 34th St. and 42nd St. 0.4148 miles: Time in seconds	Miles per hour	Between 42nd St. and 59th St. 0.8522 miles: Time in seconds	Miles per hour	Between Battery Pl. and 59th St. 4.7727 miles: Time in seconds	Miles per hour	Stops for passengers: Number for trip	Duration of stops for trip in seconds	Stops for other causes: Number for trip	Duration of stops for trip in seconds	Stops for all causes: Number for trip	Duration of stops for trip in seconds
Jan. 19	150	7	07	00 A.M.				405	10.61	503	8.81	187	9.03	240	8.53	165	9.05	360	8.54	1860	9.23						
" "	166	7	27	30				438	9.82	577	7.94	217	7.77	296	6.93	182	8.21	398	7.71	2110	8.13					14	
" "	150	8	21	00				578	7.43	652	7.02	255	6.62	255	8.04	188	7.94	442	6.95	2370	7.25						
" "	8	8	56	10				608	7.07	732	6.26	260	6.50	267	7.68	198	7.53	355	8.64	2420	7.10					44	
" "	2673	9	54	00				810	5.31	1080	4.24	255	6.62	330	6.22	135	11.75	405	7.59	3015	5.70						
" "	176	10	39	45				687	6.25	753	6.09	290	5.82	315	6.52	205	7.27	6.15	4.99	2865	6.00					47	
" "	2673	11	33	30				810	5.31	660	6.94	300	5.63	330	6.22	225	6.63	420	7.31	2925	5.86						
" "	35	12	59	15 P.M.				643	6.68	572	8.02	245	6.89	315	6.52	223	6.70	392	7.88	2390	7.19					33	
" "	38	1	59	00				750	5.74	705	6.50	315	5.36	353	5.76	232	6.43	525	5.85	2680	5.95						
" "	21	2	33	25				890	4.84	652	7.02	317	5.33	380	5.40	201	7.44	447	6.88	2887	5.94					60	
" "	17	3	39	00				900	4.78	735	6.23	285	5.92	330	6.22	315	4.74	435	7.05	3000	5.72						
" "	161	4	27	20				686	6.25	910	5.04	310	5.45	444	4.63	285	5.24	508	6.05	3023	5.69					54	
" "	17	5	24	30				1020	4.21	960	4.67	375	4.51	345	5.94	240	6.22	450	6.82	3390	5.07						
" "	147	6	15	30				538	8.00	677	6.75	245	6.89	340	6.03	220	6.79	410	7.48	2430	7.06					27	
" "	109	9	4	30				428	10.01	461	9.94	206	8.18	298	6.93	183	8.16	357	8.62	1933	8.89					43	
" "	60				6	49	48 A.M.	430	10.00	475	9.65	220	7.68	213	9.65	162	9.22	292	10.54	1782	9.64					9	
" "	150				7	38	15	540	7.95	686	6.69	300	5.63	214	9.61	255	5.86	330	9.32	2325	7.38						
" "	8				8	09	37	685	6.26	660	6.94	288	5.86	248	8.23	298	5.01	333	9.22	2388	7.18					41	
" "	2673				9	01	00	1080	3.98	690	6.64	255	6.62	315	6.52	188	7.94	352	8.74	2880	5.75						
" "	2638				9	45	50	752	5.71	723	6.33	263	6.42	266	7.72	179	8.34	377	8.15	2560	6.70					48	
" "	2673				10	44	30	825	5.21	645	7.11	300	5.63	360	5.70	202	7.41	338	9.09	2670	6.42						
" "	176				11	28	45	677	6.35	608	7.41	320	5.28	300	6.85	230	6.50	415	7.41	2550	6.72					52	
" "	38				1	11	00 P.M.	780	5.52	660	6.94	210	8.05	330	6.22	225	6.64	393	7.81	2595	6.60						
" "	2672				1	39	50	736	5.83	646	7.10	280	6.03	298	6.88	218	6.85	484	7.09	2612	6.59					64	
" "	17				2	49	00	780	5.52	690	6.64	345	4.90	360	5.70	195	7.65	360	8.55	2700	6.36						
" "	51				3	26	10	935	4.60	755	6.07	313	5.40	372	5.51	285	5.23	545	5.64	3205	5.36					49	
" "	17				4	29	30	1135	3.79	545	8.41	270	6.26	330	6.22	225	6.64	465	6.60	3030	5.67						
" "	2638				5	25	58	836	5.13	706	6.50	286	5.92	300	6.85	232	6.44	402	7.64	2762	6.21					62	
" "	17				6	22	30	510	8.43	510	8.98	210	8.05	270	7.60	180	8.29	435	7.06	2115	8.12						
" "	109				8	26	45	428	10.03	437	10.48	240	7.03	253	8.10	222	6.73	375	8.19	1955	8.80					30	
" 20	63	7	41	25 A.M.				455	9.45	685	6.69	225	7.51	270	7.60	185	8.08	325	9.45	2145	8.01					56	
" "	127	7	50	00				480	8.96	630	7.27	270	6.26	270	7.60	180	8.29	450	6.82	2280	7.52						
" "	33	9	12	35				722	5.95	748	6.12	247	6.85	298	6.88	188	7.94	387	7.94	2590	6.63					36	
" "	74	9	14	45				720	5.97	780	5.87	263	6.42	262	7.82	195	7.65	405	7.58	2625	6.54						
" "	118							—		660	6.94	338	4.99	262	7.82	225	6.63	398	7.71	—							
" "	37	11	00	15				1021	4.22	584	7.85	270	6.26	326	6.29	244	6.12	406	7.55	2851	6.02					50	
"	118	12	21	30 P.M.				705	6.10	690	6.64	233	7.25	322	6.37	225	6.63	405	7.58	2580	6.65						
" "	2609	1	11	20				601	7.13	736	6.22	403	4.18	340	6.03	249	6.00	289	10.31	2738	6.28					58	
" "	16	2	52	20				813	5.28	739	6.19	308	5.47	330	6.22	260	5.75	422	7.28	2872	5.98					51	
" "	118	2	54	00				855	5.02	720	6.36	328	5.23	337	6.66	240	6.22	450	6.82	2925	5.73						
" "	153	4	41	15				803	5.36	697	6.57	360	4.70	405	5.06	225	6.63	525	5.85	3015	5.69						
" "	103	5	9	40				888	4.45	887	5.17	310	5.44	385	5.33	237	6.30	598	5.14	3305	5.19					63	
" "	5	6	20	00				563	7.63	667	6.86	270	5.94	315	6.52	195	7.65	330	9.32	2340	7.34						

Continued on Sheet Nº 3^b.

THE MERCHANTS ASSOCIATION
OF
NEW YORK.
COMMITTEE ON ENGINEERING AND SANITATION.

SURFACE RAILWAY TRANSPORTATION
BOROUGH OF MANHATTAN
NEW YORK CITY

TRIP SPEEDS AND STOPS
ON
BROADWAY LINE.

TABULATED BY C.M.B.

SHEET Nº 3^b

TABLE 5.

SPEED IN-MILES PER HOUR OF CERTAIN CARS ON BROADWAY.

DATE 1903	CAR NUMBER	NORTH BOUND FROM BATTERY PL. AT HR.	MIN.	SEC.	SOUTH BOUND FROM 59TH ST. AT HR.	MIN.	SEC.	BETWEEN BATTERY PLACE AND CANAL ST. 1.1945 MILES TIME IN SECONDS	MILES PER HOUR	BETWEEN CANAL ST. AND 14TH ST. 1.2714 MILES TIME IN SECONDS	MILES PER HOUR	BETWEEN 14TH ST. AND 23RD ST. 0.4697 MILES TIME IN SECONDS	MILES PER HOUR	BETWEEN 23RD ST. AND 34TH ST. 0.5701 MILES TIME IN SECONDS	MILES PER HOUR	BETWEEN 34TH ST. AND 42ND ST. 0.4148 MILES TIME IN SECONDS	MILES PER HOUR	BETWEEN 42ND ST. AND 59TH ST. 0.8528 MILES TIME IN SECONDS	MILES PER HOUR	BETWEEN BATTERY PL. AND 59TH ST. 4.7727 MILES TIME IN SECONDS	MILES PER HOUR	STOPS. FOR PASSENGERS NUMBER FOR TRIP	DURATION OF STOPS FOR TRIP IN SECONDS	FOR OTHER CAUSES NUMBER FOR TRIP	DURATION OF STOPS FOR TRIP IN SECONDS	FOR ALL CAUSES NUMBER FOR TRIP	DURATION OF STOPS FOR TRIP IN SECONDS
JAN. 20	61				7	06	47	467	9.22	482	9.51	182	9.33	226	9.08	180	8.29	273	11.25	1810	9.49					59	
" "	118				8	28	35	796	5.41	672	6.82	230	7.34	244	8.40	213	7.00	282	10.90	2437	7.03					45	
" "	33				9	56	20	779	5.55	818	5.60	228	7.40	260	7.89	203	7.35	357	8.61	2645	6.50					25	
" "	118				9	59	30	—		810	5.66	225	7.50	240	8.53	210	7.11	315	9.74	—							
" "	118				11	32	00	787	5.47	728	6.29	270	6.26	300	6.85	210	7.11	360	8.53	2655	6.46						
" "	37				11	48	34	708	6.08	632	7.24	318	5.32	344	5.97	215	6.95	371	8.28	2588	6.38					59	
" "	154				1	57	40	905	4.75	515	7.45	260	6.49	335	6.12	235	6.35	410	7.49	2760	6.22					69	
" "	118				2	04	00	810	5.31	690	6.64	270	6.26	330	6.22	217	6.89	443	6.93	2760	6.22						
" "	153				3	47	08	878	4.90	615	7.45	465	3.63	315	6.52	240	6.21	397	7.73	2910	5.90					55	
" "	2667				4	10	50	818	5.26	750	6.11	320	5.27	278	7.39	212	7.04	370	8.29	2748	6.25						
" "	5				5	32	30	600	7.17	735	6.23	270	6.26	315	6.52	225	6.63	405	7.59	2550	6.73						
" "	—				7	04	00	450	9.56	540	8.49	225	7.50	255	8.06	240	6.21	450	6.82	2160	7.95						
FEB. 11	—	4	00	15				923	4.66	705	6.49	317	5.34	358	5.73	296	5.04	421	7.29	3020	5.68	22	84	3	12	25	96
" "	147	5	29	00				665	6.47	1137	4.02	323	5.23	374	5.48	271	5.50	—	—	—	—	41	259	12	139	53	398
" "	104				4	00	00	760	5.66	775	5.90	425	3.98	275	7.45	225	6.65	345	8.89	2805	6.12	36	156	8	82	44	238
" "	113				5	31	05	639	6.74	1019	4.49	302	5.60	334	6.15	262	5.71	376	8.16	2932	5.86	24	178	7	122	31	300
" 13	166	7	02	15				447	9.62	488	9.38	198	8.56	242	8.48	170	8.80	304	10.09	1849	9.27	11	42	2	11	13	53
" "	3	8	29	00				570	7.54	630	7.26	268	6.31	368	5.57	194	7.70	480	6.39	2510	6.84	13	63	4	70	17	133
" "	157	10	02	20				775	5.54	694	6.59	309	5.45	294	6.97	246	6.08	366	8.38	2684	6.38	32	143	8	60	40	203
" "	2617	11	29	00				846	5.08	724	6.31	310	5.44	348	5.90	245	6.09	367	8.37	2840	6.04	35	168	6	34	41	202
" "	95	1	01	23				735	5.83	632	7.25	258	6.54	277	7.50	226	6.60	426	7.20	2554	6.70	32	116	3	17	35	133
" "	39	2	29	15				895	4.80	870	5.26	310	5.44	323	6.34	222	6.74	445	6.90	3065	5.60	29	156	7	46	36	202
" "	158	3	59	30				745	5.77	1035	4.42	358	4.72	336	6.10	223	6.70	465	6.60	3162	5.42	25	118	12	101	37	219
" "	116	5	28	00				660	6.52	1095	4.18	367	4.61	383	5.35	213	7.01	432	7.10	3150	5.44	28	177	20	105	48	282
" "	165				7	00	00	532	8.09	531	8.60	205	8.26	215	9.54	175	8.54	310	9.89	1968	8.72	20	85	2	3	22	88
" "	72				8	30	50	553	5.03	752	6.08	325	5.20	288	7.13	221	6.76	379	8.11	2818	6.08	15	64	5	17	20	81
" "	2615				10	01	20	1025	4.19	737	6.21	333	5.08	318	6.45	188	7.94	384	8.00	2985	5.74	46	192	10	79	56	271
" "	16				11	30	04	792	5.42	716	6.40	311	5.45	268	7.65	213	7.01	374	8.22	2674	6.41	35	134	2	12	37	146
" "	2670				12	59	30	772	5.57	854	5.35	279	6.08	263	7.80	195	7.66	375	8.16	2738	6.28	21	99	8	269	29	368
" "	19				2	31	32	816	5.27	755	6.06	327	5.18	340	6.03	200	7.48	398	7.71	2836	6.05	35	179	5	34	40	213
" "	36				3	59	30	730	5.88	938	4.88	357	4.73	325	6.31	260	5.74	370	8.28	2980	5.76	8	46	11	119	19	165
" "	175				5	30	54	642	6.69	784	5.84	313	5.40	303	6.77	232	6.43	362	8.46	2636	6.51	20	88	1	2	21	90
" 14	42	7	02	00				452	9.51	438	10.45	176	9.60	257	7.99	172	8.69	373	8.22	1868	9.19	18	73	4	28	22	101
" "	15	8	31	30				551	7.80	594	7.70	242	7.00	363	5.65	168	8.89	370	8.28	2268	7.50	38	159	2	47	40	206
" "	9	10	00	48				770	5.58	800	5.72	330	5.12	333	6.16	166	9.00	391	7.84	2790	6.14	15	42	5	57	20	99
" "	117	11	30	15				1280	3.36	660	6.94	235	7.20	270	7.59	228	6.54	382	8.03	3055	5.61	44	197	10	258	54	455
" "	86	1	00	03				706	6.09	649	7.05	281	6.01	370	5.54	255	5.85	431	7.11	2692	6.37	24	154	6	125	30	279
" "	94	2	29	40				670	6.41	700	6.54	245	6.99	335	6.12	240	6.21	410	7.47	2600	6.60	64	397	2	27	66	424
" "	19				7	05	00	531	8.10	499	9.18	175	9.65	210	9.77	180	8.29	320	9.57	1915	9.00	16	61	-		16	61
" "	18				8	29	54	1139	3.78	597	7.68	284	5.96	255	8.04	197	7.58	361	8.50	2833	6.06	16	59	10	234	26	293
" "	2653				9	58	40	840	5.12	658	6.96	292	5.80	349	5.88	251	5.96	350	8.76	2740	6.25	34	138	3	28	37	166
" "	4				11	30	42	744	5.78	649	7.06	331	5.11	366	5.61	221	6.76	361	8.51	2672	6.42	24	77	3	57	27	134
" "	171				12	58	00	695	6.19	605	7.55	270	6.26	315	6.52	207	7.21	403	7.61	2495	6.88	32	145	1	1	33	146
" "	2605				2	32	29	733	5.87	768	5.96	262	6.45	312	6.58	240	6.22	335	9.14	2650	6.47	42	289	3	12	45	301

Continued from Sheet No 3a.

Note
For averages see sheet No 41 (8)

—THE MERCHANTS ASSOCIATION—
—OF—
—NEW YORK.—
—COMMITTEE ON ENGINEERING AND SANITATION.—

—SURFACE RAILWAY TRANSPORTATION—
—BOROUGH OF MANHATTAN—
—NEW YORK CITY—

TRIP SPEEDS AND STOPS
ON
BROADWAY LINE.

TABULATED BY L.M.R.

SHEET No 3b.

TABLE 6.

Speed in Miles per Hour of Certain Cars on Broadway

Date 1903	Car Number	North Bound from Battery Place at Hr.	Min.	Sec.	South Bound from 59th St. at Hr.	Min.	Sec.	Between Battery Place and Canal St. 1.1945 Miles: Time in Seconds	Miles per Hour	Between Canal St. and 14th St. 1.2714 Miles: Time in Seconds	Miles per Hour	Between 14th St. and 23rd St. 0.4697 Miles: Time in Seconds	Miles per Hour	Between 23rd St. and 34th St. 0.5701 Miles: Time in Seconds	Miles per Hour	Between 34th St. and 42nd St. 0.4148 Miles: Time in Seconds	Miles per Hour	Between 42nd St. and 59th St. 0.8522 Miles: Time in Seconds	Miles per Hour	Between Battery Place and 59th St. 4.7727 Miles: Time in Seconds	Miles per Hour	Stops for Passengers: Number per Trip	Duration of Stops per Trip in Seconds	Stops for Other Causes: Number per Trip	Duration of Stops per Trip in Seconds
Feby. 11.		4	00	15 P.M.				923	4.66	705	6.49	317	5.34	358	5.73	296	5.04	421	7.29	3020	5.68	22	84	3	12
" "	147	5	29	00 "				665	6.47	1137	4.02	323	5.23	374	5.48	271	5.50	—	—	—	—	41	259	12	139
" "	104				4	00	00 P.M.	760	5.66	775	5.90	425	3.98	275	7.45	225	6.65	345	8.89	2805	6.12	36	156	8	82
" "	113				5	31	05 "	639	6.74	1019	4.49	302	5.60	334	6.15	262	5.71	376	8.16	2932	5.86	24	178	7	122
" 13	166	7	02	15 A.M.				447	<u>9.62</u>	488	9.38	198	8.56	242	8.48	170	8.80	304	<u>10.09</u>	1849	<u>9.27</u>	11	42	2	11
" "	3	8	29	00 "				570	7.54	630	7.26	268	6.31	368	5.57	194	7.70	480	6.39	2510	6.84	13	63	4	70
" "	157	10	02	20 "				775	5.54	694	6.59	309	5.45	294	6.97	246	6.08	366	8.38	2684	6.38	32	143	8	60
" "	2617	11	29	00 "				846	5.08	724	6.31	310	5.44	348	5.90	245	6.09	367	8.37	2840	6.04	35	168	6	34
" "	95	1	01	23 P.M.				735	5.83	632	7.25	258	6.54	277	7.50	226	6.60	426	7.20	2554	6.70	32	116	3	17
" "	39	2	29	15 "				895	4.80	870	5.26	310	5.44	323	6.34	222	6.74	445	6.90	3065	5.60	29	156	7	46
" "	158	3	59	30 "				745	5.77	1035	4.42	358	4.72	336	6.10	223	6.70	465	6.60	3162	5.42	25	118	12	101
" "	116	5	28	00 "				660	6.52	1095	4.18	367	4.61	383	5.35	213	7.01	432	7.10	3150	5.44	28	177	20	105
" "	165				7	00	00 A.M.	532	8.09	531	8.60	205	8.26	215	9.54	175	8.54	310	9.89	1968	8.72	20	85	2	3
" "	72				8	30	50 "	553	5.03	752	6.08	325	5.20	288	7.13	221	6.76	379	8.11	2818	6.08	15	64	5	17
" "	2615				10	01	20 "	1025	4.19	737	6.21	333	5.08	318	6.45	188	7.94	384	8.00	2985	5.74	46	192	10	79
" "	16				11	30	04 "	792	5.42	716	6.40	311	5.45	268	7.65	213	7.01	374	8.22	2674	6.41	35	134	2	12
" "	2670				12	59	30 A.M.	772	5.57	854	5.35	279	6.08	263	7.80	195	7.66	375	8.16	2738	6.28	21	99	8	269
" "	19				2	31	32 "	816	5.27	755	6.06	327	5.18	340	6.03	200	7.48	398	7.71	2836	6.05	35	179	5	34
" "	36				3	59	30 "	730	5.88	938	4.88	357	4.73	325	6.31	260	5.74	370	8.28	2980	5.76	8	46	11	119
" "	175				5	30	54 "	642	6.69	784	5.84	313	5.40	303	6.77	232	6.43	362	8.46	2636	6.51	20	88	1	2
" 14	42	7	02	00 A.M.				452	9.51	438	<u>10.45</u>	176	9.60	257	7.99	172	8.69	373	8.22	1868	9.19	18	73	4	28
" "	15	8	31	30 "				551	7.80	594	7.70	242	7.00	363	5.65	168	8.89	370	8.28	2288	7.50	38	159	2	47
" "	9	10	00	48 "				770	5.58	800	5.72	330	5.12	333	6.16	166	<u>9.00</u>	391	7.84	2790	6.14	15	42	5	57
" "	117	11	30	15 "				1280	3.36	660	6.94	235	7.20	270	7.59	228	6.54	382	8.03	3055	5.61	44	197	10	258
" "	86	1	00	03 P.M.				706	6.09	649	7.05	281	6.01	370	5.54	255	5.85	431	7.11	2692	6.37	24	154	6	125
" "	94	2	29	40 "				670	6.41	700	6.54	245	6.99	335	6.12	240	6.21	410	7.47	2600	6.60	64	397	2	27
" "	19				7	05	00 A.M.	531	8.10	499	9.18	175	<u>9.65</u>	210	<u>9.77</u>	180	8.29	320	9.57	1915	9.00	16	61	—	—
" "	18				8	29	54 "	1139	3.78	597	7.68	284	5.96	255	8.04	197	7.58	361	8.50	2833	6.06	16	59	10	234
" "	2653				9	58	40 "	840	5.12	658	6.96	292	5.80	349	5.88	251	5.96	350	8.76	2740	6.25	34	138	3	28
" "	4				11	30	42 "	744	5.78	649	7.06	331	5.11	366	5.61	221	6.76	361	8.51	2672	6.42	24	77	3	57
" "	171				12	58	00 P.M.	695	6.19	605	7.55	270	6.26	315	6.52	207	7.21	403	7.61	2495	6.88	32	145	1	1
" "	2605				2	32	29 "	733	5.87	768	5.96	262	6.45	312	6.58	240	6.22	335	9.14	2650	6.47	42	289	3	12

Number of Trips	Stops for Passengers: Number	Time in Seconds	Stops for Other Causes: Number	Time in Seconds
32	895	4338	185	2208
Average per Trip	27.9	135.5	5.7	69
Average Time in Seconds per Stop	1	4.8	1	11.9
	6.06			

Average Speed in Miles per Hour of a Number of Cars on Broadway

Starting Hour	Number of Trips Averaged	Battery Pl. and Canal St.	Canal St. and 14th St.	14th St. and 23rd St.	23rd St. and 34th St.	34th St. and 42nd St.	42nd St. and 59th St.	Battery Pl. and 59th St.	Average Running Time between Battery Pl. and 59th St. in Minutes
7 A.M.	2 N.	9.56	9.91	9.08	8.235	8.74	9.15	9.23	30.98
	2 S.	8.09	8.89	8.95	9.655	8.41	9.73	8.86	32.36
8³⁰ "	2 N.	7.67	7.48	6.65	5.61	8.29	7.33	7.17	39.98
	2 S.	4.40	6.88	5.58	7.58	7.17	8.30	6.07	47.09
10 "	2 N.	5.56	6.65	5.28	6.56	7.54	8.11	6.46	45.62
	2 S.	4.65	6.58	5.44	6.16	6.95	8.38	5.99	47.71
11³⁰ "	2 N.	4.22	6.62	6.32	6.74	6.31	8.20	5.82	49.13
	2 S.	5.60	6.73	5.28	6.63	6.88	8.36	6.41	44.55
1 P.M.	2 N.	5.96	7.15	6.27	6.47	6.22	7.15	6.53	43.72
	2 S.	5.88	6.45	6.17	7.16	7.43	7.88	6.58	43.61
2³⁰ "	2 N.	5.60	5.90	6.17	6.23	6.47	7.18	6.10	47.21
	2 S.	5.57	6.02	5.81	6.30	6.85	8.42	6.26	45.72
4 "	2 N.	5.21	5.45	5.03	5.91	5.87	6.94	5.55	51.52
	2 S.	5.77	5.39	4.35	6.88	6.19	8.58	5.94	48.21
† 5³⁰ "	2 N.	6.49	4.10	4.92	5.41	6.25	* 7.10	* 5.44	* 52.50
	2 S.	6.71	5.16	5.50	6.46	6.07	8.31	6.18	46.40
† Average of all Trips	16 N.	6.28	6.66	6.21	6.39	6.96	* 7.68	* 6.42	* 44.59
	16 S.	5.83	6.51	5.88	7.09	6.99	8.49	6.44	44.46
Maximum { Any Trip		9.62	10.45	9.65	9.77	9.00	10.09	9.27	
Minimum { Any Trip		3.36	4.02	3.98	5.35	5.04	6.39	5.42	

Note:—The trips referred to above include all trips tabulated on this sheet in Table of Speed of Certain Cars.

† Entries of North Bound Car Records, marked thus *, are based on one less trip than stated in 2nd column.

Note that a Saturday (Feb. 14th) record is included.

Diagram of the Average Movement of Cars on Broadway Line

Based on all trips tabulated on this sheet.

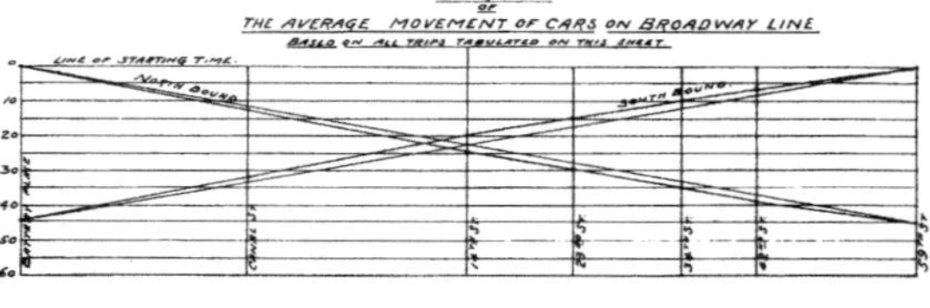

—The Merchants Association of New York—

—Committee on Engineering and Sanitation—

Surface Railway Transportation

Borough of Manhattan

New York City

—Trip Speeds and Stops on Broadway Line—

Tabulated by E.M.R.

Observations taken under direction of E. M. Rosenberg, M.E.

—Sheet No 3c

TABLE 7.

AVERAGE SPEED IN MILES PER HOUR OF A NUMBER OF CARS ON BROADWAY.

FROM OBSERVATIONS OF JANUARY 19TH & 20TH 1903 and FEBUARY 11TH, 13TH & 14TH 1903.

HOUR	NUMBER OF TRIPS AVERAGED	Speed in Miles per Hour between: Battery Pl. and Canal	Canal and 14th St	14th St and 23rd St	23rd St and 34th St	34th St and 42nd St	42nd St and 59th St	Battery Pl. and 59th St	AVERAGE RUNNING TIME BETWEEN BATTERY PL. AND 59TH ST IN MINUTES.
7 A.M. TO 8	10	9.24	8.69	8.30	8.72	8.30	9.46	8 75	32.7
9 . 12	21	5.35	6.43	6.02	6 73	7 38	8.01	6 25	45.8
1 P.M. TO 3	15	5.75	6 77	6 10	6.25	6.60	7.56	6.36	45.0
3 5	13	5.21	6 20	5.17	6.09	6 12	7.25	5.80	49.3
5 6.30	9	6.37	5.87	5.85	6.28	6.65	7.27	6.12	46.8
9 9	2	10.02	10.21	7.60	7 61	7.45	8.40	8.84	32 4
AVERAGE OF ALL TRIPS	70	6 23	6.82	6.23	6 76	7.03	7 90	6.62	44.2
MAXIMUM ANY TRIP		10.61	10.48	9.65	9.77	11 75	11.25	9.64	56 0
MINIMUM ANY TRIP		3 79	4.18	3.63	4.63	4.74	4.99	5.07	29.7

NOTE
The trips referred to above, include about an equal number of trips northward and trips southward

AVERAGE SPEED IN MILES PER HOUR OF A NUMBER OF CARS ON BROADWAY.

FROM OBSERVATIONS OF FEB 11TH, 13TH & 14TH 1903

	NUMBER OF TRIPS AVERAGED	Speed in Miles per Hour between: Battery Pl. and Canal.	Canal and 14th St	14th St and 23rd St.	23rd St and 34th St	34th St and 42nd St	42nd St and 59th St.	Battery Pl. and 59th St	AVERAGE RUNNING TIME BETWEEN BATTERY PL. AND 59TH ST IN MINUTES
† AVERAGE OF ALL TRIPS	16N	6.28	6.66	6.21	6.39	6.96	*7.68	*6.42	*44.59
	16S	5.83	6 51	5.88	7 09	6.99	*8.49	6.44	44.46
MAXIMUM ANY TRIP		9.62	10.45	9.65	9.77	9.00	10.09	9.27	
MINIMUM ANY TRIP		3.36	4.02	3.98	5.35	5.04	6.39	5.42	

NOTE
The trips referred to above, include all trips tabulated on sheet No 3 in table q speed of certain cars
† Entries of North Bound Car Records, marked thus * are based on one less trip than stated in 2nd Column

AVERAGE SPEED IN MILES PER HOUR OF A NUMBER OF CARS ON BROADWAY.

FROM OBSERVATIONS OF JANUARY 19TH & 20TH & FEBRUARY 11TH 13TH & 14TH 1903

	NUMBER OF TRIPS AVERAGED	Speed in Miles per Hour, between: Battery Pl. and Canal	Canal and 14th St.	14th St and 23rd St.	23rd St and 34th St	34th St and 42nd St	42nd St and 59th St	Battery Pl. and 59th St.	AVERAGE RUNNING TIME BETWEEN BATTERY PL. AND 59TH ST. IN MINUTES
AVERAGE OF ALL TRIPS	74	6 17	6.76	6. 12	6 71	7.00	*7.90	*6.46	*44. 35
MAXIMUM ANY TRIP		10.61	10.48	9.65	9.77	11.75	11.25	9.64	
MINIMUM ANY TRIP		3.36	4 02	3.98	4.63	4 74	4.99	5.07	

NOTE
Entries of Car Records marked thus * are based on one less trip than stated in 2nd column

AVERAGE SPEED IN MILES PER HOUR OF A NUMBER OF CARS ON BROADWAY.

FROM OBSERVATIONS OF JANUARY 19TH & 20TH & FEBRUARY 11TH 13TH & 14TH 1903.

	NUMBER OF TRIPS AVERAGED	Speed in Miles per Hour. between: Battery Pl. and Canal	Canal and 14th St.	14th St. and 23rd St.	23rd St. and 34th St.	34th St and 42nd St.	42nd St. and 59th St.	Battery Pl. and 59th St.	AVERAGE RUNNING TIME BETWEEN BATTERY PL. AND 59TH ST. IN MINUTES
AVERAGE OF ALL TRIPS	87	**6.25	6.80	6.20	6.79	7.00	*7.91	***6.54	***43.80
MAXIMUM ANY TRIP		10.61	10.48	9.65	9.77	11.75	11.28	9.64	
MINIMUM ANY TRIP		3.36	4.02	3.63	4.63	4.74	4.99	5.07	

NOTE. See sheets No 3a & 3e
Entries of Car Records marked *, or **, or *** are based respectively, on one, or two or three less trips than stated in second column.

—THE MERCHANTS ASSOCIATION—
—OF—
—NEW YORK.—
—COMMITTEE ON ENGINEERING AND SANITATION.—

—SURFACE RAILWAY TRANSPORTATION—
—BOROUGH OF MANHATTAN—
—NEW YORK CITY—

—TRIP SPEEDS AND STOPS—
—ON—
—BROADWAY LINE.—

SHEET No 41.

TABLE 8.

SPEED IN MILES PER HOUR
OF
CERTAIN CARS ON SIXTH AVE. ROUTE.

DATE 1903	CAR NUMBER	NORTH BOUND FROM BATTERY PLACE AT Hr.	Min.	Sec.	SOUTH BOUND FROM 59TH ST. AT Hr.	Min.	Sec.	BETWEEN BATTERY PLACE & CANAL ST. 1.246 MILES Time in Seconds	Miles per Hour	BETWEEN CANAL ST. & 14TH ST. 1.360 MILES Time in Seconds	Miles per Hour	BETWEEN 14TH ST. & 23RD ST. 0.438 MILE Time in Seconds	Miles per Hour	BETWEEN 23RD ST. & 34TH ST. 0.547 MILE Time in Seconds	Miles per Hour	BETWEEN 34TH ST. & 42ND ST. 0.399 MILE Time in Seconds	Miles per Hour	BETWEEN 42ND ST. & 59TH ST. 0.840 MILE Time in Seconds	Miles per Hour	BETWEEN BATTERY PLA. & 59TH ST. 4.825 MILES Time in Seconds	Miles per Hour	STOPS FOR PASSENGERS Number for Trip	Duration of Stops for Trip in Seconds	STOPS FOR OTHER CAUSES Number for Trip	Duration of Stops for Trip in Seconds
FEB. 27	2059	7	08	33				788	5.70	592	8.23	198	8.20	237	8.26	210	6.82	452	6.67	2477	7.00	18	92	3	114
" "	1677	8	39	01				819	5.48	748	6.52	303	5.36	276	7.08	223	6.43	420	7.17	2789	6.22	57	243	4	45
" "	2000	10	10	08				988	4.55	903	5.40	335	4.85	374	5.23	240	5.97	514	5.86	3354	5.17	34	185	3	72
" "	1980	11	39	45				745	6.03	780	6.25	270	6.01	305	6.41	201	7.11	461	6.53	2762	6.29	50	189	5	26
" "	1872	1	02	08				894	5.02	796	6.12	292	5.56	330	5.92	205	6.99	437	6.90	2954	5.88	28	124	3	61
" "	1862	2	35	15				961	4.67	749	6.51	360	4.51	354	5.52	236	6.07	485	6.21	3145	5.51	41	163	5	93
" "	2056	4	04	58				928	4.83	928	5.26	371	4.38	388	5.03	302	4.75	503	5.96	3420	5.08	53	508	3	117
" "	1990	5	30	50				1039	4.32	947	5.15	358	4.54	398	4.91	271	5.29	497	6.07	3510	4.95	93	506	2	68
" "	1986				7	03	21	751	5.97	794	6.12	238	6.83	296	6.61	202	7.11	381	7.91	2662	6.51	28	88	18	185
" "	2071				8	35	50	1172	3.83	803	6.04	278	5.85	282	6.94	216	6.63	483	6.23	3234	5.37	32	163	8	97
" "	1980				10	05	50	1750	2.67	1329	3.67	301	5.40	302	6.49	256	5.60	1042	2.88	4980	3.48	48	250	14	1817
" "	2074				11	33	57	968	4.64	857	5.69	314	5.18	289	6.77	335	4.28	330	9.14	3093	5.61	44	269	4	47
" "	2038				1	00	04	1065	4.21	756	6.46	322	5.05	296	6.61	234	6.12	428	7.04	3101	5.59	47	179	5	104
" "	2030				2	36	08	1414	3.17	898	5.43	313	5.19	289	6.77	268	5.34	457	6.60	3639	4.77	29	204	7	248
" "	1986				4	02	15	1025	4.37	810	5.60	270	6.01	371	5.28	324	4.43	535	5.63	3395	5.11	49	278	4	135
" "	xxxx				5	36	12	703	6.48	863	5.64	313	5.19	291	6.73	317	4.52	524	5.75	3011	5.77	36	189	8	106

NUMBER OF TRIPS	STOPS FOR PASSENGERS Number	Time in Seconds	STOPS FOR OTHER CAUSES Number	Time in Seconds
15	639	3380	82	1518
AVERAGE FOR ONE TRIP	42.6	225.3	5.6	101.2
AVERAGE TIME IN SECONDS PER STOP	1	5.3	1	18.5
	6.79			

NUMBER OF TRIPS	STOPS. FOR PASSENGERS Number	Time in Seconds	STOPS. FOR OTHER CAUSES Number	Time in Seconds
✦ 1	48	250	14	1817
AVERAGE TIME IN SECONDS PER STOP	1	5.2	1	129.78
	33.33			

AVERAGE SPEED IN MILES PER HOUR
OF
A NUMBER OF CARS ON SIXTH AVENUE ROUTE.

	NUMBER OF TRIPS AVERAGED	SPEED IN MILES PER HOUR, BETWEEN BATTERY PLACE AND CANAL ST.	CANAL ST. AND 14TH ST.	14TH ST. AND 23RD ST.	23RD ST. AND 34TH ST.	34TH ST. AND 42ND ST.	42ND ST. AND 59TH ST.	BATTERY PL. AND 59TH ST.	AVERAGE RUNNING TIME BETWEEN BATTERY PL. AND 59TH ST., IN MINUTES.
AVERAGE OF ALL NORTH BOUND TRIPS	8	5.01	6.07	5.21	5.88	6.07	6.39	5.68	50.85
AVERAGE OF SEVEN SOUTH BOUND TRIPS	7	4.42	5.85	5.53	6.49	5.29	6.72	5.47	52.70
MAXIMUM ANY TRIP INCLUDED		6.48	8.23	8.20	8.26	7.11	9.14	7.00	
MINIMUM ANY TRIP INCLUDED		3.17	5.15	4.38	4.91	4.28	5.63	4.77	

NOTE

THE TRIPS REFERRED TO ABOVE, INCLUDE ALL TRIPS TABULATED ON THIS SHEET IN TABLE OF SPEED OF CERTAIN CARS,

✦ EXCEPT THE SOUTH BOUND TRIP OF CAR Nº 1980 STARTING AT 59TH STREET AT 10-05-50 A.M. EXCLUDED BECAUSE OF EXCEPTIONAL DELAYS.

DIAGRAM
OF
THE AVERAGE MOVEMENT OF CARS ON SIXTH AVENUE ROUTE
BASED ON ALL TRIPS AVERAGED ON THIS SHEET

LINE OF STARTING TIME.
NORTH BOUND CARS
SOUTH BOUND CARS
TIME IN MINUTES.
BATTERY PLACE
CANAL STREET
14TH STREET
23RD STREET
34TH STREET
42ND STREET
59TH STREET

—THE MERCHANTS ASSOCIATION—
—OF—
—NEW YORK—
—COMMITTEE ON ENGINEERING AND SANITATION—

—SURFACE RAILWAY TRANSPORTATION—
—BOROUGH OF MANHATTAN—
—NEW YORK CITY—

—TRIP SPEEDS AND STOPS—
—ON—
—SIXTH AVE. ROUTE.—

TABULATED BY L.M.R.   OBSERVATIONS TAKEN UNDER DIRECTION OF E.M. Rosenberg, M.E.

SHEET Nº 32

TABLE 9.

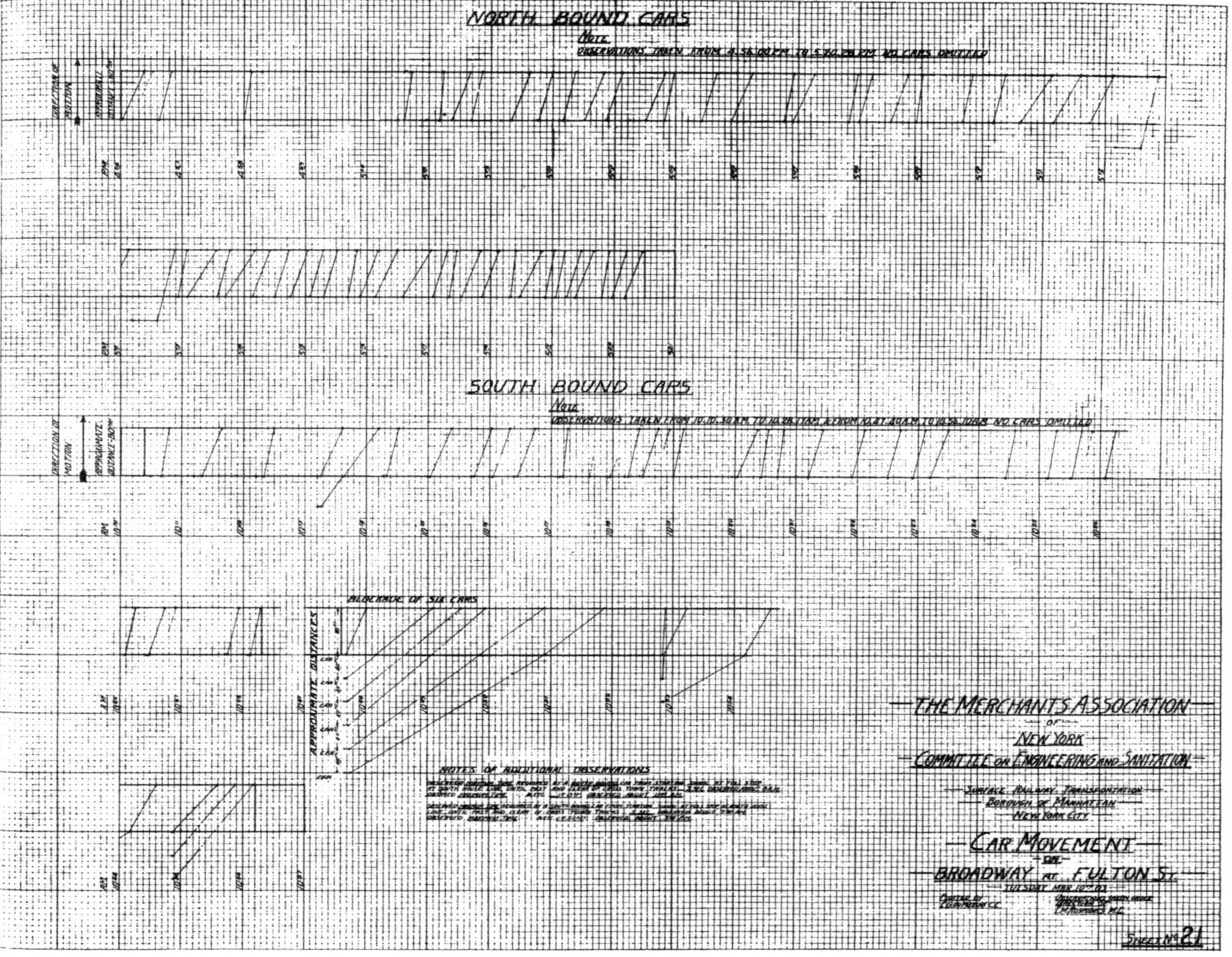

DIAGRAM 10.

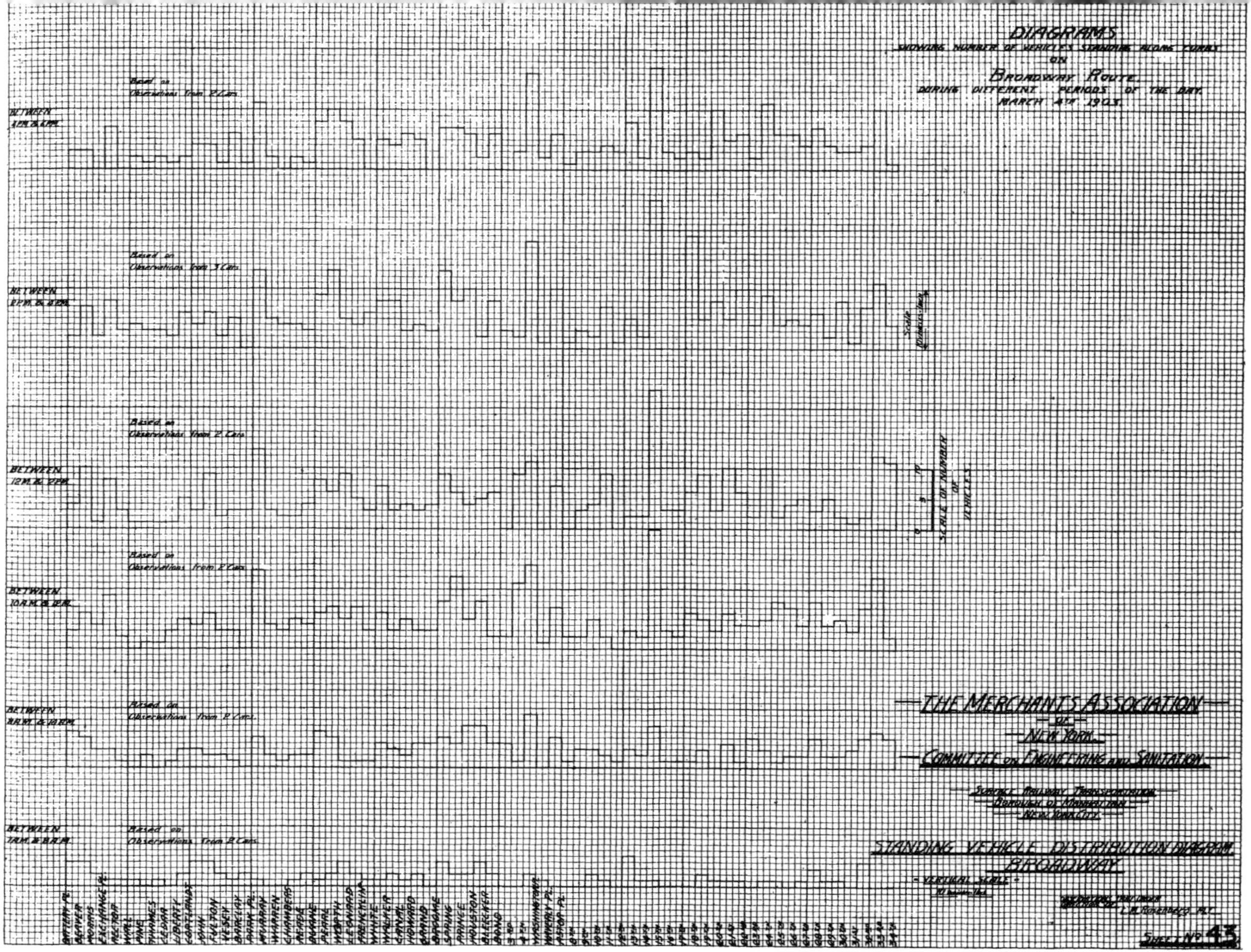

DIAGRAMS
SHOWING NUMBER OF VEHICLES STANDING ALONG CURBS
ON
BROADWAY ROUTE
DURING DIFFERENT PERIODS OF THE DAY.
MARCH 4TH 1903.

BETWEEN 4 P.M. & 6 P.M. — Based on Observations from 2 Cars.

BETWEEN 2 P.M. & 4 P.M. — Based on Observations from 3 Cars.

BETWEEN 12 M. & 2 P.M. — Based on Observations from 2 Cars.

BETWEEN 10 A.M. & 12 M. — Based on Observations from 2 Cars.

BETWEEN 8 A.M. & 10 A.M. — Based on Observations from 2 Cars.

BETWEEN 7 A.M. & 8 A.M. — Based on Observations from 2 Cars.

SCALE OF NUMBER OF VEHICLES

THE MERCHANTS ASSOCIATION
OF
NEW YORK.
COMMITTEE ON ENGINEERING AND SANITATION.

SURFACE RAILWAY TRANSPORTATION
BOROUGH OF MANHATTAN
NEW YORK CITY.

STANDING VEHICLE DISTRIBUTION DIAGRAM
BROADWAY

SHEET NO 43

171

DIAGRAM 43.

THIRTY FOURTH STREET FERRY BRANCH OF TWENTY THIRD STREET CROSSTOWN LINE
– East bound Cars –
April 11 at 23rd St. & 8th Ave.
April 11 at 23rd St. & Lexington Ave.
Note:– The west-bound cars cannot be distinguished from the cars of the main 23rd St. Line.
TWENTY THIRD STREET CROSSTOWN LINE
– East bound Cars –
April 11 at 23rd St. & 8th Ave.
April 11 at 23rd St. & Lexington Ave.
– West bound Cars –
April 11 at 23rd St. & 8th Ave.
April 11 at 23rd St. & Lexington Ave.
0 ½ 1 1½ 2
7 A.M. 7³⁰ 8 8³⁰ 9 9³⁰ 10 10³⁰ 11 11³⁰ 12 2 P.M. 2³⁰ 3 3³⁰ 4 4³⁰ 5 5³⁰ 6 6³⁰ 7

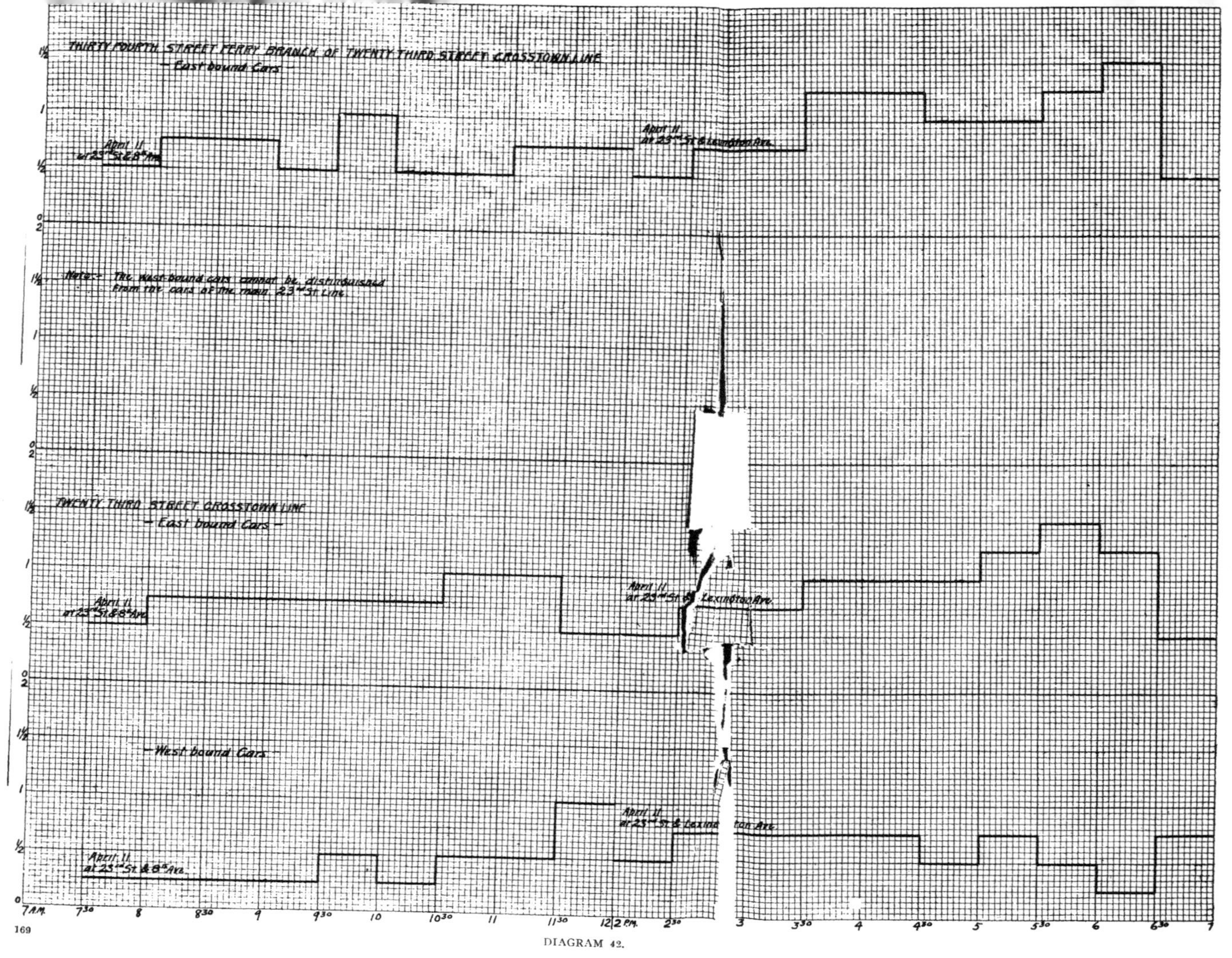

DIAGRAM 42.

CENTRAL CROSSTOWN LINE
East bound Cars
March 20 at Christopher St. Ferry
March 19 at E. 23rd St. Ferry
April 8 at 14th St. & 6th Ave.
West bound Cars
14th STREET FERRY AND UNION SQUARE BRANCH LINE (CENTRAL CROSSTOWN)
April 9 at 14th St. & 9th Ave.
1 represents Seating Capacity of Cars
7 AM
7 30
8
8 30
9
9 30
10
10 30
11
11 30
12
2 P.M.
2 30
3
3 30
4
4 30
5
5 30
6
6 30
7

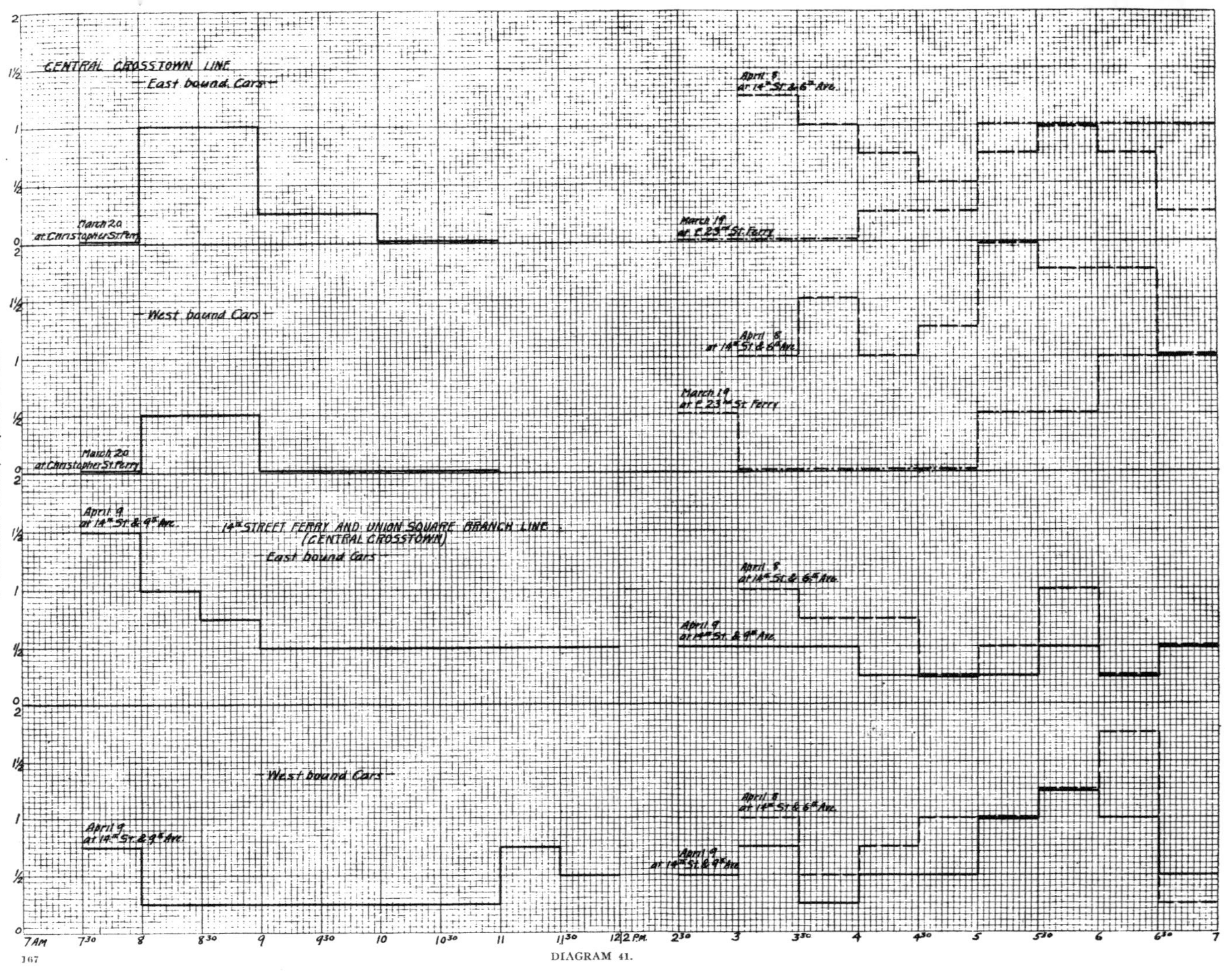

DIAGRAM 41.

BLEECKER STREET AND FULTON FERRY LINE
—East bound Cars—
—West bound Cars—
14th STREET FERRY AND GRAND STREET FERRY LINE
—East bound Cars—
—West bound Cars—
April 9
at 14th St. & 9th Ave.
April 8
at 14th St. & 6th Ave.
7 A.M.
7 30
8
8 30
9
9 30
10
10 30
11
11 30
12
2 P.M.
2 30
3
3 30
4
4 30
5
5 30
6
6 30
7

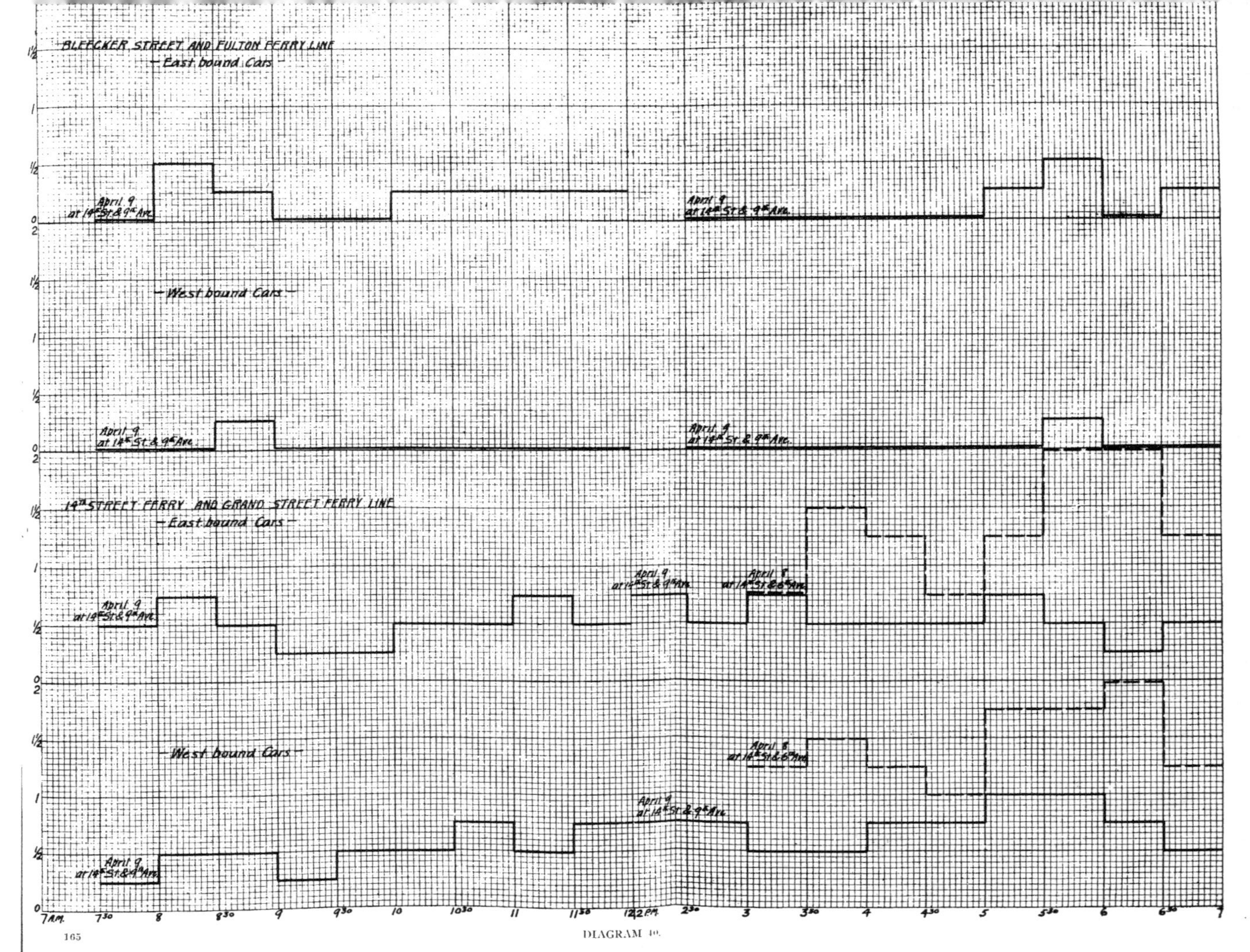

DIAGRAM 40.

CHAMBERS STREET AND ROOSEVELT STREET FERRY LINE
-East bound Cars-
March 13
at Roosevelt St. Ferry
March 14
at Chambers & Duane Sts.
March 13
at Chambers & Duane Sts.
-West bound Cars-
March 14
at Chambers & Duane Sts.
March 13
at Roosevelt St. Ferry
March 13
at Chambers & Duane Sts.
CHAMBERS STREET AND GRAND STREET FERRY LINE
-East bound Cars-
March 14
at Chambers & Duane Sts.
March 13
at Chambers & Duane Sts.
-West bound Cars-
March 14
at Chambers & Duane Sts.
March 13
at Chambers & Duane Sts.
1 represents Seating Capacity of Cars.
7 A.M.
8
9
10
11
12
2 P.M.
3
4
5
6
7

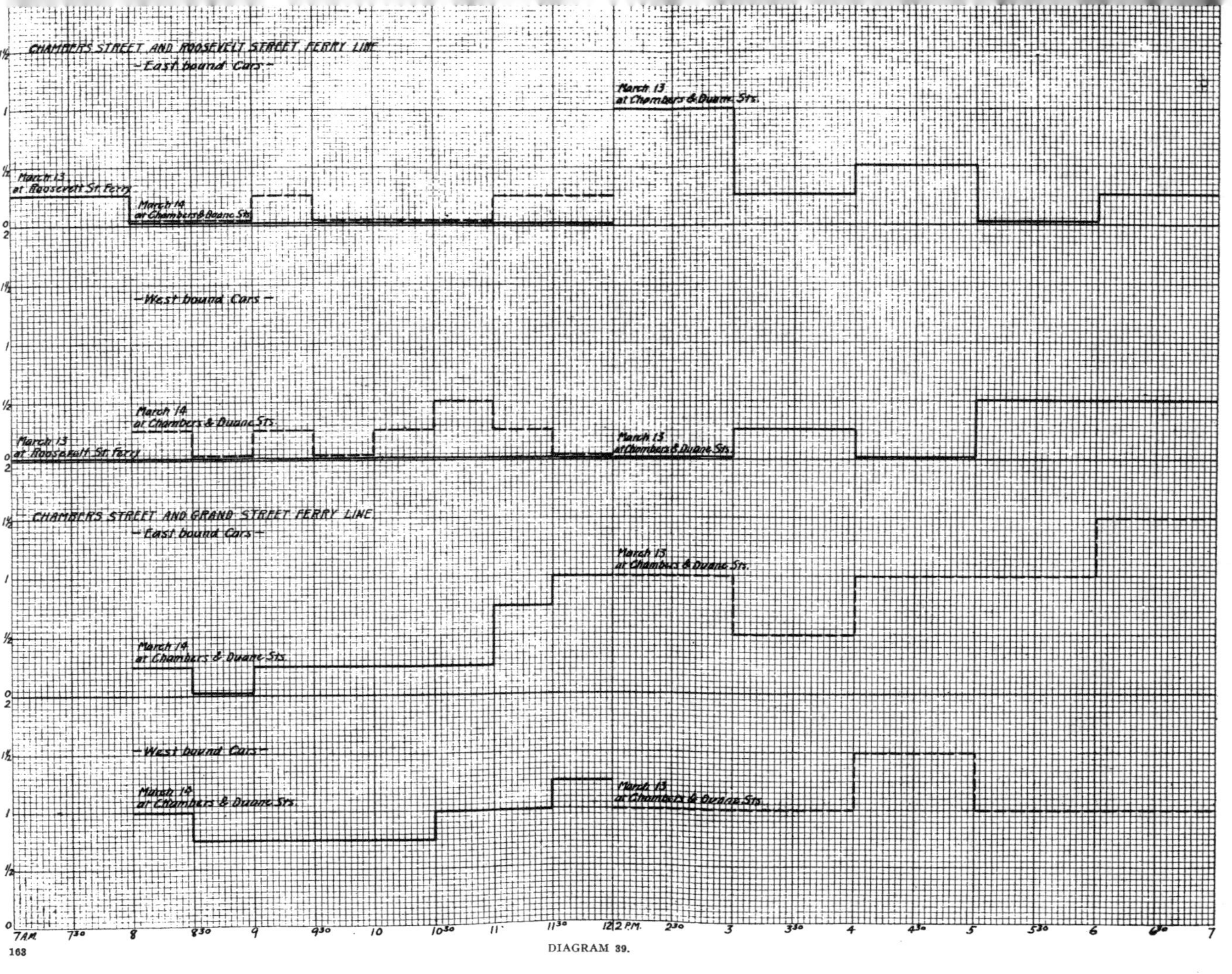

DIAGRAM 39.

Average Load of Cars in terms of Seating Capacity, represented by 1

Car Line	Date of Observation	Place of Observation	A.M. 7-7:30 N or E bound	7-7:30 S or W bound	7:30-8 N or E bound	7:30-8 S or W bound	8-8:30 N or E bound	8-8:30 S or W bound	8:30-9 N or E bound	8:30-9 S or W bound	9-9:30 N or E bound	9-9:30 S or W bound	9:30-10 N or E bound	9:30-10 S or W bound	10-10:30 N or E bound	10-10:30 S or W bound	10:30-11 N or E bound	10:30-11 S or W bound	11-11:30 N or E bound	11-11:30 S or W bound	11:30-12 N or E bound	11:30-12 S or W bound
Belt Line – Eastern Division	-1903- March 11	Grand & Corlears Sts.	1/4	3/4	1/4	3/4	1/4	3/4	1/4	3/4	1/4	1/4	1/4	1/4	1/4	1/4	1/4	1/4	1/4	1/4	1/4	1/4
Belt Line – Western Division	March 19	South Ferry			1/4	1/4	1/2	1/4	1/2	1/4	1/4	1/4	1/4	1/4	1/4	1/2	1/4	1/2	0	0	0	0
" "	April 10	Desbrosses & West Sts.	3/4	1/2	1/2	3/4	1/4	3/4	3/4	1/2	1/4	1/2	0	1/4	1/4	1/4	0	1/4	1/2	1/4	1/4	1/4
Avenue B Line	March 18	34th St. Ferry			1/2	1/4	1/2	1/4	1/2	1/4												
" "	March 21	Canal St. & Broadway					1/4	3/4	0	3/4	1/4	3/4	1/4	3/4	1/2	1/2	1/2	1/4	1	3/4		
Avenue D Line	March 18	E. 23rd St. Ferry									0	1/4	0	1/4	1/4	0	1/4	0	0	0	0	0
" "	March 21	Canal St. & Broadway					1/4	1	0	1	1/4	1/2	1/4	3/4	1/4	1/2	3/4	3/4	1/2	1/2		
Chambers St. & Grand St. Ferry Line	March 14	Chambers & Duane Sts.					1/4	1	0	3/4	1/4	3/4	1/4	3/4	1/4	3/4	1/4	1	3/4	1	1	1 1/4
Chambers St. & Roosevelt St. Ferry Line	March 13	Roosevelt St. Ferry	1/4	0	1/4	0	0	0	0	0	0	0	0	0	0	0	0	0	0	0	0	0
" "	March 14	Chambers & Duane Sts.					0	1/4	0	0	1/4	1/4	0	0	0	1/4	0	1/2	1/4	1/4	1/4	0
Bleecker St. & Fulton Ferry Line	April 9	14th St. & 9th Ave.			0	0	1/2	0	1/4	1/4	0	0	0	0	1/4	0	1/4	0	1/4	0	1/4	0
Desbrosses St. & Grand St. Line	March 11	Grand St. & Bowery	1/2	1	1/2	1	3/4	3/4	3/4	3/4	1	1	1	1					1/2	1/2	1/2	1/2
" "																						
Spring St. Line	March 10	Spring St. & Broadway			1/4	1	1/4	1/4	1/4	3/4	1/4	1/4	1/4	3/4	1/4	1/4	1/4	1/4	1/4	1/4	1/4	1/4
Houston St. & Prince St. Line	March 11	Houston St. & Bowery		1 1/2		1 1/2		1 1/2		1 1/2		1		1		1		1/2		1/2		1/2
" "	April 10	Desbrosses & West Sts.			1/4	0	0	0	1/4	0	1/4	1/4	1/4	0	0	1/4	1/4	0	1/2	0	1/4	1/4
6th Ave. & Desbrosses St. Ferry Line	April 10	Desbrosses & West Sts.			1/4	1/4	0	0	0	0	0	0	1/4	0	1/4	0	1/4	0	1/4	0	1/4	0
Christopher St., 8th St. & 10th St. Line	March 12	Christopher St. Ferry	1	1/2	1	1/2	1	0	1	0	1 1/2	0	1/2	0	1/2	1/4	1/2	1/4	0	0	0	0
14th St. Ferry & Grand St. Ferry Line	April 9	14th St. & 9th Ave.			1/2	1/4	3/4	1/2	1/2	1/2	1/4	1/4	1/4	1/2	1/2	1/2	1/2	3/4	3/4	1/2	1/2	3/4
" "																						
14th St. Ferry & Union Sq. Branch Line	April 9	14th St. & 9th Ave.			1 1/2	3/4	1	1/4	3/4	1/4	1/2	1/4	1/2	1/4	1/2	1/4	1/2	1/4	1/2	3/4	1/2	1/2
" "																						
Central Crosstown Line	March 20	Christopher St. Ferry			0	0	1	1/2	1	1/2	1/4	0	1/4	0	0	0	0	0				
" "																						
23rd St. Crosstown Line	April 11	23rd St. & 8th Ave.			1/2	1/4	3/4	1/4	3/4	1/4	3/4	1/4	3/4	1/2	3/4	1/4	1	1/2	1	1/2	1/2	1
34th St. Ferry Branch of 23rd St. Line	April 11	23rd St. & 8th Ave.			1/2		3/4		3/4		1/2		1		1/2		1/2		3/4		3/4	
28th & 29th Sts. Crosstown Line	March 10	W. 23rd St. Ferry	1/2	1/2	1/2	1/2	1/2	1/2	1/2	1/2	1/4	1/4	1/4	1/4	1/4	1/4	1/4	1/4	0	0	0	0
34th St. Crosstown Line	March 13	34th St. Ferry	3/4	1 1/2	3/4	1 1/2	0	3/4	0	3/4	1/4	3/4	1/4	3/4	1/4	1/4	1/4	1/4	1/4	1/4		
" "	March 14	34th St. & Madison Ave.	3/4	1 1/2	3/4	1 1/2	3/4	1 1/2	3/4	1 1/2	3/4	3/4	3/4	3/4	3/4	3/4	3/4	3/4	3/4	3/4	3/4	3/4
42nd St. Line	March 16	42nd St. & Broadway					1/2	3/4	1/2	3/4	1/2	1/4	1/2	1/4	1/4	1/2	1/2	1/2	1/2	1/2	1/2	3/4
"																						
10th Ave. Line	March 16	42nd St. & Broadway					3/4	3/4	3/4	3/4	1/2	3/4	3/4	3/4	3/4	1/2	3/4	1/2	1/2	3/4	1/2	1/2
" "	March 17	34th St. Ferry					0	1/2	0	0	0	1/2	1/4	0	1/4	1/4	0	1/4	0	1/4	1/4	1/4
Boulevard Branch Line	March 16	42nd St. & Broadway					1	1/2	1	3/4	1	1/2	3/4	3/4	3/4	3/4	3/4	1/2	3/4	3/4	1/2	1/2
" "	March 17	34th St. Ferry							1/4	1/2	1/4	1/4	0	1/4	0	1/4	1/2	1/4	1/4	1/4	1/4	1/4

Car Line	Date of Observation	Place of Observation	2-2:30 N or E bound	2-2:30 S or W bound	2:30-3 N or E bound	2:30-3 S or W bound	3-3:30 N or E bound	3-3:30 S or W bound	3:30-4 N or E bound	3:30-4 S or W bound	4-4:30 N or E bound	4-4:30 S or W bound	4:30-5 N or E bound	4:30-5 S or W bound	5-5:30 N or E bound	5-5:30 S or W bound	5:30-6 N or E bound	5:30-6 S or W bound	6-6:30 N or E bound	6-6:30 S or W bound	6:30-7 P.M. N or E bound	6:30-7 P.M. S or W bound
Belt Line – Eastern Division	-1903- March 10	8th St. & Ave. D											1/4	1/4	1/4	1/4	1/4	1 1/2	1/4	1 1/2	1/4	1/4
Belt Line – Western Division	March 18	53rd St. & 10th Ave.					1/4	1/4	1/4	1/4	1/2	1/2	1/2	1/2	1/2	1/2	1/2	1/2	1/2	1/2	1/2	1/2
" "	April 10	Desbrosses & West Sts.	1/2	1/2	3/4	1/2	1/2	3/4	1/2	1/2	1/2	1/2	3/4	3/4	3/4	1	3/4	1	3/4	3/4	1/2	1/4
Avenue B Line	March 17	Ann St. & Park Row			1/4	1/4	1/4	1/4	1/4	0	1/4	1/4	1/2	1/4	1/2	1/4	1/2	1/4	1/2	0	1/4	0
" "																						
Avenue D Line	March 17	Ann St. & Park Row			1/4	0	1/4	1/2	1/4	0	1/4	0	1/2	1/4	1/4	1/4	3/4	0	3/4	1/4	0	0
" "																						
Chambers St. & Grand St. Ferry Line	March 13	Chambers & Duane Sts.	1	1	1	1	1/2	1	1/2	1	1	1 1/2	1	1 1/2	1	1	1	1	1 1/2	1	1 1/2	1
Chambers St. & Roosevelt St. Ferry Line	March 13	Chambers & Duane Sts.	1	0	1	0	1/4	1/4	1/4	1/4	1/2	0	1/2	0	0	1/2	0	1/2	1/4	1/2	1/4	1/2
" "																						
Bleecker St. & Fulton Ferry Line	April 9	14th St. & 9th Ave.			0	0	0	0	0	0	0	0	0	0	1/4	0	1/2	1/2	0	0	1/4	0
Desbrosses St. & Grand St. Line	March 10	Grand St. & Broadway													1	3/4	1	3/4	1	1	1	1
" "	March 11	Grand St. & Bowery					1/2	1/2	1/2	1/2	1/2	1/2	1/2	1/2	1	1	1	1	1	1	1	1
Spring St. Line	March 10	Spring St. & Bowery			1/4	1/4	3/4	3/4	3/4	3/4	3/4	3/4	3/4	3/4	3/4	1/4	3/4	1/4	3/4	1/4	3/4	1/4
Houston St. & Prince St. Line	March 11	Houston St. & Broadway		1/2		1/2		1/4		1		1/4		1/4		1		1		1		1
" "	April 10	Desbrosses & West Sts.	0	1/4	1/4	1/4	0	0	0	0	1/4	0	0	0	1/4	1/4	1/4	0	1/4	1/4	1/4	1/4
6th Ave. & Desbrosses St. Ferry Line	April 10	Desbrosses & West Sts.	1/4	0	1/4	0	1/4	1/4	0	0	1/4	0	0	0	1/4	1/4	0	1/4	0	1/4	0	0
Christopher St., 8th St. & 10th St. Line	March 12	Christopher St. Ferry	1/4	0	1/4	0	0	1/2	0	1/2	1/2	0	1/2	0	1 1/2	1/4	1 1/2	1/4	1	1/2	1	1/2
14th St. Ferry & Grand St. Ferry Line	April 9	14th St. & 9th Ave.	3/4	3/4	1/2	3/4	3/4	1/2	1/2	1/2	1/2	3/4	1/2	3/4	3/4	1	1/2	1	1/4	3/4	1/2	1/2
" "	April 8	14th St. & 6th Ave.					3/4	1 1/4	1 1/2	1 1/2	1 1/4	1 1/4	3/4	1	1 1/4	1 3/4	2	1 3/4	2	2	1 1/4	1 1/4
14th St. Ferry & Union Sq. Branch Line	April 9	14th St. & 9th Ave.			1/2	1/2	1/2	3/4	1/2	1/4	1/4	1/2	1/4	1/2	1/4	1	1/2	1 1/4	1/4	1	1/2	1/2
" "	April 8	14th St. & 6th Ave.					1	1	3/4	1/2	3/4	3/4	1/4	1	1/2	1	1	1 1/4	1/4	1 3/4	1/2	1/4
Central Crosstown Line	March 19	E. 23rd St. Ferry			0	1/2	0	0	0	0	1/4	0	1/4	0	1	1/2	1	1/2	1	1	1	1
" "	April 8	14th St. & 6th Ave.					1 1/4	1	1	1 1/2	3/4	1	1/2	1 1/4	3/4	2	1	1 3/4	3/4	1 3/4	1/4	1
23rd St. Crosstown Line	April 11	23rd St. & Lexington Ave.	1/2	1/2	3/4	3/4	3/4	3/4	1	3/4	1	3/4	1	1/2	1 1/4	3/4	1 1/2	1/2	1 1/4	1/4	1/2	3/4
34th St. Ferry Branch of 23rd St. Line	April 11	23rd St. & Lexington Ave.	1/2		3/4		3/4		1 1/4		1 1/4		1		1		1 1/4		1 1/2		1/2	
28th & 29th Sts. Crosstown Line	March 9	W. 23rd St. Ferry			0	0	1/4	1/4	1/4	1/4	1/4	1/4	1/4	1/4	1/4	1/4	1/2	1/2	1/2	1/2	1/2	1/2
34th St. Crosstown Line	March 13	42nd St. Ferry					1/4	1/4	1/4	0	1/4	3/4	3/4	3/4	3/4	3/4	3/4	3/4	3/4	3/4	3/4	3/4
" "	March 14	34th St. & Lexington Ave.	1 1/4	1 1/2									1 1/4	3/4	1 1/4	3/4	1 1/2	3/4	1 1/2	3/4	1 1/2	3/4
42nd St. Line	March 16	42nd St. & 10th Ave.			1/2	1/4	1/4	1/2	1/4	1/2	1/4	1/4	1/2	1/2	1/2	1/2	1/2	3/4	1/4	1/2	1/4	1/2
"	March 14	42nd St. & 3rd Ave.						1/2	3/4	1/2	3/4	1/2	3/4	3/4	1	3/4	1 1/2	3/4	1/4	1/2	1/4	1/2
10th Ave. Line	March 16	42nd St. & 10th Ave.			1/2	1/2	1/2	3/4	3/4	3/4	1/2	3/4	1/2	3/4	3/4	3/4	1	1	3/4	1	1/2	3/4
" "	March 14	42nd St. & 3rd Ave.						3/4	1/2	1/2	1/2	3/4	1 1/4	3/4	1	1	1 1/4	1/2	1/4	3/4	1/2	1/4
Boulevard Branch Line	March 14	42nd St. & 3rd Ave.							3/4	1/2	1/4	1	1/2	1/2	3/4	3/4	1 1/4	3/4	1/4	1/2	1/4	1/4
" "																						

Car Line	Date of Observation	Place of Observation	A.M. 6-6:30 N or E bound	6-6:30 S or W bound	6:30-7 N or E bound	6:30-7 S or W bound	7-7:30 N or E bound	7-7:30 S or W bound	7:30-8 N or E bound	7:30-8 S or W bound	8-8:30 N or E bound	8-8:30 S or W bound	8:30-9 N or E bound	8:30-9 S or W bound			11-11:30 N or E bound	11-11:30 S or W bound	11:30-12 N or E bound	11:30-12 S or W bound	12-12:30 N or E bound	12-12:30 S or W bound
59th St. Crosstown Line	May 21	59th St. & 8th Ave.									1 1/4	1	1 1/4	1								
116th St. Line	May 5	116th St. & 8th Ave.			1 1/4	1 1/4	1 1/4	1 1/4	1 1/4	1 1/4	1 1/4	1 1/4	1 1/4	1 1/4								
St. Nicholas Ave. Line	April 23	Fort Lee Ferry	1/4	1/4	1/2	1/4	0	0	0	0	0	0	0	0								
125th St. Line	April 20	125th St. & 3rd Ave.	1	1	1	1	1/2	1	3/4	1	1/2	3/4	1/4	1			1/2	1/2	1/2	3/4	1/4	1/2
" "	April 21	125th St. & 8th Ave.	1	1	1	1	1	1/2	1	1	1/2	1/2	1/2	1/2			3/4	1/2	1/4	1/2	1/2	3/4
135th St. & Port Morris Line	April 15	135th St. & 8th Ave.	1/4	1	1/2	1 1/4	3/4	1 1/4	1/2	1 1/4	1/2	1 1/4	1/2	1			1/4	1/2	1/4	1/4	1/4	1/4
" "	April 16	135th St. & 8th Ave.	1/2	1	1	1	1	1 1/4	1	1	1	1 1/4	1	1 1/4			1/2	1	1	3/4	1/2	1
" "	April 17	135th St. & 8th Ave.	1/4	1	1	1 1/4	1	1 1/4	1	1 1/4	1/2	1	1/2	1			1/4	1/2	1/4	1/4	1/4	1

Car Line	Date of Observation	Place of Observation	12:30-1 N or E bound	12:30-1 S or W bound	1-1:30 N or E bound	1-1:30 S or W bound	1:30-2 N or E bound	1:30-2 S or W bound			4-4:30 N or E bound	4-4:30 S or W bound	4:30-5 N or E bound	4:30-5 S or W bound	5-5:30 N or E bound	5-5:30 S or W bound	5:30-6 N or E bound	5:30-6 S or W bound	6-6:30 N or E bound	6-6:30 S or W bound	6:30-7 P.M. N or E bound	6:30-7 P.M. S or W bound
59th St. Crosstown Line	May 5	59th St. & 5th Ave.									1	1	1 1/4	1 1/4	1 1/4	1 1/4	1 1/4	1 1/4	1 1/4	1 1/4	1 1/4	1 1/4
116th St. Line																						
St. Nicholas Ave. Line	April 23	Fort Lee Ferry			0	0	0	0			0	0	0	0	0	0	0	0	0	0	0	0
125th St. Line	April 20	125th St. & 3rd Ave.	1/4	1/2	3/4	1	1/2	1			1	1	1	1	1	1	1 1/4	1 1/4	1 1/4	1 1/4	1 1/4	1 1/4
" "	April 21	125th St. & 8th Ave.	1/2	1/2	1	1	1/2	1			1 1/4	1 1/4	1 1/4	1 1/4	1 1/4	1 1/4	1 1/4	1 1/4	1 1/4	1 1/4	1 1/4	1 1/4
135th St. & Port Morris Line	April 15	135th St. & 8th Ave.	1/4	1/4	1/4	1/4	1/4	1/2			3/4	1/2	1/2	1/2	1	1	1 1/4	1 1/4	1 1/4	1	1	1
" "	April 16	135th St. & 8th Ave.	1/2	1	1	1	1	1 1/4			1	1/2	1	1	1 1/4	1/2	1 1/4	1	1 1/4	1/2	1 1/4	1
" "	April 17	135th St. & 8th Ave.	1/4	1/2	1/2	1	1/4	1/2			1/4	1/2	1/2	1/2	1 1/4	1/2	1 1/4	1	1 1/4	1/2	1 1/4	1/2

TABLE 38.

THIRTY-FOURTH STREET FERRY BRANCH
OF
TWENTY-THIRD STREET CROSSTOWN LINE
April 11, 1903
April 11
April 11, 1903
April 11
TWENTY-THIRD STREET CROSSTOWN LINE
CHRISTOPHER STREET AND TENTH STREET LINE
March 12
March 12
7 A.M. 7³⁰ 8 8³⁰ 9 9³⁰ 10 10³⁰ 11 11³⁰ 12 2 P.M. 2³⁰ 3 3³⁰ 4 4³⁰ 5 5³⁰ 6 6³⁰ 7
0 1 2 3 4 5 6 7

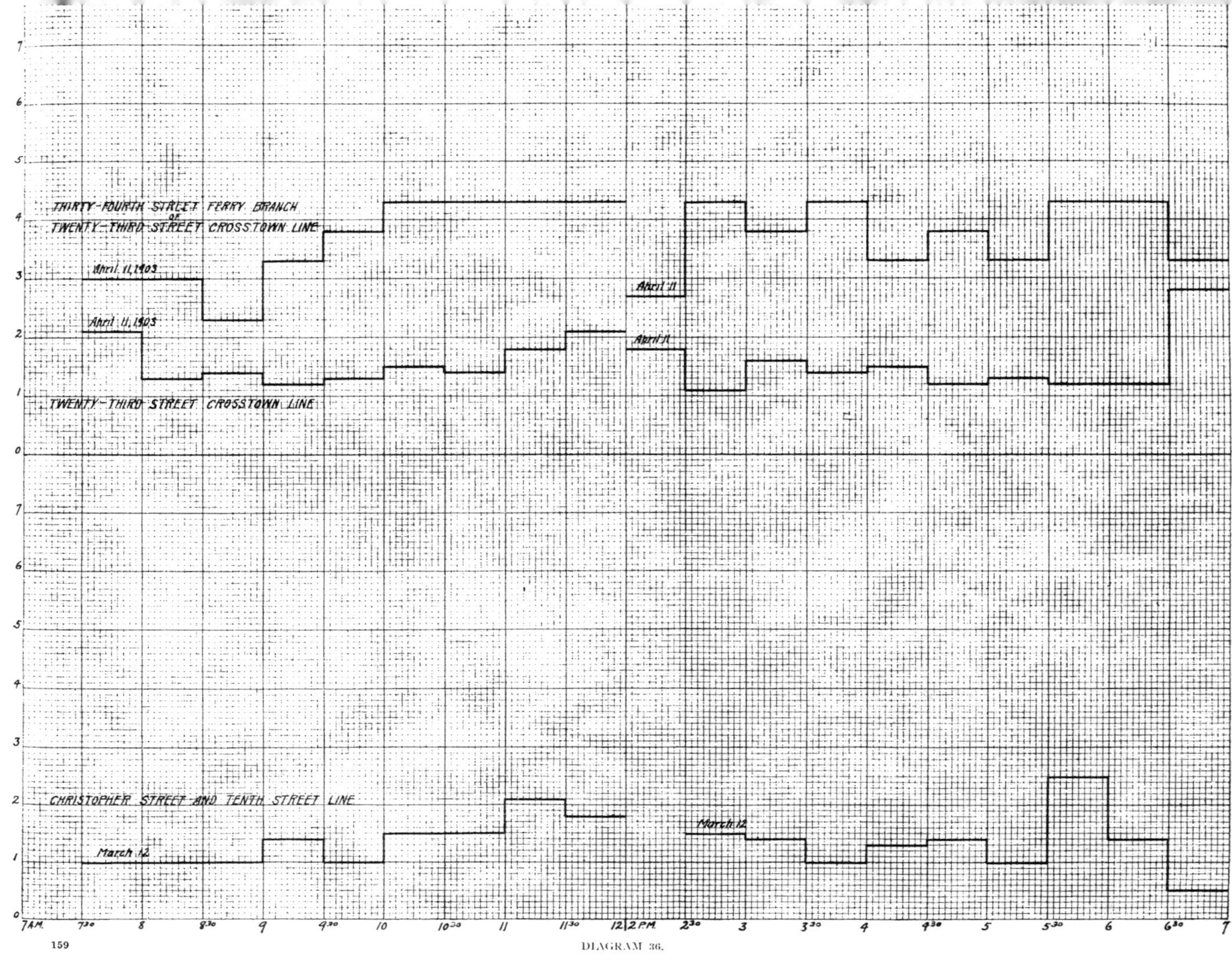

DIAGRAM 36.

CENTRAL CROSSTOWN LINE
March 20
March 19
April 8
14th STREET FERRY AND UNION SQUARE BRANCH LINE
(CENTRAL CROSSTOWN)
April 9
April 9
April 8
8
7
6
5
4
3
2
1
0
7
6
5
4
3
2
1
0
7 A.M.
7 30
8
8 30
9
9 30
10
10 30
11
11 30
12 2 P.M.
2 30
3
3 30
4
4 30
5
5 30
6
6 30
7

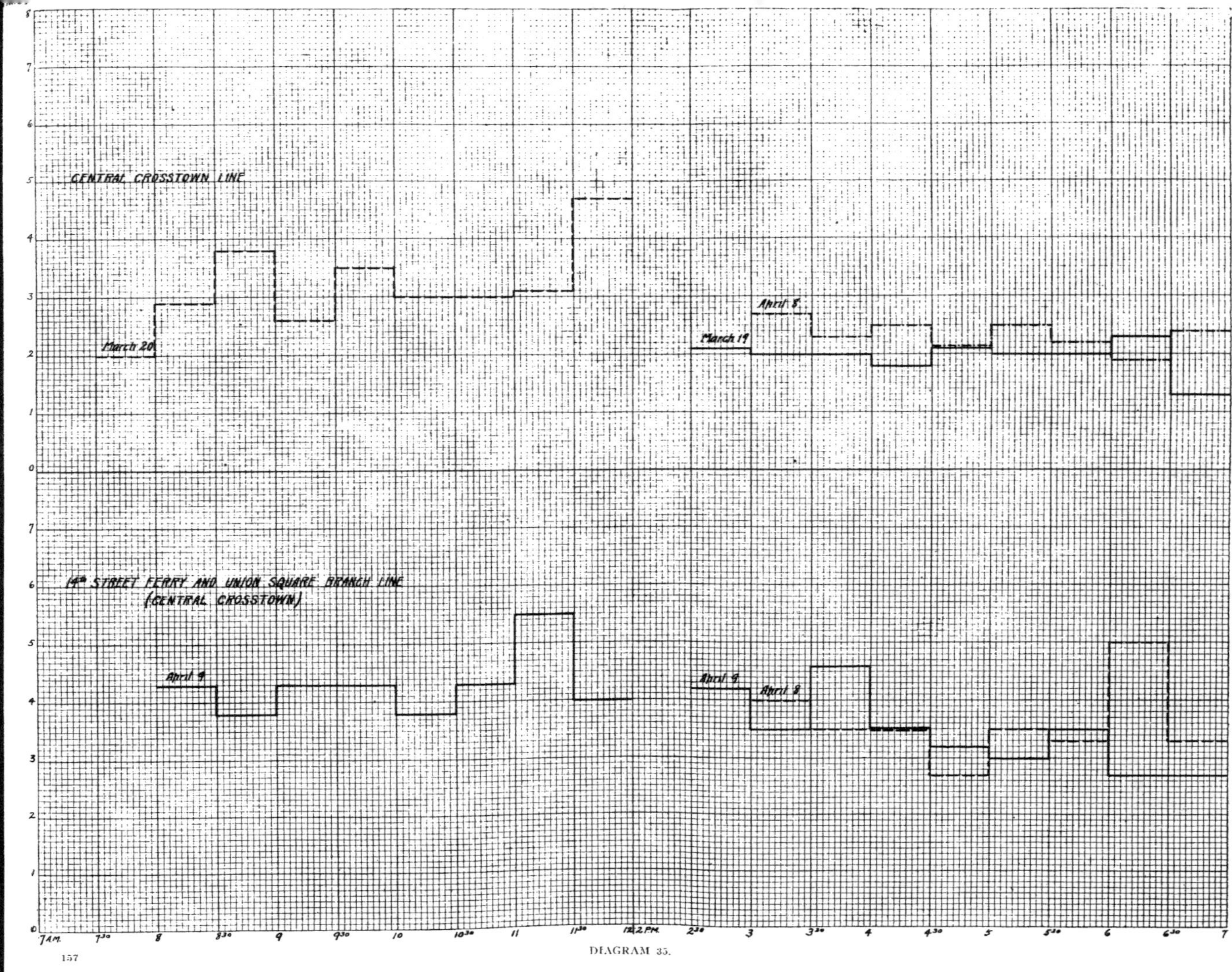

DIAGRAM 35.

SIXTH AVENUE AND DESBROSSES STREET FERRY LINE
April 10
April 10
AVENUE C LINE
(HOUSTON ST. & PRINCE ST. LINE)
April 10
March 11
March 10
April 10
March 11
March 9
8
7
6
5
4
3
2
1
0
7
6
5
4
3
2
1
0
7 A.M.
7³⁰
8
8³⁰
9
9³⁰
10
10³⁰
11
11³⁰
12
2 P.M.
2³⁰
3
3³⁰
4
4³⁰
5
5³⁰
6
6³⁰
7

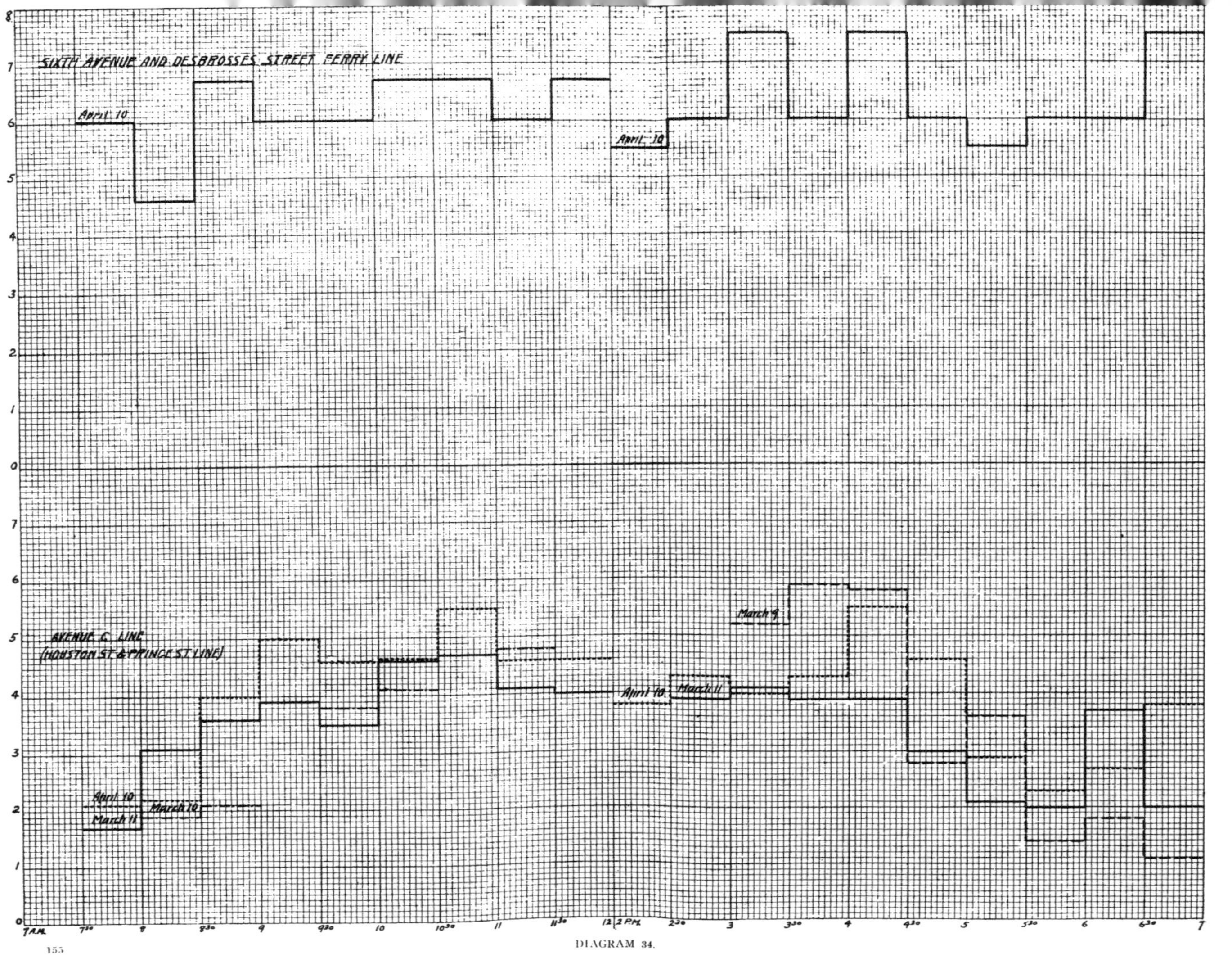

DIAGRAM 34.

SPRING STREET LINE
March 9
March 10
March 7
March 10
DESBROSSES and GRAND STREET LINE
March 11
March 7
March 6
March 10
March 11
7 A.M.
7³⁰
8
8³⁰
9
9³⁰
10
10³⁰
11
11³⁰
12
2 P.M.
2³⁰
3
3³⁰
4
4³⁰
5
5³⁰
6
6³⁰
7

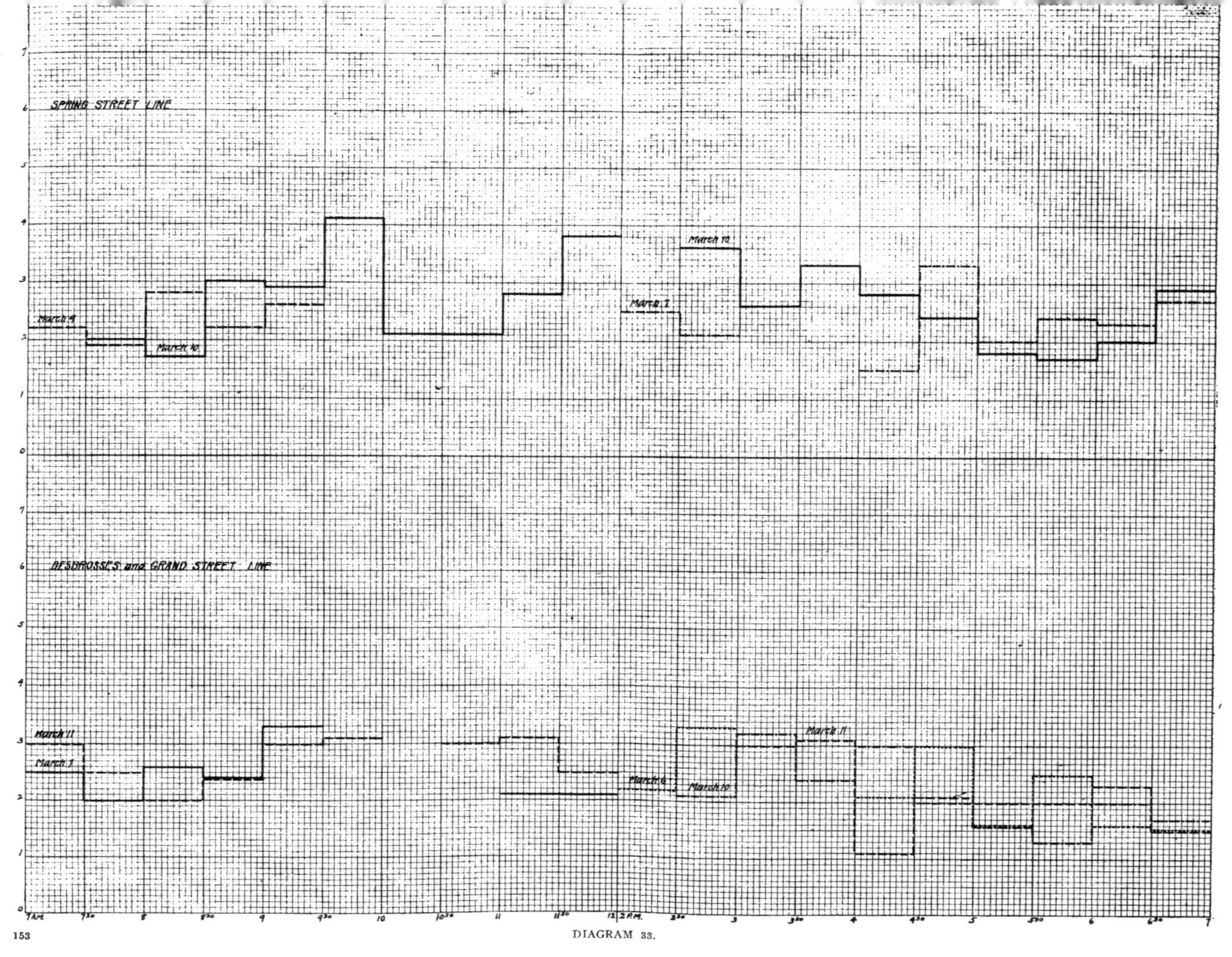

DIAGRAM 33.

Car Line	Date of Observation	Place of Observation	7 AM to 7:30	7:30 to 8	8 to 8:30	8:30 to 9	9 to 9:30	9:30 to 10	10 to 10:30	10:30 to 11	11 to 11:30	11:30 to 12	Date of Observation	Place of Observation	2 PM to 2:30	2:30 to 3	3 to 3:30	3:30 to 4	4 to 4:30	4:30 to 5	5 to 5:30	5:30 to 6	6 to 6:30	6:30 to 7
	Average Headway in Minutes and tenths													Average Headway in Minutes and tenths										
Belt Line – Eastern Division	—1903— March 7	59th St & 1st Ave.	4.0	4.1	7.3	7.5			6.0	6.3	7.5		—1903— March 6	South Ferry						3.1	4.0	6.5	5.2	4.8
″ ″ ″	March 11	Grand & Corlears Sts.	4.4	5.8	6.7	7.4	7.6	7.7	8.0	4.8	7.3	5.2	March 10	8th St & Ave D						6.9	4.9	5.8	6.4	7.4
Belt Line – Western Division	March 19	South Ferry		6.0	4.0	4.3	5.0	5.7	3.9	4.2	6.5	5.0	March 18	53rd St & 10th Ave		2.0	2.3	4.8	3.0	5.0	3.3	4.9	4.3	4.8
″ ″ ″	April 10	Desbrosses & West Sts	4.0	4.3	4.0	4.6	4.3	5.0	4.0	5.0	4.6	4.6	April 10	Desbrosses & West Sts.	4.3	4.3	4.6	4.0	4.0	4.6	4.3	4.6	5.0	3.8
Fulton St. Line	March 6	Fulton & West Sts		5.0	4.7	4.5	5.2	4.8	5.2	5.2	6.0	5.0	March 6	Fulton St & Broadway		30.0	4.3	3.3	3.9	4.1	3.9	8.0	6.0	7.5
Avenue B Line	March 18	34th St Ferry		5.0	5.0	4.1							March 17	Ann St & Park Row		4.6	4.6	6.0	4.3	4.6	5.5	3.8	5.0	4.6
″ ″	March 21	Canal St. & E. Broadway			3.3	4.0	5.5	5.5	6.0	4.6	8.0													
Avenue D Line	March 18	E. 23rd St. Ferry					28.0	10.0	11.0	10.0	20.0	9.0	March 17	Ann St. & Park Row		10.0	10.0	12.0	15.0	10.0	8.6	6.7	6.7	7.5
″ ″	March 21	Canal St. & E. Broadway			6.7	5.5	6.7	8.6	20.0	7.5														
Chambers St. & Grand St Ferry Line	March 7	Chambers St. Ferry	2.0	1.8	2.6	2.1	2.4	2.1	3.2	3.2	3.6	2.0	March 7	Chambers St. & B'way		2.1	2.8	1.7	1.4	3.0	2.3	2.0	1.7	2.0
″ ″ ″	March 14	Chambers & Duane Sts.			2.5	3.4	3.2	3.8	3.9	4.1	4.1	4.8	March 13	Chambers & Duane Sts	3.0	2.6	2.9	4.5	3.7	2.7	2.9	2.3	3.7	3.2
Chambers St. & Roosevelt St Ferry Line	March 13	Roosevelt St. Ferry		7.7	6.5	7.0	6.8	8.3	5.2	5.3	8.9	5.8	March 13	Chambers & Duane Sts.		9.5	8.0	11.0	8.3	7.0	6.4	7.5	5.6	5.0
″ ″ ″	March 14	Chambers & Duane Sts			5.6	8.6	8.2	8.3	7.0	9.3	7.8	12.0												
Cortlandt St & Grand St Ferry Line	March 9	Cortlandt St. Ferry	2.6	3.0	2.6	4.9	2.1	3.1	3.8	3.8	4.2	3.4	March 9	Cortlandt St. Ferry		4.0	5.8	3.7	6.6	2.5	3.6	5.0	3.3	6.0
Bleecker St. & Fulton Ferry Line	April 9	14th St. & 9th Ave.			5.5	7.5	6.0	6.7	12.0	10.0	6.7	10.0	April 9	14th St & 9th Ave.		6.6	8.6	20.0	6.0	5.5	7.5	6.7	7.5	6.0
Desbrosses & Grand St. Line.	March 7	Desbrosses St. Ferry	2.5	2.0	2.6	2.4	3.3				2.1	2.1	March 6	Desbrosses St. Ferry	2.2	3.3			2.1	3.0	1.6	2.5	1.6	1.5
″ ″ ″	March 11	Grand St. & Bowery	3.0	2.5	2.0	2.4	3.0	3.1		3.0	3.1	2.5	March 11	Grand St. & Bowery			3.0	3.1	1.1	2.1	2.0	2.0	2.3	1.5
″ ″ ″													March 10	Grand St. & Broadway		2.1	3.2	2.4	3.0	2.0	1.6	1.3	2.0	1.7
Spring St. Line	March 9	Desbrosses St Ferry	2.2	1.9	2.8	2.2	2.6						March 7	Desbrosses St. Ferry	2.5	2.1			1.5	3.3	2.0	2.4	2.3	2.7
″ ″	March 10	Spring St. & B'way		2.0	1.7	3.0	2.9	4.1	2.1	2.1	2.8	3.8	March 10	Spring St. & Bowery		3.6	2.6	3.3	2.8	2.4	1.8	1.7	2.0	2.9
Houston St. & Prince St. Line	March 10	23rd St. & 1st Ave.			1.9	2.1		3.8	4.1		4.8		March 9	Chambers St Ferry			5.2	5.9	5.8	2.8	3.6	1.4	1.8	1.1
″ ″ ″	March 11	Houston St. & Bowery		1.7	3.1	3.6	3.9	3.5	4.6	4.7	4.1	4.0	March 11	Houston St & Broadway		3.9	4.1	3.9	3.9	3.0	2.1	2.0	3.7	2.0
″ ″ ″	April 10	Desbrosses & West Sts		2.1	2.2	4.0	5.0	4.6	4.6	5.5	4.6	4.6	April 10	Desbrosses & West Sts.	3.8	4.3	4.0	4.3	5.5	4.6	2.9	2.3	2.7	3.8
6th Ave. & Desbrosses St Ferry Line	April 10	Desbrosses & West Sts		6.0	4.6	6.7	6.0	6.0	6.7	6.7	6.0	6.7	April 10	Desbrosses & West Sts	5.5	6.0	7.5	6.0	7.5	6.0	5.5	6.0	6.0	7.5
Christopher St. 8th St & 10th St. Line	March 12	Christopher St. Ferry		1.0	1.0	1.0	1.4	1.0	1.5	1.5	2.1	1.8	March 12	Christopher St Ferry		1.5	1.4	1.0	1.3	1.4	1.0	2.5	1.4	0.5
14th St Ferry & Grand St Ferry Line	April 9	14th St. & 9th Ave.		2.0	2.3	2.6	2.6	3.3	2.9	3.0	4.6	3.0	April 9	14th St. & 9th Ave.	3.0	2.7	2.6	2.7	2.6	2.6	2.5	2.3	2.6	2.7
″ ″ ″													April 8	14th St. & 6th Ave.				3.5	3.2	2.6	2.3	2.1	3.0	4.6
14th St. Ferry & Union Square Branch Line	April 9	14th St & 9th Ave.			4.3	3.8	4.3	4.3	3.8	4.3	5.5	4.0	April 9	14th St. & 9th Ave		4.2	3.5	4.6	3.5	3.2	3.0	3.5	2.7	2.7
″ ″ ″													April 8	14th St. & 6th Ave.			4.0	3.5	3.5	2.7	3.5	3.3	5.0	3.3
Central Crosstown Line	March 20	Christopher St. Ferry		2.0	2.9	3.8	2.6	3.5	3.0	3.0	3.1	4.7	March 19	E. 23rd St. Ferry		2.1	2.0	2.0	1.8	2.1	2.0	2.0	2.3	1.3
″ ″													April 8	14th St & 6th Ave.			2.7	2.3	2.5	2.1	2.5	2.2	1.9	2.4
23rd St. Crosstown Line	April 11	23rd St. & 8th Ave.		2.1	1.3	1.4	1.2	1.3	1.5	1.4	1.8	2.1	April 11	23rd St. & Lexington Ave.	1.8	1.1	1.6	1.4	1.5	1.2	1.3	1.2	1.2	2.8
34th St. Ferry Branch of 23rd St. Line	April 11	23rd St. & 8th Ave.		3.0	3.0	2.3	3.3	3.8	4.3	4.3	4.3	4.3	April 11	23rd St & Lexington Ave	2.7	4.3	3.8	4.3	3.3	3.8	3.3	4.3	4.3	4.3
28th & 29th Sts Crosstown Line	March 10	W. 23rd St Ferry	2.7	2.7	2.3	2.0	3.9	3.7	3.4	3.6	3.0	3.3	March 9	W. 23rd St Ferry		3.3	3.1	3.0	3.0	3.6	2.0	2.0	2.6	2.0
34th St. Crosstown Line	March 13	34th St Ferry	1.8	2.1	1.9	1.8	2.1	2.5	2.3	2.5	2.8		March 13	42nd St. Ferry			2.3	3.0	2.9	2.2	2.2	1.9	1.9	2.2
″ ″	March 14	34th St. & Madison Ave	2.2	1.9	1.9	2.2	2.8	1.7	2.3	2.2	2.3	1.9	March 14	34th St & Lexington Ave	2.5	2.7	2.9	1.9	2.2	1.8	2.1	1.5	2.3	2.1
42nd St. Line	March 16	42nd St & Broadway			1.7	3.8	3.3	3.5	2.9	3.2	7.5	5.5	March 16	42nd St. & 10th Ave.		6.0	3.8	4.3	3.8	5.0	3.2	4.6	4.0	5.5
″ ″													March 14	42nd St. & 3rd Ave				4.0	6.7	3.2	4.2	3.6	3.0	6.0
10th Ave. Line	March 16	42nd St. & Broadway			2.8	6.0	4.6	4.6	4.6	4.6	5.5	5.5	March 16	42nd St. & 10th Ave.		4.9	3.8	3.8	4.6	4.6	3.8	4.6	3.2	3.8
″ ″													March 14	42nd St & 3rd Ave.			6.7	8.6	6.7	5.0	3.1	4.4	6.0	8.6
Boulevard Branch Line	March 16	42nd St & Broadway			2.5	5.5	5.5	4.0	3.8	4.3	5.5	6.0	March 14	42nd St. & 3rd Ave.				6.7	4.6	2.6	2.9	2.9	3.3	5.5
″ ″ ″	March 17	34th St. Ferry				4.0	6.0	5.0	3.3		5.5	7.5	March 17	42nd St. & 3rd Ave.					3.0	3.8	2.3	2.6		
86th St Crosstown Line	March 9	8th Ave & 85th St.	2.5	1.6	1.5	2.8		3.0			3.0		March 7	85th St & 8th Ave						2.6	1.9	1.6	1.7	1.9

TABLE 32.

AWP.

HEADWAY SHEET No. 1a

Car Line	Date of Observation	Place of Observation	Average Headway in Minutes and tenths: 6 AM to 6^{30}	6^{30} to 7	7 to 7^{30}	7^{30} to 8	8 to 8^{30}	8^{30} to 9		11 to 11^{30}	11^{30} to 12	12 to 12^{30}	Date of Observation	Place of Observation	Average Headway in Minutes and tenths: 12^{30} to 1	1 to 1^{30}	1^{30} to 2		4 to 4^{30}	4^{30} to 5	5 to 5^{30}	5^{30} to 6	6 to 6^{30}	6^{30} to 7
59th St. Crosstown Line	1903 May 21	59th St. & 8th Ave.					1.1	1.3					1903 May 5	59th St. & 5th Ave.					1.0	1.1	0.9	0.8	0.9	0.8
116th St. Line	May 5	116th St. & 8th Ave.		2.2	2.1	2.1	2.1	2.2																
" "					2.2	2.3																		
St. Nicholas Ave. Line	April 23	Fort Lee Ferry	Headway		10	minutes							April 23	Fort Lee Ferry	Headway		10	minutes						
125th St. Line	April 20	125th St. & 3rd Ave.	Headway		3	minutes							April 20	125th St. & 3rd Ave.	Headway		3	minutes						
" "	April 21	125th St. & 8th Ave.		"	"	"							April 21	125th St. & 8th Ave.		"	"	"						
135th St. & Port Morris Line	April 15	135th St. & 8th Ave.	2.3	2.2	1.9	2.3	1.9	2.3		2.5	2.6	2.7	April 15	135th St. & 8th Ave.	2.9	3.2	2.9		2.4	2.2	2.5	2.3	2.0	2.0
" " "	April 16	135th St. & 8th Ave.	2.1	2.2	2.3	2.3	2.3	2.1		2.3	2.4	2.4	April 16	135th St. & 8th Ave.	2.5	2.7	2.4		2.1	1.9	2.1	2.0	2.0	1.8
" " "	April 17	135th St. & 8th Ave.	2.2	2.2	1.9	2.3	1.9	2.4		2.9	2.5	2.6	April 17	135th St. & 8th Ave.	2.6	3.2	2.6		1.9	2.1	2.1	2.0	1.8	1.7

TABLE 31.

—THE MERCHANTS ASSOCIATION—
—OF—
—NEW YORK—

—COMMITTEE ON ENGINEERING AND SANITATION—

—SURFACE RAILWAY TRANSPORTATION—
—BOROUGH OF MANHATTAN—
—NEW YORK CITY—

—HEADWAY—
—ON—
—CROSSTOWN AND HORSE CAR LINES—

Sheets No. 1a & 2a and 1b – 15b (inclusive)

CASE V.
NINTH AVE. SOUTH BOUND
APRIL 1ST 1903 10PM.
CASE VI.
8TH AVE. NORTH BOUND
CASE VII.
8TH AVE. NORTH BOUND
APRIL 1ST 1903 10PM.
CASE VIII.
8TH AVE. NORTH BOUND.
MARCH 18TH 1903 9 P.M.
—THE MERCHANTS ASSOCIATION—
—OF—
—NEW YORK.—
—COMMITTEE ON ENGINEERING AND SANITATION.—
—START AND STOP DIAGRAMS.—
—STREET CAR MOVEMENTS.—
SHEET Nº 47

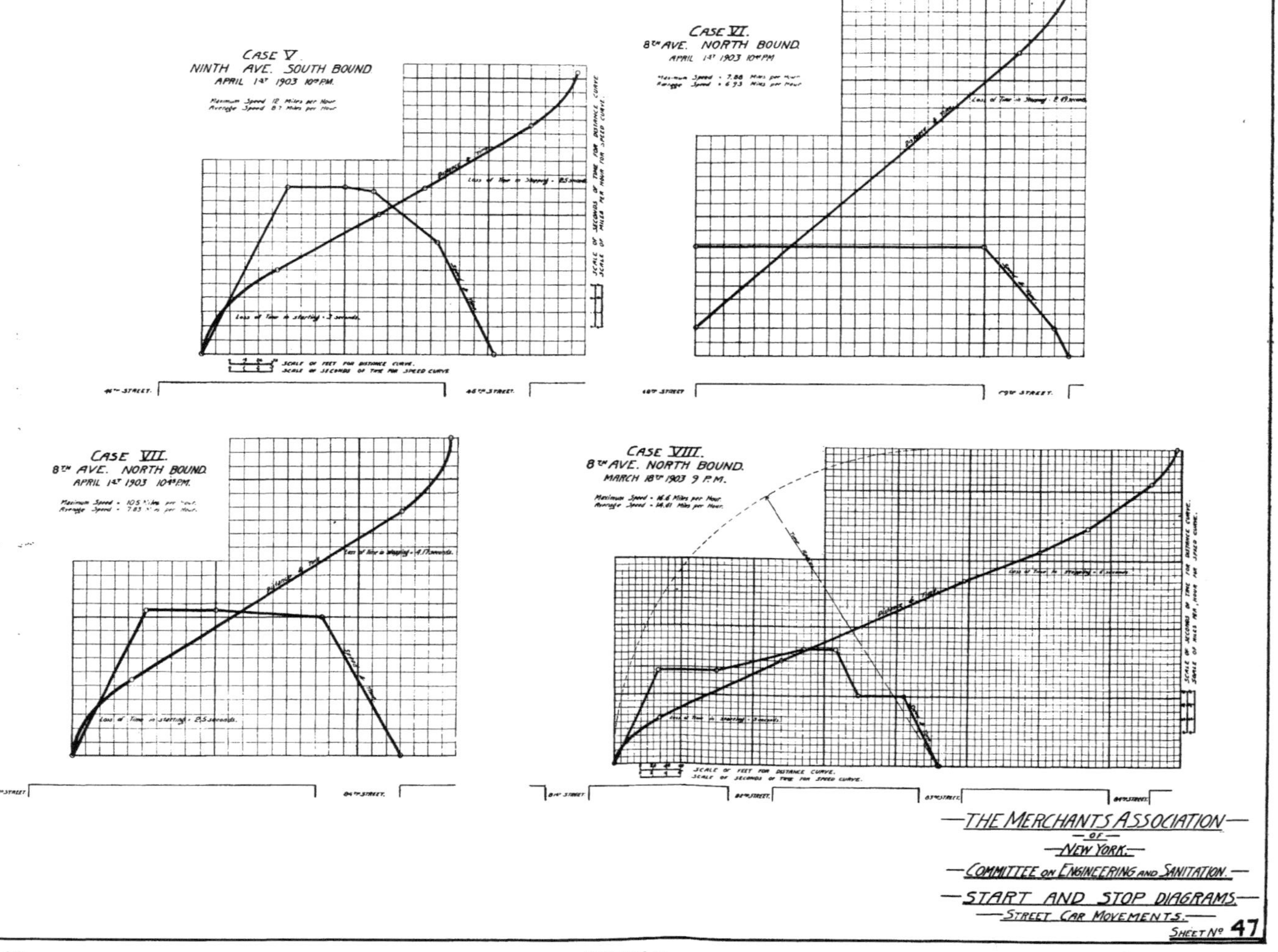

DIAGRAM 30.

CASE I.
SIXTH AVE. NORTH BOUND.
APRIL 1ST 1903 - - 9.30 PM
SCALE OF FEET FOR DISTANCE CURVE.
SCALE OF SECONDS OF TIME FOR SPEED CURVE.
43D STREET.
44TH STREET.
CASE II.
AMSTERDAM AVE. NORTH BOUND
APRIL 1ST 1903 EVENING.
89TH STREET.
90TH STREET.
CASE III.
AMSTERDAM AVE. NORTH BOUND
APRIL 1ST 1903 EVENING.
Maximum speed - 11 Miles per hour
Average speed - 7¾ Miles per hour.
84TH STREET.
85TH STREET.
CASE IV.
AMSTERDAM AVE. NORTH BOUND
APRIL 1ST 1903 EVENING.
MAXIMUM Speed - 11.2 Miles per hour.
Average Speed - 8.9 Miles per hour.
87TH STREET.
88TH STREET.
THE MERCHANTS ASSOCIATION
OF
NEW YORK.
COMMITTEE ON ENGINEERING AND SANITATION.
START & STOP DIAGRAMS
STREET CAR MOVEMENTS.
SHEET NO 46.

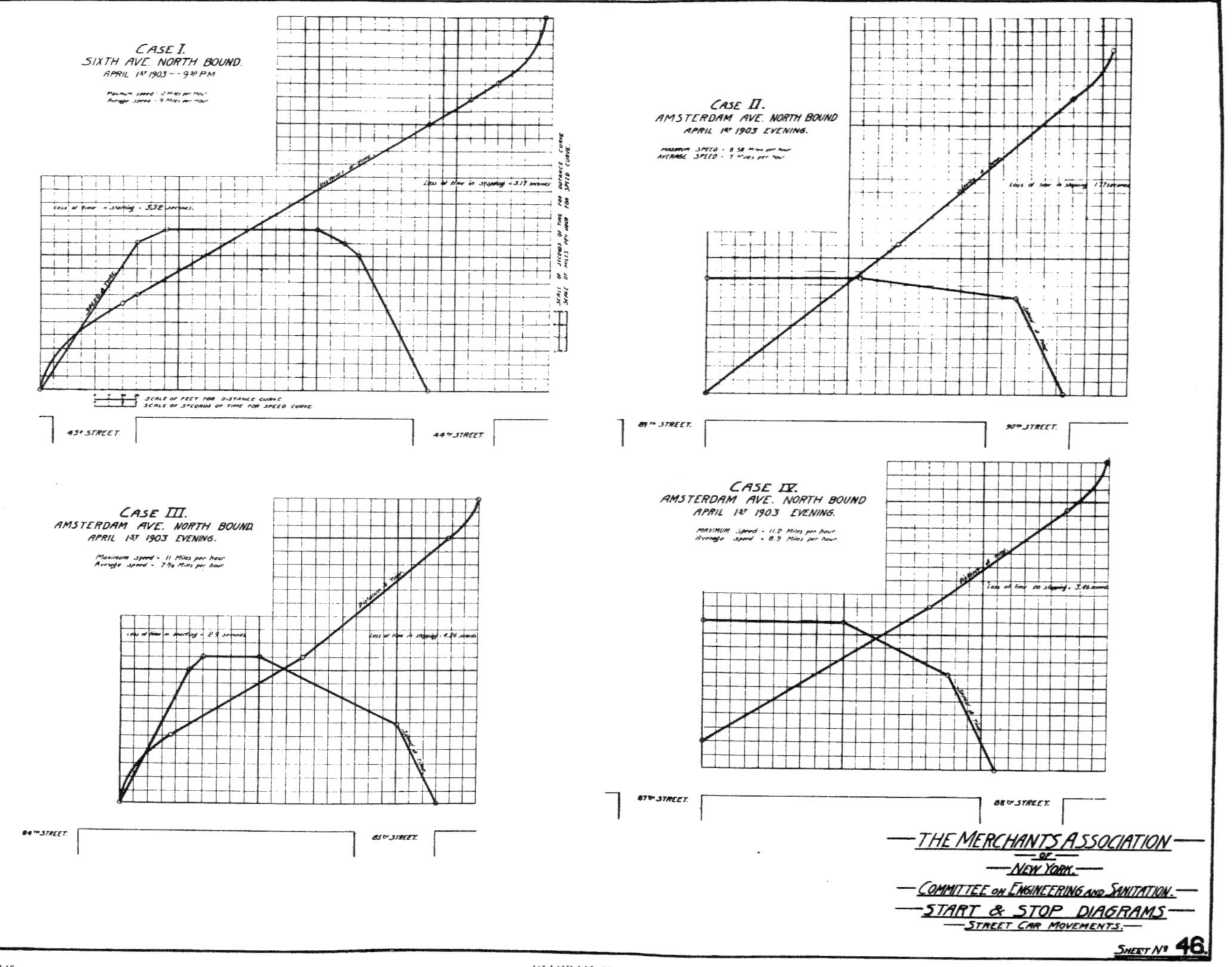

DIAGRAM 29.

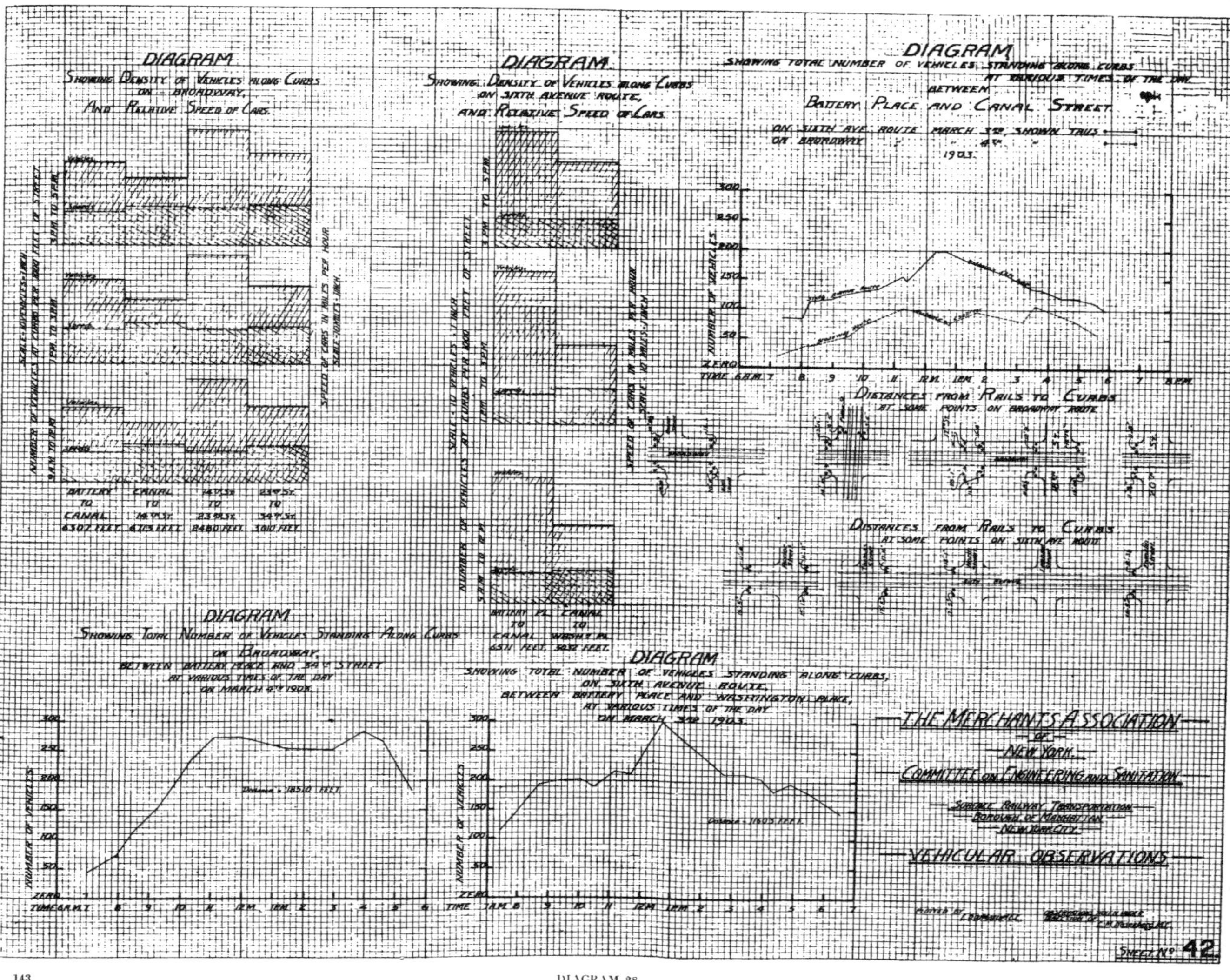

DIAGRAM 28.

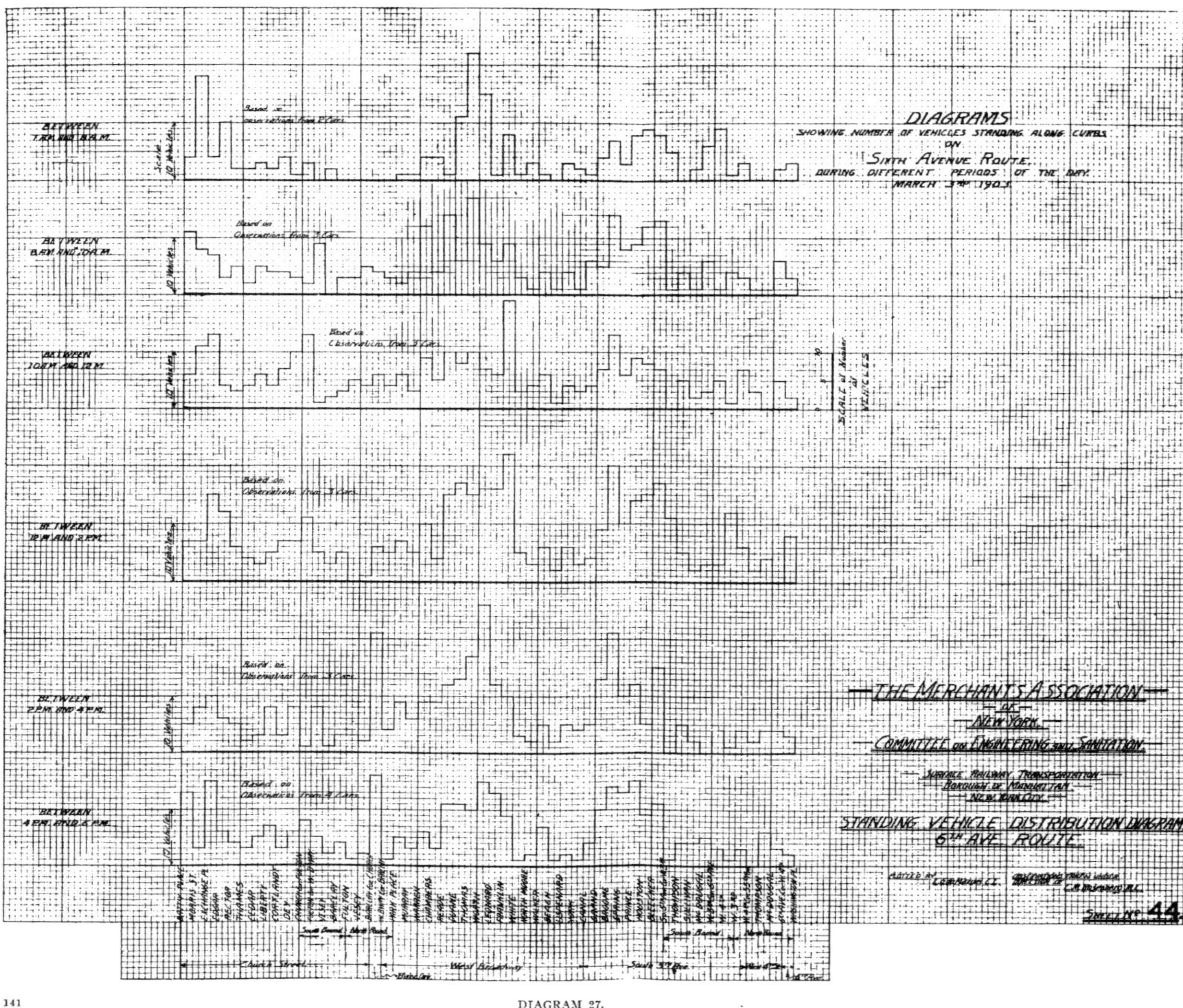

DIAGRAM 27.

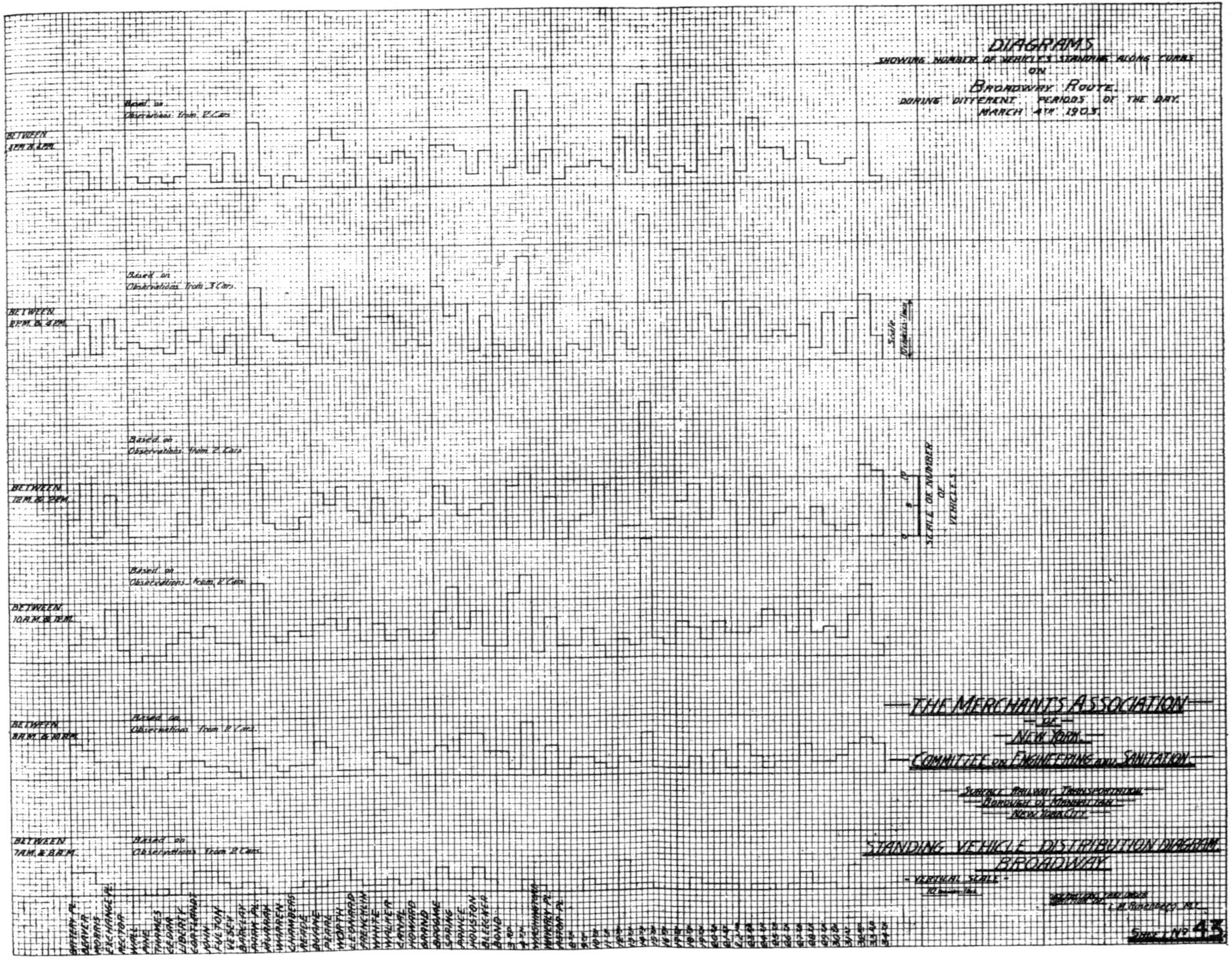

DIAGRAMS
SHOWING NUMBER OF VEHICLES STANDING ALONG CURBS
ON
BROADWAY ROUTE.
DURING DIFFERENT PERIODS OF THE DAY.
MARCH 4TH 1903.

BETWEEN 4 P.M. & 6 P.M. — Based on Observations from 2 Cars.

BETWEEN 2 P.M. & 4 P.M. — Based on Observations from 3 Cars.

BETWEEN 12 M. & 2 P.M. — Based on Observations from 2 Cars.

BETWEEN 10 A.M. & 12 M. — Based on Observations from 2 Cars.

BETWEEN 8 A.M. & 10 A.M. — Based on Observations from 2 Cars.

BETWEEN 7 A.M. & 8 A.M. — Based on Observations from 2 Cars.

SCALE OF NUMBER OF VEHICLES: 0, 5, 10

BATTERY PL., BEAVER, MORRIS, EXCHANGE PL., RECTOR, WALL, PINE, THAMES, CEDAR, LIBERTY, CORTLANDT, JOHN, FULTON, VESEY, BARCLAY, PARK PL., MURRAY, WARREN, CHAMBERS, READE, DUANE, PEARL, WORTH, LEONARD, FRANKLIN, WHITE, WALKER, CANAL, HOWARD, GRAND, BROOME, SPRING, PRINCE, HOUSTON, BLEECKER, BOND, 3RD, 4TH, WASHINGTON, WAVERLY PL., ASTOR PL.

THE MERCHANTS ASSOCIATION
OF
NEW YORK
COMMITTEE ON ENGINEERING AND SANITATION.

SURFACE RAILWAY TRANSPORTATION
BOROUGH OF MANHATTAN
NEW YORK CITY.

STANDING VEHICLE DISTRIBUTION DIAGRAM.
BROADWAY

VERTICAL SCALE

SHEET No. 43

DIAGRAM 26.

—Vehicle Record—

Form 2.

—Vehicles Standing on Curbs—

Observers Stationed on Cars

of

—Broadway Line—

Wednesday, March 4th 1903

Vehicles standing between	Car No. 2644 (North bound, arrived at 34th St 7-22-53 A.M.)			Car No. 73 (South bound, started from 34th St 7-40-43 A.M.)			Car No. 27 (North bound, arrived at 34th St 8-46-58 A.M.)			Car No. 2619 (South bound, started from 34th St 8-52-08 A.M.)		
	Westerly curbing	Easterly curbing	E+W	Westerly curbing	Easterly curbing	E+W	Westerly curbing	Easterly curbing	E+W	Westerly curbing	Easterly curbing	E+W
34th St												
33rd St										5		5
32nd St							4	2	6			
31st St	3	1	4				1	4	5	1	1	2
30th St							1	2	3			
29th St		1	1					2	2			
28th St				1		1	2		2			
27th St	1		1	1	2	3	2	2	4	1	4	5
26th St				1		1		2	2	1		1
25th St							2		2	1		1
24th St	1		1				1		1			
23rd St				1		1	3		3	1		1
22nd St							1		1		5	5
21st St				1		1	1		1	1		1
20th St		1	1	1		1	1	3	4		3	3
19th St		1	1									
18th St		2	2	1	1	2				1	2	3
17th St								1	1	1		1
16th St							1		1	1		1
15th St							1		1			
14th St				1		1	3	1	4	4	3	7
13th St		1	1		1	1				1	1	2
12th St	1	1	2	4	1	5	2		2	3		3
11th St							1		1	1		1
10th St					1	1		2	2		2	2
9th St		2	2				1		1	2	1	3
8th St											3	3
Astor Pl								1	1			
Waverly Pl							3		3	5		5
Wash. Pl				1		1						
4th St					2	2		1	1		9	9
3rd St											1	1
Bond								4	4		2	2
Bleecker	2		2	1	1	2	2		2	3	1	4
Houston	1		1	4		4	1		1	5	2	7
Prince	1	1	2		1	1	1	2	3	4	3	7
Spring		2	2		1	1	1	3	4	1	2	3
Broome				2	2	4	3	2	5	4		4
Grand							1		1	2	2	4
Howard		1	1	1	1	2		1	1	4		4
Canal					1	1		2	2			
Walker		1	1	1	1	2	1		1	3		3
White				1		1	2		2	4		4
Franklin		1	1	1		1				1		1
Leonard		2	2	1	1	2	1		1	1		1
Worth	2	2	4	1		1					1	1
Thomas, Pearl	2		2		1	1	1	1	2	4	1	5
Duane		1	1	1		1				4	2	6
Reade	1		1		1	1	1	1	2		2	2
Chambers		1	1							1	1	2
Warren										1		1
Murray										2		2
Park Pl				1		1				4	1	5
Barclay				2		2						
Vesey, Ann	1		1				1		1		1	1
Fulton		2	2		1	1		2	2		1	1
Dey, John	1	1		1	3	4		1	1	1	1	2
Cortlandt	2		2	4		4				3		3
Liberty		1	1	1	1	2		3	3	1	2	3
Cedar								1	1			
Thames	1		1									
Pine								2	2			
Wall					1	1						
Rector				1		1		1	1	1		1
Exch. Pl				1		1	2	1	3	1		1
Morris				2		2	3		3	1		1
Beaver					4	4		5	5		4	4
Batt'y Pl				4		4	6		6	4		4
	Started from Batt'y Pl 7-03-59 A.M.			Arrived at Batt'y Pl 8-09-58 A.M.			Started from Batt'y Pl 8-16-58 A.M.			Arrived at Batt'y Pl 9-36-43 A.M.		

Vehicles standing between	Car No. 6 (North bound, arrived at 34th St 10-34-38 A.M.)			Car No. 2634 (South bound, started from 34th St 10-42-05 A.M.)			Car No. 2632 (North bound, arrived at 34th St 12-26-38 P.M.)			Car No. 47 (South bound, started from 34th St 12-12-02 P.M.)			Car No. 37 (North bound, arrived at 34th St 2-13-43 P.M.)		
	Westerly curbing	Easterly curbing	E+W	Westerly curbing	Easterly curbing	E+W	Westerly curbing	Easterly curbing	E+W	Westerly curbing	Easterly curbing	E+W	Westerly curbing	Easterly curbing	E+W
34th St															
33rd St	1		1	1		1		1	1	10	1	11	1	3	4
32nd St	10	2	12	1	3	4	10	2	12	2	1	3	10	1	11
31st St	2	5	7	2	4	6	2		2		2	2	2	5	7
30th St		2	2	3		3	1		1				1		1
29th St	2		2	1	4	5	1		1	1	1	2		3	3
28th St	1	1	2	4		4	3		3	4	1	5		1	1
27th St	5	3	8	2	2	4	2	1	3	1		1	3	2	5
26th St	1	1	2	4		4	3	2	5	2		2		2	2
25th St	4		4	6	1	7	3	1	4	1	2	3		3	3
24th St	4		4	8		8	2		2				3		3
23rd St	5		5		1	1	8	2	10	6		6	4		4
22nd St	1	1	2	2	2	4		2	2		1	1		2	2
21st St	4		4	3	1	4	3	1	4	4	2	6	2	3	5
20th St	3	3	6	3	1	4	4	6	10	7	1	8		1	1
19th St				3		3	2	1	3	1	1	2		1	1
18th St	3	1	4	4	1	5	5	4	9	4	2	6	1	2	3
17th St	1		1	5	1	6	4	2	6	5		5	1	18	19
16th St	1		1	2		2	3		3	1		1			
15th St	2		2	3		3	2		2	3		3			
14th St	5	15	20	9	7	16	8	15	23	6	13	19	2	2	4
13th St	1	1	2		1	1	1		1		2	2	1		1
12th St		2	2	2	1	3	1	1	2				1	2	3
11th St													1		1
10th St	1	1	2		1	1	1	2	3	1	8	9		7	7
9th St				3	2	5	1		1	3	1	4	2		2
8th St		2	2	2		2	1	2	3	2		2			
Astor Pl		2	2												
Waverly Pl	7		7	6		6	6		6	7		7	4		4
Wash. Pl	1		1	1		1									
4th St	3	6	9	1	15	16		11	11	1	6	7		12	12
3rd St		11	11	1	1	2	3	6	9	1		1	1		1
Bond		1	1		2	2								3	3
Bleecker	1	1	2		1	1	2	1	3	6		6	3	2	5
Houston	2	1	3	6	2	8	2	1	3	4	1	5	2		2
Prince	3		3	3	2	5	2	2	4		3	3	4		4
Spring	2	10	12	5	4	9	1	5	6	1	4	5	1	7	8
Broome	4	4	8	2	5	7	5	4	9	2	1	3	2	3	5
Grand	1	2	3	1	1	2		3	3	1	3	4	1	1	2
Howard				2	1	3		3	3	1	1	2	1	3	4
Canal				3	2	5	1	1	2	3	1	4		2	2
Walker		1	1	3		3		3	3	2		2	2	6	8
White		2	2	4	2	6	5	2	7	1		1	5	3	8
Franklin	1	1	2	2	1	3	2	1	3		1	1	4	1	5
Leonard	4	1	5	6	1	7	4		4	4	1	5	1	2	3
Worth	3	2	5	2	1	3	4	5	9	2	4	6	1	1	2
Thomas, Pearl	3	2	5	2	5	7	4	2	6	1	1	2	5	4	9
Duane	2	3	5	2	4	6	3	5	8	4	2	6	1	1	2
Reade		2	2	2	2	4		2	2	2	2	4	2	1	3
Chambers	1	2	3	3	2	5				1	1	2		1	1
Warren	2		2	3		3	2		2	1		1			
Murray	2		2	4		4				3		3	1		1
Park Pl	1	3	4	1	12	13	1	12	13	1	10	11	1	12	13
Barclay							2		2	1		1			
Vesey, Ann	1		1	3		3	2	1	3	1		1	4		4
Fulton		3	3					2	2		1	1			
Dey, John	1	1	2	3	3	6	4	5	9	1	1	2	2	4	6
Cortlandt	1	3	4	2		2	2	1	3		1	1	2	1	3
Liberty	2	3	5	1		1		1	1	4	1	5		1	1
Cedar	1	2	3	2	1	3		1	1		1	1		2	2
Thames	1		1	1		1				1		1			
Pine		1	1								1	1		3	3
Wall								1	1		1	1		4	4
Rector				2		2	1		1	3		3			
Exch. Pl	1	1	2	4	5	9	1		1	4	4	8	3	5	8
Morris	4		4	4		4	1		1	1		1	1		1
Beaver		6	6		4	4		10	10		3	3		7	7
Batt'y Pl	2	1	3	3		3	4		4	3		3	2		2
	Started from Batt'y Pl 9-51-03 A.M.			Arrived at Batt'y Pl 11-29-32 A.M.			Started from Batt'y Pl 11-31-38 A.M.			Arrived at Batt'y Pl 12-30-38 P.M.			Started from Batt'y Pl 1-32-45 P.M.		

Vehicles standing between	Car No. 2647 (South bound, started from 34th St 2-38-30 P.M.)			Car No. 120 (North bound, arrived at 34th St 4-08-38 P.M.)			Car No. 42 (South bound, started from 34th St 4-16-34 P.M.)			Car No. — (North bound, arrived at 34th St 6-10-31 P.M.)		
	Westerly curbing	Easterly curbing	E+W	Westerly curbing	Easterly curbing	E+W	Westerly curbing	Easterly curbing	E+W	Westerly curbing	Easterly curbing	E+W
34th St												
33rd St		1	1					1	1			
32nd St		2	2	10		10	10		10	10		10
31st St		6	6	1	2	3	1	3	4			
30th St				1		1		3	3			
29th St	4	4	8	1	3	4	1	2	3			
28th St		2	2				3	1	4	3	1	4
27th St	3	3	6	2	3	5	2	5	7	2		2
26th St	2		2	1	3	4	4		4	3	1	4
25th St	1		1	3		3	1	2	3	5	1	6
24th St	4		4	4		4	4		4	5	1	6
23rd St	5		5	9		9	5	1	6	11		11
22nd St		2	2	1	3	4		2	2			
21st St	5	2	7	4	6	10	2	4	6	2		2
20th St	2	1	3	3	2	5	4	1	5	1	1	2
19th St	1	4	5	2	6	8	8	2	10	2		2
18th St	3	2	5	3	2	5		2	2	2		2
17th St	3	2	5	1	3	4	3		3		1	1
16th St	2		2	2	8	10	2		2			
15th St	2		2	3	7	10	3		3			
14th St	5	20	25	4	2	6	1	16	17	1	16	17
13th St				1	1	2	1	1	2			
12th St	1		1	4	1	5	4	4	8		2	2
11th St				1		1	3		3	2		2
10th St		2	2		1	1					4	4
9th St				1	1	2	2	1	3		1	1
8th St				1	2	3	1	2	3	1	1	2
Astor Pl		1	1					1	1			
Waverly Pl	10		10	6		6	6		6	4		4
Wash. Pl	1		1				2		2			
4th St	2	15	17	2	16	18	1	15	16	1	6	7
3rd St	2		2				1		1	1	2	3
Bond					1	1		1	1			
Bleecker	6		6	7	1	8	5	1	6	3	1	4
Houston	1	1	2	1		1	2		2	1	1	2
Prince	5	5	10	2	1	3	2	4	6	3	2	5
Spring	3	4	7	2	4	6	2	5	7	1	4	5
Broome	5	8	13	2		2	3	4	7	1	6	7
Grand	1	2	3	1	2	3						
Howard	1	3	4	1	2	3	1	4	5		3	3
Canal				2	1	3	3	3	6	4	3	7
Walker	1	1	2	4	3	7	1	2	3	2	2	4
White	5	1	7	5	1	6	3	2	5		3	3
Franklin	1		1	4	2	6						
Leonard	3	1	4		2	2	4	1	5	3		3
Worth	2	3	5		4	4	6	2	8	1	2	3
Thomas, Pearl	8	5	13	5	7	12	5	4	9	6	4	10
Duane	3	4	7	6	3	9	6	2	8	4		4
Reade		1	1		2	2					1	1
Chambers	3	1	4				2		2			
Warren				4		4						
Murray	5		5	1		1				2		2
Park Pl	3		3	2	11	13	2	7	9		11	11
Barclay							1		1			
Vesey, Ann	5		5	4		4	4	2	6		1	1
Fulton					2	2		1	1		1	1
Dey, John	2	2	4	4	1	5		2	2	3	1	4
Cortlandt				4		4		4	4	1	2	3
Liberty	5	1	6	2		2	2		2	1		1
Cedar	2		2	2		2				1		1
Thames				3		3	2		2	1		1
Pine		2	2		2	2					1	1
Wall					1	1		1	1		2	2
Rector	1		1	3		3						
Exch. Pl	3	3	6	3	1	4	4	3	7	3		3
Morris				2		2						
Beaver		1	1		4	4		3	3			
Batt'y Pl	1		1		2	2	3		3			
	Arrived at Batt'y Pl 3-17-52 P.M.			Started from Batt'y Pl 3-25-10 P.M.			Arrived at Batt'y Pl 4-38-34 P.M.			Started from Batt'y Pl 5-27-34 P.M.		

—The Merchants Association—
— of —
—New York—
—Committee on Engineering and Sanitation—

—Surface Railway Transportation—
—Borough of Manhattan—
—New York City—

—Vehicle Count—
—from—
—Broadway Cars—

Sheet No 20.

TABLE 25.

—Vehicle Record—

Form 2.

—Vehicles standing on Curbs.—

Observers stationed on cars of

—Sixth Avenue Line.—

Tuesday, March 3rd 1903

Vehicles standing at / between	Car # 2026 North bound, arrived at Wash. Pl. 7-30-03 A.M.			Car # 2070 South bound, started from Wash. Pl. 7-37-45 A.M.			Car # 2070 North bound, arrived at Wash. Pl. 8-30-23 A.M.			Car # 1905 South bound, started from Wash. Pl. 8-39-23 A.M.			Car # 1905 North bound, arrived at Wash. Pl. 9-34-11 A.M.			Car # 2048 South bound, started from Wash. Pl. 9-42-30 A.M.			Car # 2048 North bound, arrived at Wash. Pl. 10-45-35 A.M.			Car # 1674 South bound, started from Wash. Pl. 10-57-30 A.M.			Car # 1674 North bound, arrived at Wash. Pl. 11-52-50 A.M.			Car # 2056 South bound, started from Wash. Pl. 12-02-01 P.M.		
	West curb	East curb	E+W	West curb	East curb	E+W	West curb	East curb	E+W	West curb	East curb	E+W	West curb	East curb	E+W	West curb	East curb	E+W	West curb	East curb	E+W	West curb	East curb	E+W	West curb	East curb	E+W	West curb	East curb	E+W
Wash. Pl.																														
6th & W. 4th St.	3		3				2	1	3				1	2	3				2		2				1		1			
McDougal	2		2				4	2	6				2	4	6				4	1	5				2	2	4			
Thompson							1		1																					
W. 3rd S. Av.													1		1				1		1				3		3			
W. 3rd St.	1	2	3				1		1				2	1	3				5	2	7				2	2	4			
W. 4th St.				1		1				3	1	4					2	2					1	1					2	2
W. S. 6th Av.				3W	1	4				1		1				2		2				4	1	5						
McDougal					6	6				4	2	6				2		2					3	3				1	2	3
Sullivan					2	2					1	1				1	3	4				1	1	2				2		2
Thompson										1	3	4					1	1				2W	3	5				2	3	5
S. 5th Av. 3rd				5		5				1		1				1	1	2										5	6	11
Bleecker	4	4	8		2	2	5	7	12	5+	8	13	7	10	17	4	5+	9	1+	6	7	3	4	7	2	3	5		1	1
Houston	2	2	4	3	6	9	5	7	12	5	6	11	3	8	11	3	6	9	4	9	13	3	5	8	5	3	8	4	3	7
Prince	2W	1	3	2	6	8		6	6	5	4+	7	6	3+	9	3	2	5	2	3+	5	1	7	8	3	6	9	3+	5	8
Spring		2	2	2	1	3		2	2	2	6	8	4	2	6	1	5	6	1	1+	2	2	3	5	2	4	6	1	4	5
Broome	1		1	7		7	4	5	9	8	6	14	8	6	14	7	11	18	3+	4	7	6	1	7	8	5	13	11	6	17
Grand	1	3	4	3	1	4	1	2	3	3	2	5	2+		2	3	4	7	3	3	6	3	4	7	2	4	6	4	5	9
Canal		2	2		1	1	2	2	4		3	3	3	3	6		5	5		1	1	1	2	3	3	1	4	1	3	4
York	2+		2				1+		1				1+		1				3+		3								3	3
Lispenard					3	3		4	4		1	1		3	3		2	2		4	4		2	2		4	4		6	6
Beach										1		1	1		1	4	1	5	1		1	1		1	1		1	1		1
Walker		1	1		1	1		2+	2	1+		1		4	4								6	6		4	4		2	2
N. Moore				3		3	1		1							2		2	4		4	2		2	2		2	2		2
White					1+	1					1	1	2	1	3								3	3					1	1
Franklin	2		2	6	2	8	7	2	9	6	1	7	5	2	7	10	4	14	4	3	7	11	6	17	13	6	19	14	8	22
Leonard		1	1							4	2	6		4	4	1	4	5	5	1	6	4		4	3		3	1	6	7
Worth	4		4		15	15	3	3	6	6+	3	9	3+	1	4	8	8	16	5+	2	7	2	1	3	2	1	3	8+	4	12
Thomas	4	18	22	3		3	3	14	17	1	4	5	1+	6	7				3	6	9		9	9	4	6	10		14	14
Duane	3	2	5	7	4	11	3	3	6	2	3	5	4	2	6	6	7	13	3	5	8	1	3	4	2	3	5	9	7	16
Reade	2	2	4		1	1	7	5	12	7	7	14	5	4	9	4	5	9	4	5	9	1	3	4	1	9	10	5	6	11
Chambers		2	2		4	4		2	2		3	3		4	4		3	3		5	5	2	3	5		5	5		3	3
Warren					4	4	4	5	9	2	6	8	3	9	12	1	1	2	2	6	8		5	5	4	5	9	1	5	6
Murray				1		1	1		1	3	1	4				1	2	3	1	1	2	2	1	3	3		3	2	1	3
Park Pl.				1		1	1		1	2		2				1	3	4	2	2	4	3	3	6	2	3	5	4	3	7
W. B'way cor. Barclay							1		1				3		3				1	1	2					4	4			
W. B'way cor. Church							1+	2	3				2	2	4				4	1	5				3	3	6			
Vesey	2		2				1		1				4	1	5				3		3				4		4			
Fulton							2		2				3		3				1	1	2				5		5			
Barclay										3		3				3	1+	4					3	3				2	3	5
Vesey																2		2				1	1	2				3		3
Fulton cor. W. B'way										7	2	9				1	1+	2					1	1				2	3	5
Church cor. Fulton				1	2	3					2	2				8		8				10	3	13				8	3	11
Dey		1	1											3	3	2	5	7	2	6	8	6	4	10	2	4	6	1	3	4
Cortlandt		1	1	2	2	4	1	2	3	1	2	3	1	3	4	4	4	8	3	4	7	3	3	6	2	2	4	5	2	7
Liberty					2	2	1	3	4	1	2	3	1	2	3	1	2	3	1	1	2	3	3	6	4		4	2	2	4
Cedar	1	1	2	1	2	3	1	3	4		2	2	3	2	5	1	1	2	3	1	4	5	1	6	4	2	6	1	1+	2
Thames	1	1	2		1	1					2	2				1	1	2	2		2	2	2	4	1		1		4	4
Rector	2		2		++		5		5	5	++	5	4	1+	5	1	++	1	3	++	3	2	+	2	3	++	5	6		6
Edgar	10		10	5		5	2		2	3		3	3		3	2		2	2		2	3		3	4		4	12		12
Exch. Pl.					4	4		6	6		7	7		3	3					3	3		13	13		4	4		15	15
Morris		18	18	3W	1	4	1	2	3	3	5	8		6	6		5	5		7	7	6		6	1	10	11	1		1
Batt'y Pl.	4		4		2	2	3	4	7	2		2	5	6	11	1	6	7		5	5	1	5	6	2	1	3	1	2	3
	Started from Batt'y Pl. [illegible]			Arrived at Batt'y Pl. [illegible]			Started from Batt'y Pl. [illegible]			Arrived at Batt'y Pl. [illegible]			Started from Batt'y Pl. [illegible]			Arrived at Batt'y Pl. [illegible]			Started from Batt'y Pl. [illegible]			Arrived at Batt'y Pl. [illegible]			Started from Batt'y Pl. [illegible]			Arrived at Batt'y Pl. [illegible]		

Vehicles standing at / between	Car # 2056 North bound, arrived at Wash. Pl. 12-53-[illegible] P.M.			Car # 195 South bound, started from Wash. Pl. 1-06-00 P.M.			Car # 1869 North bound, arrived at Wash. Pl. 2-56-01 P.M.			Car # 1887 South bound, started from Wash. Pl. 3-05-30 P.M.			Car # 1887 North bound, arrived at Wash. Pl. 4-05-36 P.M.			Car # 1669 South bound, started from Wash. Pl. 4-07-44 P.M.			Car # 1669 North bound, arrived at Wash. Pl. 5-08-[illegible] P.M.			Car # 2039 South bound, started from Wash. Pl. 5-12-17 P.M.			Car # 2039 North bound, arrived at Wash. Pl. 6-07-05 P.M.		
	West curb	East curb	E+W	West curb	East curb	E+W	West curb	East curb	E+W	West curb	East curb	E+W	West curb	East curb	E+W	West curb	East curb	E+W	West curb	East curb	E+W	West curb	East curb	E+W	West curb	East curb	E+W
Wash. Pl.																											
6th & W. 4th St.	8		8				2		2					3	3				2		2				1	1	2
McDougal							3	1	4				3		3				6		6				3		3
Thompson	4		4				3		3				4		4				6+		6				1		1
W. 3rd S. Av.	2		2				2						2														
W. 3rd St.	3	3	6				1	1	2				3	1	4				2	1	3				1	1	2
W. 4th St.				4	8	12				1		1					1	1									
W. S. 6th Av.				2	1+	3				3	1	4				1	1	2					3	3			
McDougal					1	1										3	2	5									
Sullivan					2	2					2+	2										2	2	4			
Thompson					1	1					5	5				2	2	4				2	2	4			
S. 5th Av. 3rd				++						++						+	1	1									
Bleecker	5	12	17	5	7	13	4	5	9	6	9	15	5	7	12	5	6	11	3	6	9	4	3	7	1	4	5
Houston	6	9+	15	6	2+	8		2	2	1	3	4	2	3	5	3	3	6		6	6	7	2	9	3	3	6
Prince	2	12+	14	2	7+	9	4	8	12	4	6+	10	3	1	4	3	4+	7	8	7+	15	4	3	7	2	3	5
Spring		3	3	1	9	10	1	3	4	4	3	7	6	4	10	1	3	4	1	12	13	7	3+	10	1	1	2
Broome	14+	6	20	8+	4	12	6+	4	10	12	9	21	4+	5	9	10	1	11	6	6	12	3	11	14	7	3	10
Grand	3	3+	6	5	2	7	1	3	4	2	3	5	4	9	13	4	6	10	2+	1	3	2	8+	10	4	2	6
Canal	1	3	4		4+	4	1	1	2		3	3		5	5	2	1+	3		1	1		3	3	2	2	4
York	2+		2				1		1	2+	2	4				1		1	1+		1				1+		1
Lispenard		6	6		4	4		2	2					5	5		2	2		1	1					2	2
Beach	2		2	1		1	1+		1	1		1	2		2	1		1				1		1	1		1
Walker		3	3	2	4	6		3	3		5	5		5	5		7	7		2	2		6	6		1	1
N. Moore	3		3							2		2	1		1	2		2				2		2	2		2
White		4	4		5	5					3	3		2	2		1	1									
Franklin	14	8	22	13	7	20	3		3	5	2	7	5	5	10	5		5	6	2	8	7	2	9	1	3	4
Leonard	9	4	13	8	8	16	3	4	7	3	3	6	12		12	11	2	13	5	5	10	6	2	8	1	1	2
Worth	6+	2	8	10+	6	16	3	3	6	11	15	26	3+		3	6	9	15	1+	1	2	5	6	11	4		4
Thomas	7+	8	15		10	10	6+	11	17				6+	10	16				2+	4	6		10	10	+	10	10
Duane	9	8	17	4	7	11	5	8	13	6	4	10				4	6	10	2	9	11	5	5	10	5	5+	10
Reade	5	5	10	1	14	15	2+	10	12	2+	6	8	3+	5	8	5	1	6	5+	4	9	1+	2	3	4	7	11
Chambers		4	4		1	1		1	1		3	3		9	9		2	2		3	3		1	1	+	1	1
Warren	2	8	10		4	4		9	9	2	3	5	1	3	4	2	4	6	2	4	6	1	1	2	1	2	3
Murray	2		2	3	2	5	3	3	6	3	+	3	3	1	4		1	1	1	2	3				3		3
Park Pl.	3	3	6	3	2	5	2	2	4	8	1	9	3	3	6	2	2	4	2	3	5	2	1	3	1	2	3
W. B'way cor. Barclay	1	4	5				2	2	4				1		1					1	1					1	1
W. B'way cor. Church	2	4	6				11	10	21				5	5	10				8	8	16				8	2	10
Vesey	1		1				2		2				1		1				2		2				1		1
Fulton							3		3				1		1				1		1						
Barclay					2	2					3	3				2	2	4					2	2			
Vesey											1	1					2	2									
Fulton cor. W. B'way				5		5				8		8										5		5			
Church cor. Fulton				5		3					1	1				5	3	8									
Dey	2	4	6	4	3	7	1	7	8	1	3	4		4	4		1	1	1	5	6		2	2			
Cortlandt	4	1	5	5	1	6	1		1		3	3	2	1	3	1		1				1	2	3		3	3
Liberty	2	3	5		3	3	5	3	8	3	2	5	2	1	3	4	2	6	2		2	4	2+	6	3	4	7
Cedar	1	2	3		2	2		1	1		1	1	1	2	[illegible]	3		3	3	2	5	2		2	1	1	2
Thames		1	1		2+	2		1	1	1	1+	2		1	1	2	1+	3	1		1				[illegible]		1
Rector	3	3	6	1		1	3		3				2	5+	5	1	3	4	3	++	3				1	1+	2
Edgar	11		11	7		7	6		6	2		2	2		2				1		1	6		6	5		5
Exch. Pl.		10	10		10	10		10	10		5	5					8	8		1	1		15+	15		4	4
Morris	1	6	7	5		5		2	2	3		3		8	8	1		1		1	1	1		1		3	3
Batt'y Pl.	2	4	6	5	2	7	3	1	4	1	4	5	2	2	4	1	1	2		13	13	1	2	3		2	2
	Started from Batt'y Pl. [illegible]			Arrived at Batt'y Pl. [illegible]			Started from Batt'y Pl. [illegible]			Arrived at Batt'y Pl. [illegible]			Started from Batt'y Pl. [illegible]			Arrived at Batt'y Pl. [illegible]			Started from Batt'y Pl. [illegible]			Arrived at Batt'y Pl. [illegible]			Started from Batt'y Pl. [illegible]		

W indicates a vehicle which has been left at curb after horses had been unhitched. All such vehicles are also included in the figures given.

+ indicates a large pushcart used for rag, paper or other bulky bundles. No pushcart of any type are included in the figures given.

—The Merchants Association—
—of—
—New York—
—Committee on Engineering and Sanitation—

—Surface Railway Transportation—
—Borough of Manhattan—
—New York City—

—Vehicle Count—
—from—
—Sixth Avenue Cars—

Tabulated by R. Matis. Observations taken under direction of C. M. Hoskins M.E.

Sheet No. 19.

TABLE 24.

—THE MERCHANTS' ASSOCIATION OF NEW YORK.—

COMMITTEE ON ENGINEERING AND SANITATION

SURFACE RAILWAY TRANSPORTATION — BOROUGH OF MANHATTAN, NEW YORK

CAR AND VEHICLE RECORD TAKEN AT TWO FIXED POINTS OF BROADWAY LINE

FEB-3RD-1903 — FEB-5TH-1903

OBSERVATIONS TAKEN UNDER DIRECTION OF I. M. ROSENBERG M.E.

CHAMBERS ST. — HOUSTON ST — CHAMBERS ST. — HOUSTON ST

TIME SCALE | CAR NO. | TIME P.M. (HRS. MIN. SEC.) | VEHICLES ON TRACK (S, D) | OTHER VEHICLES IN SAME DIRECTION (S, D)

ISOCHRONOUS LINES AT 5-MINUTE INTERVALS.

ARROWS INDICATE DIRECTION AND RELATIVE SPEED OF CARS.

FASTER ETC. — 8 MILES PER HOUR — SLOWER ETC.

MOVEMENT OF CARS TIMED AT ONLY ONE STATION INDICATED APPROXIMATELY BY BROKEN LINE THUS

SHEET No. 16

DIAGRAM 23.

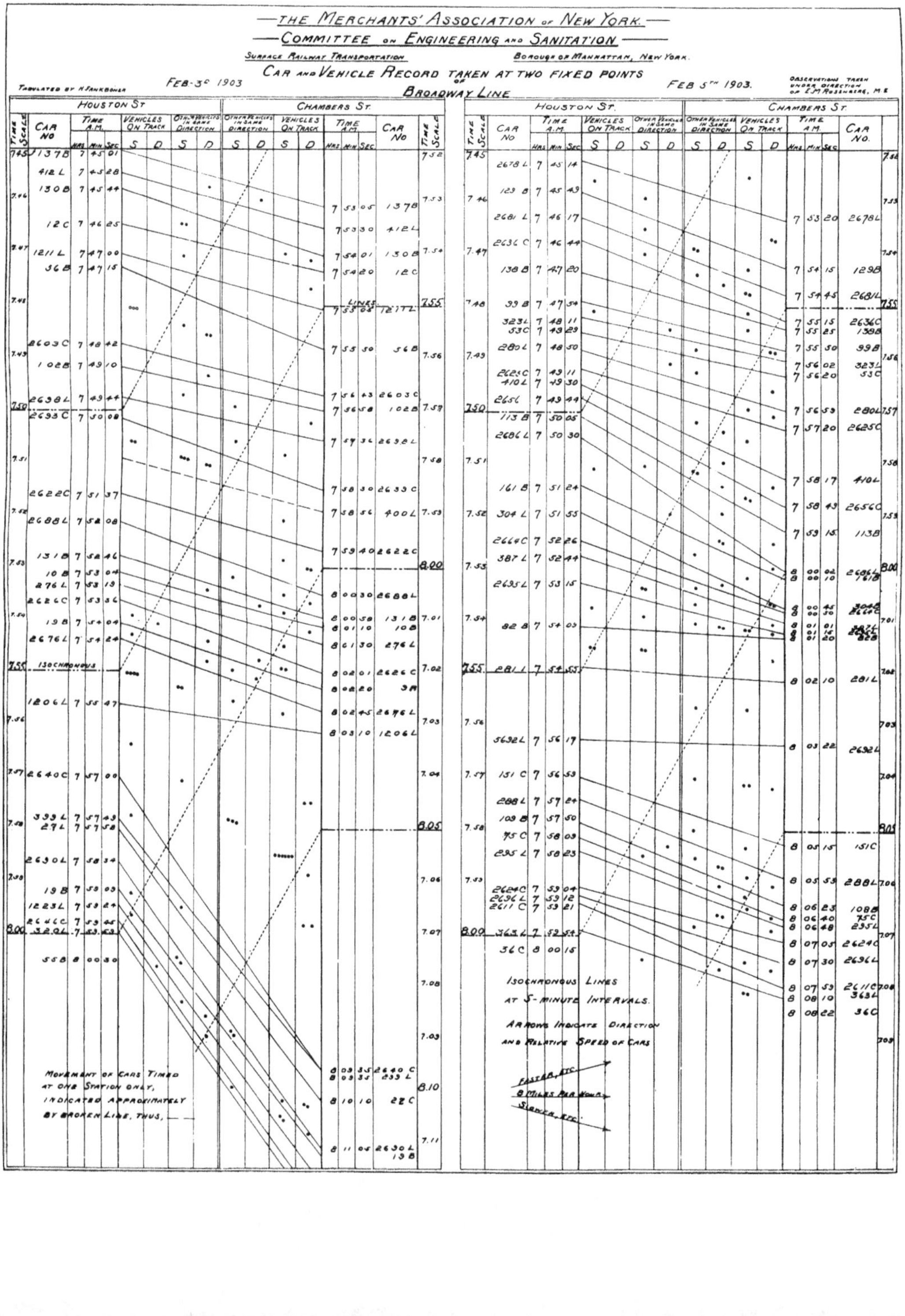

181

THE MERCHANTS' ASSOCIATION OF NEW YORK.

COMMITTEE ON ENGINEERING AND SANITATION

SURFACE RAILWAY TRANSPORTATION — BOROUGH OF MANHATTAN, NEW YORK.

CAR AND VEHICLE RECORD TAKEN AT TWO FIXED POINTS OF BROADWAY LINE

TABULATED BY H. FANKBONER

OBSERVATIONS TAKEN UNDER DIRECTION OF E. M. ROSENBERG, M. E.

FEB. 3rd 1903

Columns: Time Scale; Car No.; Time A.M.; Vehicles on Track (S, D); Other Vehicles in Same Direction (S, D).

Houston St. Car No.	Hrs	Min	Sec	Chambers St. Hrs	Min	Sec	Car No.
137B	7	45	01	7	53	05	137B
412L	7	45	28	7	53	30	412L
130B	7	45	44	7	54	01	130B
12C	7	46	25	7	54	20	12C
1211L	7	47	00	7	55	05	1211L
36B	7	47	15	7	55	50	36B
2603C	7	48	42	7	56	43	2603C
102B	7	49	10	7	56	58	102B
2638L	7	49	44	7	57	36	2638L
2633C	7	50	08	7	58	30	2633C
2622C	7	51	37	7	58	56	400L
2688L	7	52	08	7	59	40	2622C
131B	7	52	46	8	00	30	2688L
10B	7	53	04	8	00	58	131B
276L	7	53	19	8	01	10	10B
2626C	7	53	36	8	01	30	276L
19B	7	54	04	8	02	01	2626C
2676L	7	54	24	8	02	20	3R
1206L	7	55	47	8	02	45	2676L
2640C	7	57	00	8	03	10	1206L
399L	7	57	49	8	09	35	2640C
27L	7	57	58	8	09	35	233L
2630L	7	58	34	8	10	10	22C
19B	7	59	03	8	11	05	2630L 19B
1223L	7	59	24				
2646C	7	59	45				
3291L	7	59	59				
55B	8	00	30				

MOVEMENT OF CARS TIMED AT ONE STATION ONLY, INDICATED APPROXIMATELY BY BROKEN LINE, THUS, ———

FEB 5th 1903.

Houston St. Car No.	Hrs	Min	Sec	Chambers St. Hrs	Min	Sec	Car No.
2678L	7	45	14	7	53	20	2678L
123B	7	45	43	7	54	15	129B
2681L	7	46	17	7	54	45	2681L
2636C	7	46	44	7	55	15	2636C
138B	7	47	20	7	55	25	138B
39B	7	47	54	7	55	50	99B
323L	7	48	11	7	56	02	323L
53C	7	48	29	7	56	20	53C
280L	7	48	50	7	56	53	280L
2625C	7	49	11	7	57	20	2625C
410L	7	49	30	7	58	17	410L
2656	7	49	44	7	58	43	2656C
113B	7	50	05	7	59	15	113B
2686L	7	50	30	8	00	02	2686L
161B	7	51	24	8	00	10	161B
304L	7	51	55	8	00	45	304B
2664C	7	52	26	8	00	50	2664C
387L	7	52	44	8	01	01	387L
2695L	7	53	15	8	01	15	2695L
82B	7	54	03	8	01	20	82B
281L	7	54	55	8	02	10	281L
5632L	7	56	17	8	03	22	2692L
151C	7	56	53	8	05	15	151C
288L	7	57	24	8	05	53	288L
109B	7	57	50	8	06	23	108B
75C	7	58	03	8	06	40	75C
295L	7	58	23	8	06	48	235L
2624C	7	59	04	8	07	05	2624C
2696L	7	59	12	8	07	30	2696L
2611C	7	59	21	8	07	53	2611C
363L	7	59	54	8	08	10	363L
36C	8	00	15	8	08	22	36C

ISOCHRONOUS LINES AT 5-MINUTE INTERVALS.

ARROWS INDICATE DIRECTION AND RELATIVE SPEED OF CARS

FASTER, ETC.

8 MILES PER HOUR.

SLOWER, ETC.

DIAGRAM 22.

SHEET No. 8.

THE MERCHANTS ASSOCIATION OF NEW YORK
COMMITTEE ON ENGINEERING AND SANITATION.
SURFACE RAILWAY TRANSPORTATION.
BOROUGH OF MANHATTAN, NEW YORK
CAR AND VEHICLE RECORD TAKEN AT TWO FIXED POINTS
OF
BROADWAY LINE.
FEB. 3RD. 1903.
FEB. 5TH. 1903.
HOUSTON ST.
CHAMBERS ST.
TIME SCALE
CAR NO
TIME A.M.
HRS MIN SEC
VEHICLES ON TRACK
OTHER VEHICLES IN SAME DIRECTION
S
D
ARROWS INDICATE DIRECTION AND RELATIVE SPEED OF CARS
ISOCHRONOUS LINES AT 5 MINUTE INTERVALS
SHEET No. 5.

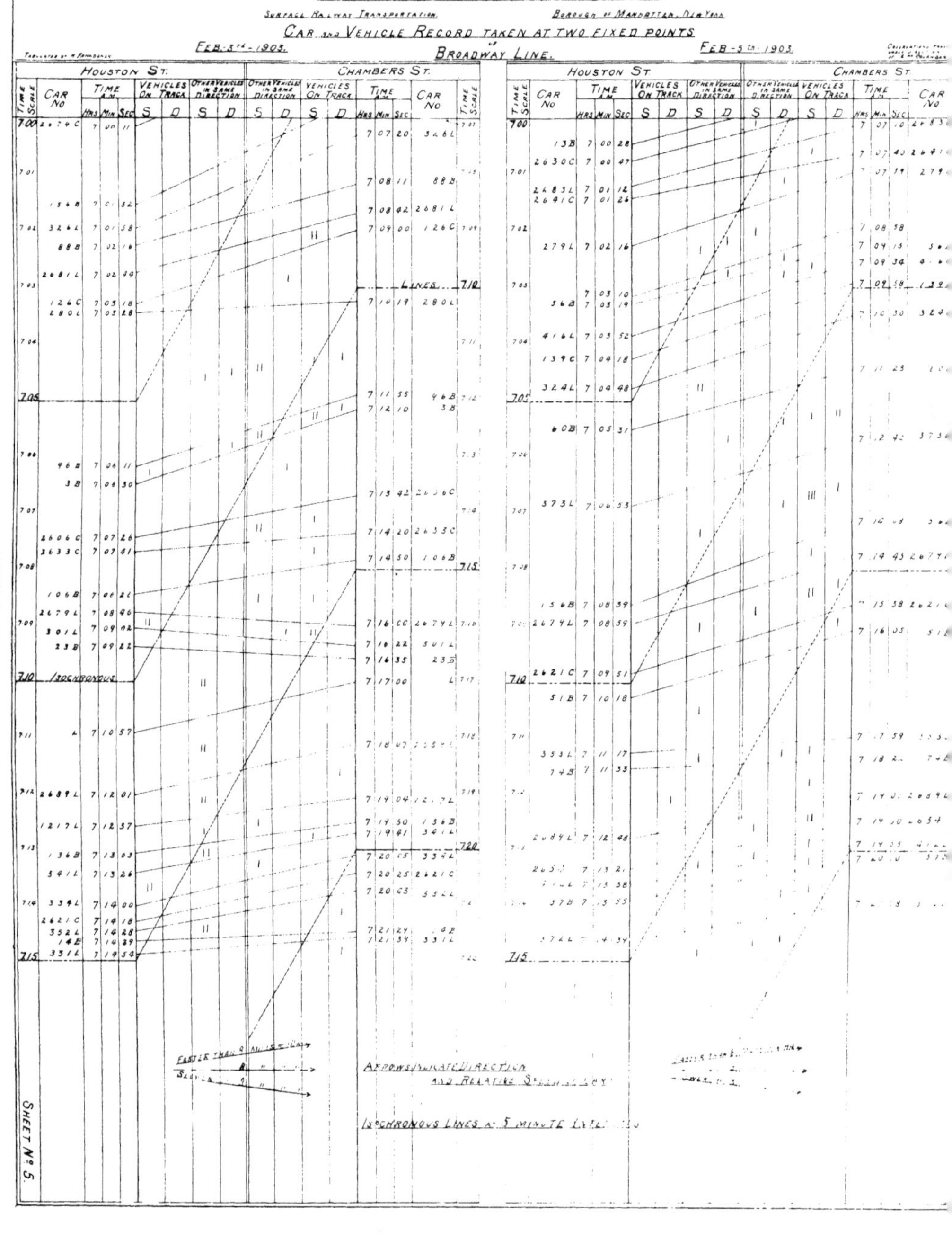

DIAGRAM 24.

Vehicle and Car Count at Intersection of —Fulton Street with Greenwich Street—

Observations taken Thursday, March 12th 1903.

Time	Cars bound North	Cars bound South	Cars bound East	Cars bound West	Cars bound East-North	Cars bound South-East	Vehicles bound North	Vehicles bound South	Vehicles bound East	Vehicles bound West	Vehicles bound North-East	Vehicles bound North-West	Vehicles bound South-East	Vehicles bound South-West	Vehicles bound East-North	Vehicles bound East-South	Vehicles bound West-North	Vehicles bound West-South	Totals: All cars and vehicles	Totals: All vehicles no cars	Totals: All cars	Crossing Greenwich traffic: Cars and vehicles	Crossing Greenwich traffic: Vehicles no cars	Crossing Greenwich traffic: Cars
7 A.M.-7.30 A.M.	21	8	6	6	-	9	25	53	7	9	3	3	0	4	5	3	9	6	183	133	50	57	36	21
7.30-8.00	24	7	7	7	1	12	39	57	3	14	6	-	6	3	1	1	3	4	207	148	58	63	36	27
8.00-8.30	19	11	5	8	1	14	61	84	18	15	11	2	10	6	3	9	3	6	274	225	58	80	54	26
8.30-9.00	30	12	6	6	1	19	86	82	24	20	3	2	14	2	4	2	6	15	325	256	69	102	75	27
9.00-9.30	18	9	8	7	1	12	88	109	15	23	15	-	15	1	3	5	4	6	337	284	53	90	64	26
9.30-10.00	20	13	9	0	1	14	98	100	27	28	25	2	28	4	5	2	10	2	402	339	63	132	102	30
10.00-10.30	21	9	6	5	3	14	103	102	26	20	13	1	16	7	3	-	20	19	382	328	54	107	83	24
10.30-11.00	23	10	7	7	-	13	115	96	21	19	16	2	14	4	2	1	21	26	391	331	60	105	78	27
11.00-11.30	12	8	7	6	-	10	72	96	19	28	17	1	18	0	3	-	17	16	334	291	43	108	85	23
11.30-12 M.	18	7	6	3	1	7	101	113	18	37	10	1	24	-	2	-	7	9	362	322	40	108	91	17
12 M.-12.30 P.M.	21	12	4	6	-	13	80	74	22	38	18	3	8	-	-	-	7	7	313	257	56	101	78	23
12.30 P.M.-1.00	21	8	5	7	1	12	66	64	18	17	18	-	14	2	2	-	8	7	269	215	54	83	58	25
1.00-1.30	20	9	8	6	1	9	77	71	20	20	16	-	17	3	3	6	26	8	320	267	53	94	70	24
1.30-2.00	23	9	6	5	1	14	75	69	19	26	24	2	12	2	3	-	11	16	333	279	58	100	78	22
2.00-2.30	24	10	6	6	2	9	106	65	18	24	18	1	16	2	2	1	9	17	350	293	57	97	74	23
2.30-3.00	16	10	8	6	-	18	92	105	18	19	14	4	16	1	1	2	21	18	369	311	58	108	76	32
3.00-3.30	24	9	4	5	-	10	128	121	21	27	16	2	15	2	4	-	21	13	422	370	52	101	82	19
3.30-4.00	19	11	4	5	-	14	83	110	3	29	13	1	15	5	3	-	13	13	336	288	48	87	64	23
4.00-4.30	29	12	8	8	-	16	131	113	13	29	30	-	16	2	2	-	19	21	445	376	69	109	81	28
4.30-5.00	21	12	7	7	-	15	95	96	17	20	19	-	13	2	-	1	12	18	353	295	62	97	68	29
5.00-5.30	22	7	4	5	-	18	83	54	19	33	24	1	19	2	1	1	11	14	315	259	56	111	84	27
5.30-6.00	22	9	5	6	-	16	73	71	6	14	24	1	7	2	-	-	19	7	293	237	58	89	62	27

Vehicle and Car Count at Intersection of —Canal Street with West Broadway—

Observations taken Friday, March 20th 1903.

Time	Cars bound North	Cars bound South	Cars bound East	Cars bound West	Cars bound West-North	Cars bound North-West	Cars bound South-East	Cars bound East-South	Vehicles bound North	Vehicles bound South	Vehicles bound East	Vehicles bound West	Vehicles bound North-East	Vehicles bound North-West	Vehicles bound South-East	Vehicles bound South-West	Vehicles bound East-North	Vehicles bound East-South	Vehicles bound West-North	Vehicles bound West-South	Totals: All cars and vehicles	Totals: All vehicles no cars	Totals: All cars	Crossing West B'way traffic: Cars and vehicles	Crossing West B'way traffic: Vehicles no cars	Crossing West B'way traffic: Cars
7 A.M.-7.30 A.M.	5	6	5	6	1	9	-	11	22	43	33	37	11	3	6	9	1	14	2	15	261	218	43	137	117	20
7.30-8.00	7	11	6	5	-	7	-	12	40	62	73	78	16	13	12	10	2	19	6	25	399	351	48	221	203	18
8.00-8.30	8	6	5	4	-	14	-	11	46	53	90	97	20	16	11	15	3	34	4	16	453	405	48	258	235	23
8.30-9.00	8	14	10	10	1	12	-	14	50	72	106	130	36	6	9	15	9	26	9	7	544	475	69	301	264	32
9.00-9.30	12	12	4	3	-	12	-	10	57	63	93	111	33	15	12	13	15	16	5	13	507	452	55	282	261	21
9.30-10.00	10	8	5	6	-	12	-	12	66	79	113	114	46	20	12	19	0	31	8	17	586	533	53	305	282	23
10.00-10.30	7	12	7	8	1	10	-	8	69	71	113	105	34	32	1	22	5	15	4	22	546	493	53	303	278	25
10.30-11.00	11	11	7	6	-	10	-	13	71	55	120	111	42	24	8	22	7	19	12	16	565	507	58	306	286	23
11.00-11.30	11	9	5	8	-	10	-	8	61	100	118	116	48	34	10	22	7	20	12	24	623	572	51	332	309	23
11.30-12 M.	8	13	3	11	1	13	-	10	84	63	110	91	37	16	6	20	7	15	10	19	547	486	61	278	249	29
12 M.-12.30 P.M.	10	11	4	6	-	11	-	11	53	41	79	78	40	15	2	13	12	10	10	16	428	375	53	223	402	21
12.30 P.M.-1.00	13	12	4	7	-	17	-	14	48	49	98	64	32	23	5	16	14	16	6	18	450	383	67	250	222	28
1.00-1.30	7	9	6	5	1	7	-	6	37	32	94	82	45	15	5	14	5	16	9	22	426	381	45	243	223	20
1.30-2.00	11	12	5	4	-	11	-	14	54	53	66	112	44	17	4	18	4	16	5	22	468	415	53	243	223	20
2.00-2.30	11	10	7	5	-	10	-	11	52	59	124	118	39	21	7	27	5	17	8	19	550	496	54	316	294	22
2.30-3.00	13	11	8	7	-	10	-	8	61	69	118	167	56	21	4	13	8	27	15	27	649	586	63	376	345	31
3.00-3.30	10	14	7	6	-	9	-	8	62	61	124	119	41	20	4	26	11	17	9	24	570	516	54	324	302	22
3.30-4.00	10	12	8	5	-	12	-	9	81	72	117	167	53	24	6	45	8	21	7	20	687	631	56	375	350	25
4.00-4.30	15	18	8	6	-	11	-	13	74	94	94	153	53	23	6	38	0	18	7	21	670	605	65	339	314	25
4.30-5.00	12	12	9	-	-	15	-	17	69	47	113	117	62	20	3	9	10	9	12	19	563	490	73	314	282	32
5.00-5.30	13	15	11	12	-	14	-	14	68	37	113	130	54	21	7	12	9	9	10	19	563	479	84	331	289	42
5.30-6.00	12	15	7	8	7	14	5	6	50	31	106	107	44	25	3	4	9	4	10	15	676	602	74	293	259	34

—THE MERCHANTS ASSOCIATION—
—OF—
—NEW YORK—
—COMMITTEE ON ENGINEERING AND SANITATION—

—SURFACE RAILWAY TRANSPORTATION—
—BOROUGH OF MANHATTAN—
—NEW YORK CITY—

—VEHICLE & CAR—
—COUNT—
—AT STREET INTERSECTIONS.—

Tabulated by [illegible] [illegible] C.H. [illegible]

Sheet No. 34

TABLE 20.

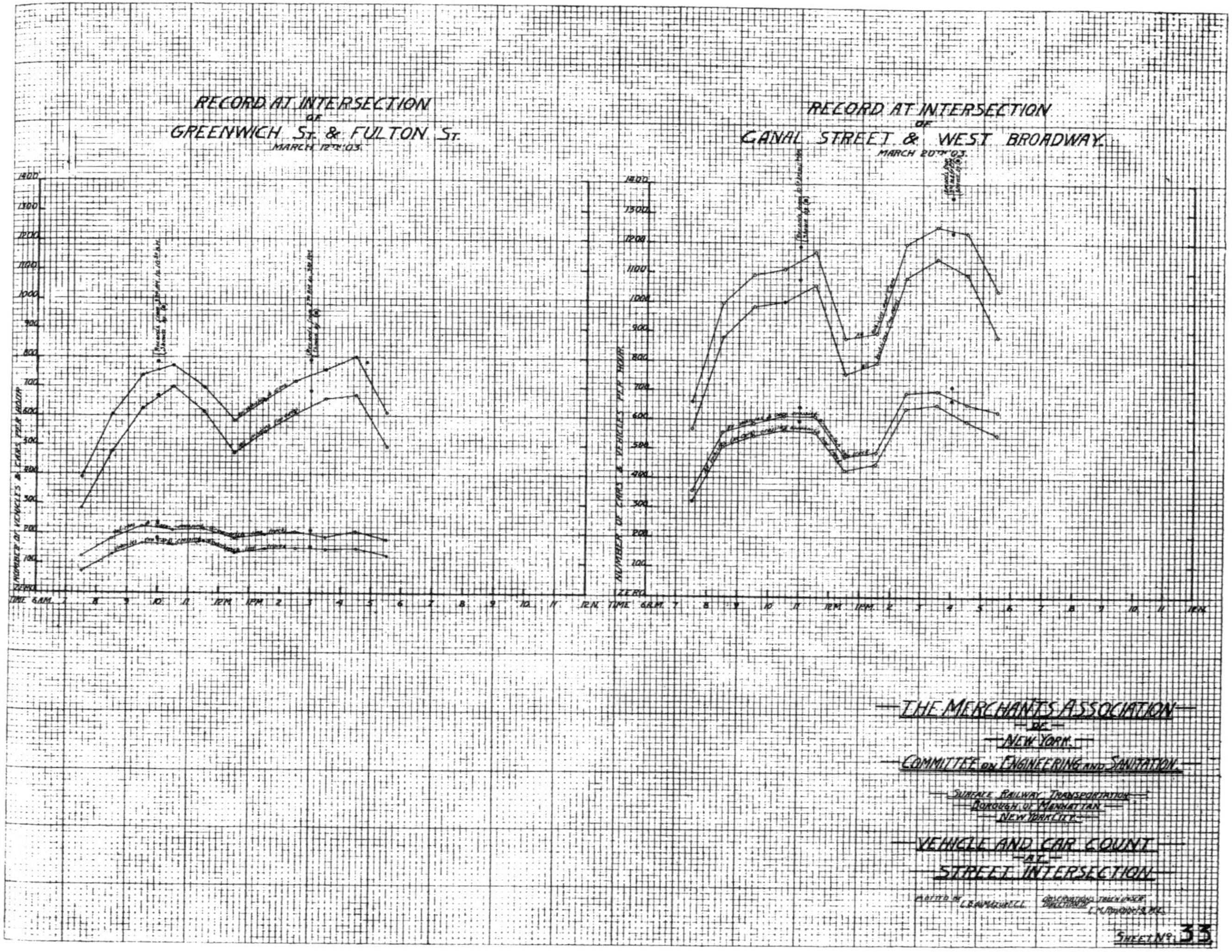

RECORD AT INTERSECTION
OF
GREENWICH ST. & FULTON ST.
MARCH 12TH 03.

NUMBER OF VEHICLES & CARS PER HOUR

1400
1300
1200
1100
1000
900
800
700
600
500
400
300
200
100
ZERO

TIME 6 A.M. 7 8 9 10 11 12 M. 1 P.M. 2 3 4 5 6 7 8 9 10 11 12 N.

RECORD AT INTERSECTION
OF
CANAL STREET & WEST BROADWAY.
MARCH 20TH 03.

NUMBER OF CARS & VEHICLES PER HOUR.

1400
1300
1200
1100
1000
900
800
700
600
500
400
300
200
100
ZERO

TIME 6 A.M. 7 8 9 10 11 12 M. 1 P.M. 2 3 4 5 6 7 8 9 10 11 12 N.

THE MERCHANTS ASSOCIATION
OF
NEW YORK.
COMMITTEE ON ENGINEERING AND SANITATION.

SURFACE RAILWAY TRANSPORTATION
BOROUGH OF MANHATTAN
NEW YORK CITY.

VEHICLE AND CAR COUNT
AT
STREET INTERSECTION

SHEET NO. 33

DIAGRAM 19.

VEHICLE AND CAR COUNT AT INTERSECTION OF

— FULTON STREET WITH BROADWAY —

OBSERVATIONS TAKEN TUESDAY, MARCH 10TH 1903.

TIME	CARS BOUND North	South	East	West	VEHICLES BOUND North	South	East	West	North-East	North-West	South-East	South-West	East-North	East-South	West-North	West-South	TOTALS All cars and vehicles	All vehicles (no cars)	All cars	Traffic crossing Broadway line tracks: Cars and vehicles	Vehicles (no cars)	Cars
7.00 A.M.-7.30 A.M.	36	38	5	6	20	41	5	8	2	1	12	10	9	2	6	—	196	111	85	41	30	11
7.30 - 8.00	46	47	6	7	32	57	19	24	4	2	10	9	10	2	10	2	283	177	106	76	63	13
8.00 - 8.30	56	61	6	5	44	94	26	25	8	—	15	20	13	2	16	4	395	267	128	94	83	11
8.30 - 9.00	55	79	6	6	74	104	17	38	8	5	14	34	14	4	6	8	472	326	146	104	96	12
9.00 - 9.30	70	57	6	6	75	127	36	36	15	2	21	45	6	5	12	9	628	449	179	122	110	12
9.30 - 10.00	65	95	6	7	102	204	47	42	11	1	19	37	25	4	16	5	686	513	173	152	139	13
10.00 - 10.30	70	90	7	6	104	199	57	42	10	1	16	41	18	2	24	12	699	526	173	159	146	13
10.30 - 11.00	58	74	4	3	88	204	37	33	14	7	34	46	7	8	18	8	642	503	139	127	120	7
11.00 - 11.30	51	78	4	5	107	118	53	41	19	1	20	19	26	6	28	3	576	460	138	152	143	9
11.30 - 12.00 M.	66	67	6	7	123	95	40	52	11	—	16	50	12	4	29	4	562	416	146	137	124	13
12.00 M. - 12.30 P.M.	67	66	7	5	95	97	34	29	6	2	15	17	7	1	28	1	477	332	145	98	86	12
12.30 P.M. - 1.00	69	65	4	10	66	86	27	43	11	3	9	19	8	3	21	3	447	299	148	107	93	14
1.00 - 1.30	54	57	7	7	83	94	34	96	10	5	9	20	16	0	11	5	464	339	125	129	115	14
1.30 - 2.00	50	54	8	7	91	82	51	30	11	4	24	28	12	4	14	3	469	350	119	135	120	15
2.00 - 2.30	49	65	5	6	79	95	32	35	6	2	17	22	15	1	10	6	425	320	105	118	107	11
2.30 - 3.00	37	60	6	7	99	135	35	35	18	7	24	29	4	1	19	7	523	413	110	125	112	13
3.00 - 3.30	58	57	5	6	102	107	48	58	10	—	20	25	5	3	21	7	530	404	126	149	138	11
3.30 - 4.00	49	61	6	7	109	129	30	44	15	7	16	26	9	1	18	4	526	403	123	123	110	13
4.00 - 4.30	65	75	6	6	107	101	60	40	7	3	19	35	7	6	20	3	550	400	150	130	118	12
4.30 - 5.00	76	75	6	7	120	86	38	38	8	2	26	33	17	3	21	2	558	394	164	136	123	13
5.00 - 5.30	63	74	6	5	39	64	50	25	16	6	24	10	12	4	17	1	430	290	148	129	118	11
5.30 - 6.00	72	71	4	6	60	41	27	34	2	5	4	15	7	1	22	3	394	241	153	93	80	10

VEHICLE AND CAR COUNT AT INTERSECTION OF

— CANAL STREET WITH BROADWAY —

OBSERVATIONS TAKEN FRIDAY, MARCH 13TH 1903.

TIME	CARS BOUND North	South	East	West	VEHICLES BOUND North	South	East	West	North-East	North-West	South-East	South-West	East-North	East-South	West-North	West-South	TOTALS All cars and vehicles	All vehicles (no cars)	All cars	Traffic crossing Broadway line tracks: Cars and vehicles	Vehicles (no cars)	Cars
7.00 A.M.-7.30 A.M.	39	20	10	4	15	34	43	39	—	5	7	9	6	16	5	2	277	176	101	115	99	16
7.30 - 8.00	42	54	11	3	37	41	30	95	—	4	3	13	11	17	2	5	395	286	110	193	176	19
8.00 - 8.30	58	73	14	5	43	58	55	75	3	8	5	18	16	15	9	5	460	310	150	183	164	19
8.30 - 9.00	58	76	12	6	52	78	66	68	6	17	12	12	12	11	7	3	510	362	152	194	176	18
9.00 - 9.30	60	69	13	4	70	81	89	119	11	20	22	36	10	12	18	11	659	496	164	289	271	17
9.30 - 10.00	61	69	12	6	93	99	77	96	7	17	10	29	32	27	13	7	655	507	148	257	239	18
10.00 - 10.30	67	65	9	4	80	114	96	97	20	20	8	45	26	18	10	3	682	537	145	263	250	13
10.30 - 11.00	58	65	11	4	100	109	84	83	17	28	19	28	17	9	13	1	646	508	138	247	232	15
11.00 - 11.30	62	67	11	5	98	135	77	100	4	20	5	28	24	6	10	6	660	515	145	248	232	16
11.30 - 12.00 M.	80	61	7	4	92	93	81	91	15	6	13	36	8	4	4	4	607	455	152	216	205	11
12.00 M. - 12.30 P.M.	63	68	8	4	75	78	87	65	9	13	10	21	9	10	13	2	533	390	143	198	186	12
12.30 P.M. - 1.00	71	63	8	3	57	54	55	54	13	19	8	13	10	2	9	2	439	294	145	157	146	11
1.00 - 1.30	54	53	11	5	77	60	83	93	15	19	11	18	11	4	8	1	523	400	123	234	218	10
1.30 - 2.00	51	41	7	3	85	42	58	95	11	22	9	19	—	1	8	5	457	355	102	199	189	10
2.00 - 2.30	56	50	9	3	88	110	89	100	18	23	7	22	8	6	14	5	610	492	118	246	234	12
2.30 - 3.00	50	56	4	9	102	116	57	75	18	23	12	37	7	10	9	2	593	475	119	191	178	13
3.00 - 3.30	46	71	6	1	113	94	76	106	16	[illegible]	15	40	12	13	6	6	650	526	124	240	233	7
3.30 - 4.00	67	76	15	4	113	105	59	100	14	26	9	33	9	12	11	4	663	503	160	227	210	17
4.00 - 4.30	67	63	5	6	133	124	92	108	19	25	9	32	5	13	13	—	714	573	141	248	237	11
4.30 - 5.00	62	74	8	2	116	107	82	79	15	28	6	34	6	10	11	11	651	505	146	222	212	10
5.00 - 5.30	66	83	8	5	114	93	74	91	20	31	3	27	4	6	12	1	638	476	162	217	204	13
5.30 - 6.00	74	73	11	4	80	83	71	95	10	32	2	20	1	3	13	3	582	415	167	219	204	15

VEHICLE AND CAR COUNT AT INTERSECTION OF

— CHAMBERS STREET WITH BROADWAY

OBSERVATIONS TAKEN FRIDAY, MARCH 6TH 1903.

TIME	CARS BOUND North	South	East	West	VEHICLES BOUND North	South	East	West	North-East	North-West	South-East	South-West	East-North	East-South	West-North	West-South	TOTALS All cars and vehicles	All vehicles (no cars)	All cars	Traffic crossing Broadway line tracks: Cars and vehicles	Vehicles (no cars)	Cars
12.00 M. - 12.30 P.M.	94	56	NO EASTBOUND CAR-TRACKS	16	109	51	23	41	42	9	18	3	1	1	23	12	499	333	166	120	104	16
12.30 P.M. - 1.00	82	54		10	102	52	17	56	35	8	16	7	3	4	26	16	482	336	146	126	116	10
1.00 - 1.30	28	51		12	43	50	27	78	15	1	20	6	—	3	14	10	360	269	91	148	136	12
1.30 - 2.00	48	52		9	94	88	33	80	31	10	14	14	1	7	13	23	519	410	109	172	163	9
2.00 - 2.30	66	48		12	107	69	46	81	47	16	15	8	2	6	15	24	562	436	126	196	184	12
2.30 - 3.00	47	46		8	121	100	31	67	38	4	15	7	3	3	15	32	537	436	101	160	152	8
3.00 - 3.30	37	52		15	113	102	23	78	32	6	16	9	2	5	14	12	516	412	104	152	137	15
3.30 - 4.00	46	52		17	100	88	30	82	34	5	16	10	2	3	18	31	532	417	115	181	164	17
4.00 - 4.30	85	64		15	152	78	38	70	88	11	10	11	3	2	13	27	667	503	164	174	159	15
4.30 - 5.00	127	79		14	174	61	35	55	95	13	28	8	7	6	12	12	726	506	220	164	150	14
5.00 - 5.30	153	75		18	173	68	42	56	102	27	25	6	5	2	17	21	784	538	246	194	176	18
5.30 - 6.00	108	49		15	107	65	27	34	50	2	30	3	—	5	13	12	520	348	172	120	105	15

VEHICLE AND CAR COUNT AT INTERSECTION OF

— 18TH STREET WITH BROADWAY —

OBSERVATIONS TAKEN SATURDAY, MARCH 7TH 1903.

TIME	CARS BOUND North	South	East	West	VEHICLES BOUND North	South	East	West	North-East	North-West	South-East	South-West	East-North	East-South	West-North	West-South	TOTALS All cars and vehicles	All vehicles (no cars)	All cars	Traffic crossing Broadway line tracks: Cars and vehicles	Vehicles (no cars)	Cars
7.00 A.M.-7.30 A.M.	28	54	NO EASTBOUND CAR-TRACKS	12	36	32	6	2	1	—	3	4	2	—	3	5	156	94	94	30	18	12
7.30 - 8.00	38	72		12	60	62	8	6	4	5	3	1	—	3	4	4	282	160	122	38	26	12
8.00 - 8.30	46	75		12	46	74	13	8	4	7	4	2	1	3	10	6	311	178	133	51	39	12
8.30 - 9.00	70	72		13	83	77	13	15	7	6	7	4	3	4	8	8	390	235	155	65	52	13
9.00 - 9.30	68	68		12	90	89	14	10	1	7	6	7	4	6	4	7	388	240	148	60	48	12
9.30 - 10.00	62	56		12	97	96	11	8	12	6	6	10	7	4	14	9	410	280	130	59	47	12
10.00 - 10.30	67	63		10	94	82	10	11	2	2	6	2	3	4	4	5	362	225	137	47	37	10
10.30 - 11.00	74	68		12	109	120	17	16	6	4	14	12	8	5	6	12	463	309	154	83	71	12
11.00 - 11.30	60	63		10	108	109	12	13	5	8	4	10	6	4	6	8	426	293	133	61	51	10
11.30 - 12.00 M.	51	56		9	96	95	11	9	4	8	4	21	7	2	4	3	384	268	116	51	42	9
12.00 M. - 12.30 P.M.	65	58		10	85	57	12	7	4	7	8	8	5	6	1	9	342	209	133	50	40	10
12.30 - 1.00	63	59		10	83	59	9	9	1	3	2	7	4	4	2	4	314	182	132	41	31	10
1.00 - 1.30	72	51		12	67	50	11	5	1	1	2	2	3	5	3	10	295	160	135	44	32	12
1.30 - 2.00	65	59		12	92	63	18	11	10	5	3	—	5	8	7	5	363	227	136	59	47	12
2.00 - 2.30	48	78		12	103	58	16	16	6	1	1	1	3	2	3	5	352	214	138	53	41	12
2.30 - 3.00	51	55		13	109	86	23	8	2	4	8	5	3	4	7	7	385	266	119	66	53	13
3.00 - 3.30	75	69		16	115	89	16	11	8	7	6	10	6	10	9	6	453	293	160	68	52	16
3.30 - 4.00	76	77		15	125	85	11	17	7	15	4	18	4	7	4	4	471	303	168	72	57	15
4.00 - 4.30	68	73		15	98	76	14	11	1	3	4	7	4	—	6	4	384	228	156	55	40	15
4.30 - 5.00	87	80		15	100	60	11	13	3	3	8	5	2	1	4	7	399	217	182	59	44	15
5.00 - 5.30	75	69		12	93	54	6	10	4	6	8	6	3	4	1	6	357	201	156	51	39	12
5.30 - 6.00	101	57		15	83	62	11	10	2	3	6	1	2	5	6	3	367	194	173	50	35	15

NOTE FOR 18TH STREET RECORD:
WEST BOUND CARS TURN SOUTH ON TO BROADWAY LINE TRACKS.

— THE MERCHANTS ASSOCIATION —
— OF —
— NEW YORK. —
— COMMITTEE ON ENGINEERING AND SANITATION —

— SURFACE RAILWAY TRANSPORTATION —
— BOROUGH OF MANHATTAN —
— NEW YORK CITY —

— VEHICLE & CAR —
— COUNT —
— AT STREET INTERSECTIONS. —

TABULATED BY A. MORRIS.   OBSERVATIONS TAKEN UNDER DIRECTION OF E. M. BOSCHOOTS M.E.

SHEET Nº 29.

TABLE 18.

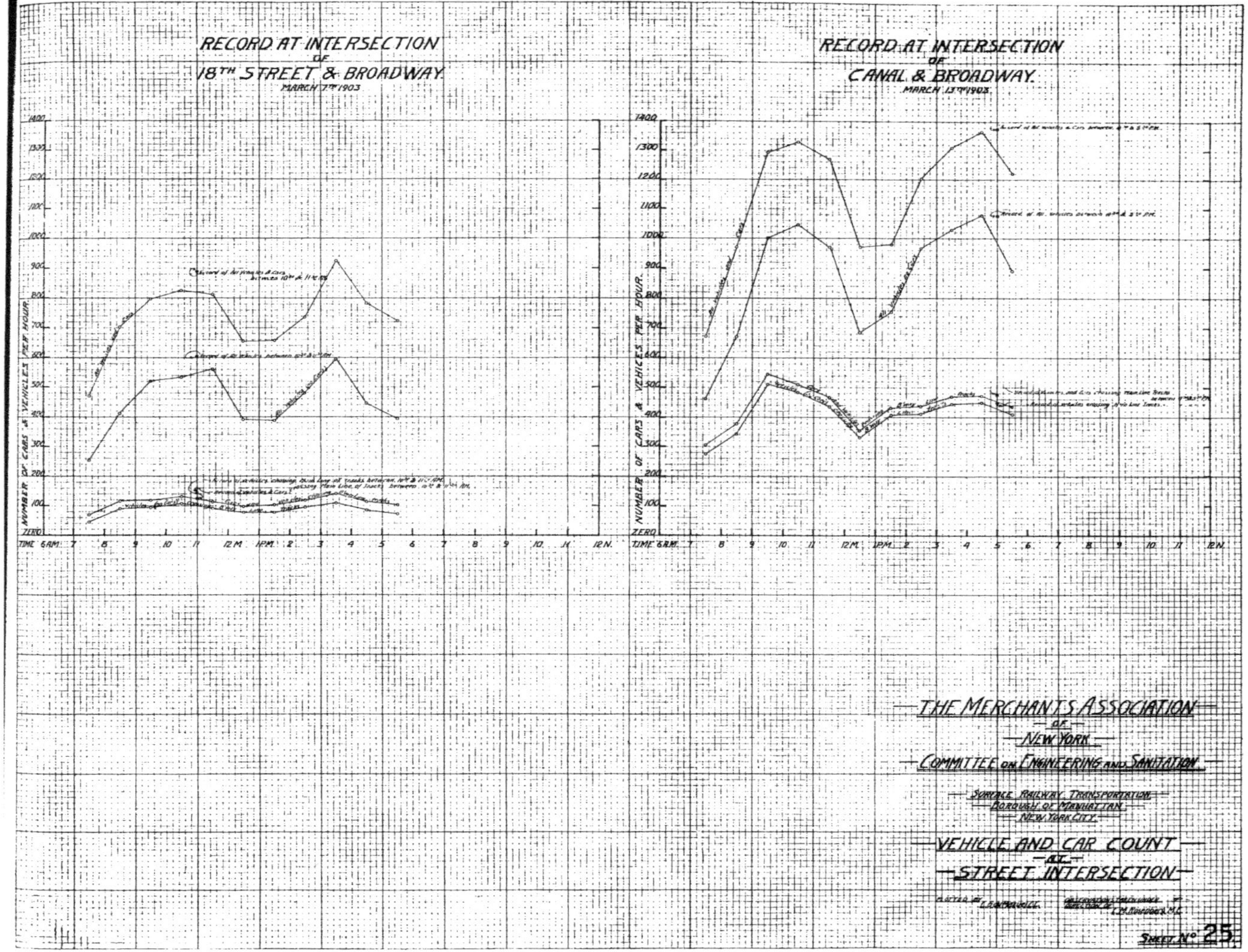

RECORD AT INTERSECTION OF 18TH STREET & BROADWAY.

MARCH 7TH 1903.

RECORD AT INTERSECTION OF CANAL & BROADWAY.

MARCH 13TH 1903.

NUMBER OF CARS & VEHICLES PER HOUR.

TIME 6 A.M. 7 8 9 10 11 12 M. 1 P.M. 2 3 4 5 6 7 8 9 10 11 12 N.

THE MERCHANTS ASSOCIATION OF NEW YORK

COMMITTEE ON ENGINEERING AND SANITATION

SURFACE RAILWAY TRANSPORTATION
BOROUGH OF MANHATTAN
NEW YORK CITY

VEHICLE AND CAR COUNT AT STREET INTERSECTION

SHEET No. 25

DIAGRAM 17.

RECORD AT INTERSECTION
OF
CHAMBERS & BROADWAY.
MARCH 6TH 1903
RECORD AT INTERSECTION
OF
FULTON & BROADWAY.
MARCH 10TH 1903
NUMBER OF CARS & VEHICLES PER HOUR.
NUMBER OF CARS AND VEHICLES PER HOUR.
THE MERCHANTS ASSOCIATION
OF
NEW YORK.
COMMITTEE ON ENGINEERING AND SANITATION
SURFACE RAILWAY TRANSPORTATION
BOROUGH OF MANHATTAN
NEW YORK CITY.
VEHICLE AND CAR COUNT
AT
STREET INTERSECTION
SHEET NO. 23

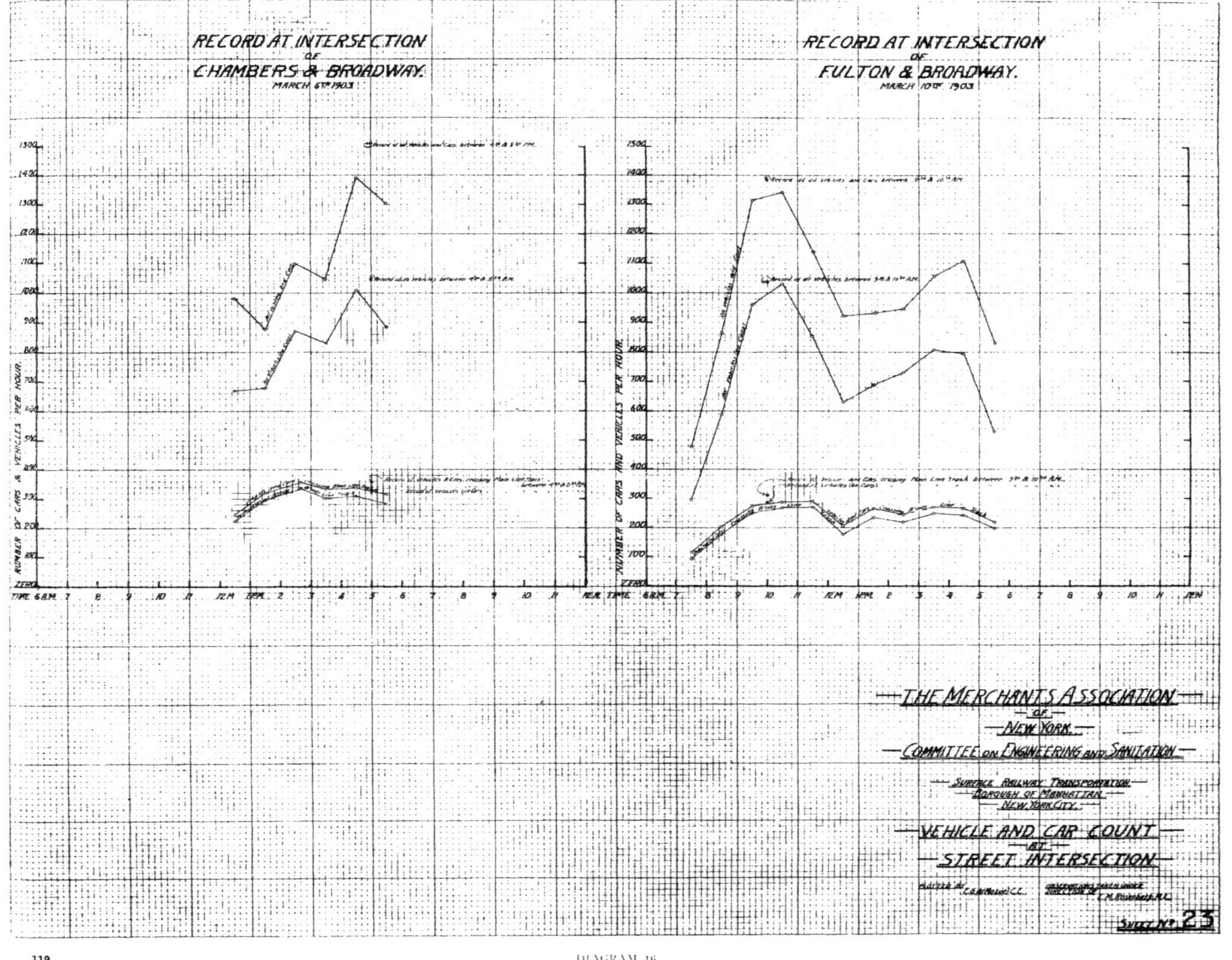

DIAGRAM 16.

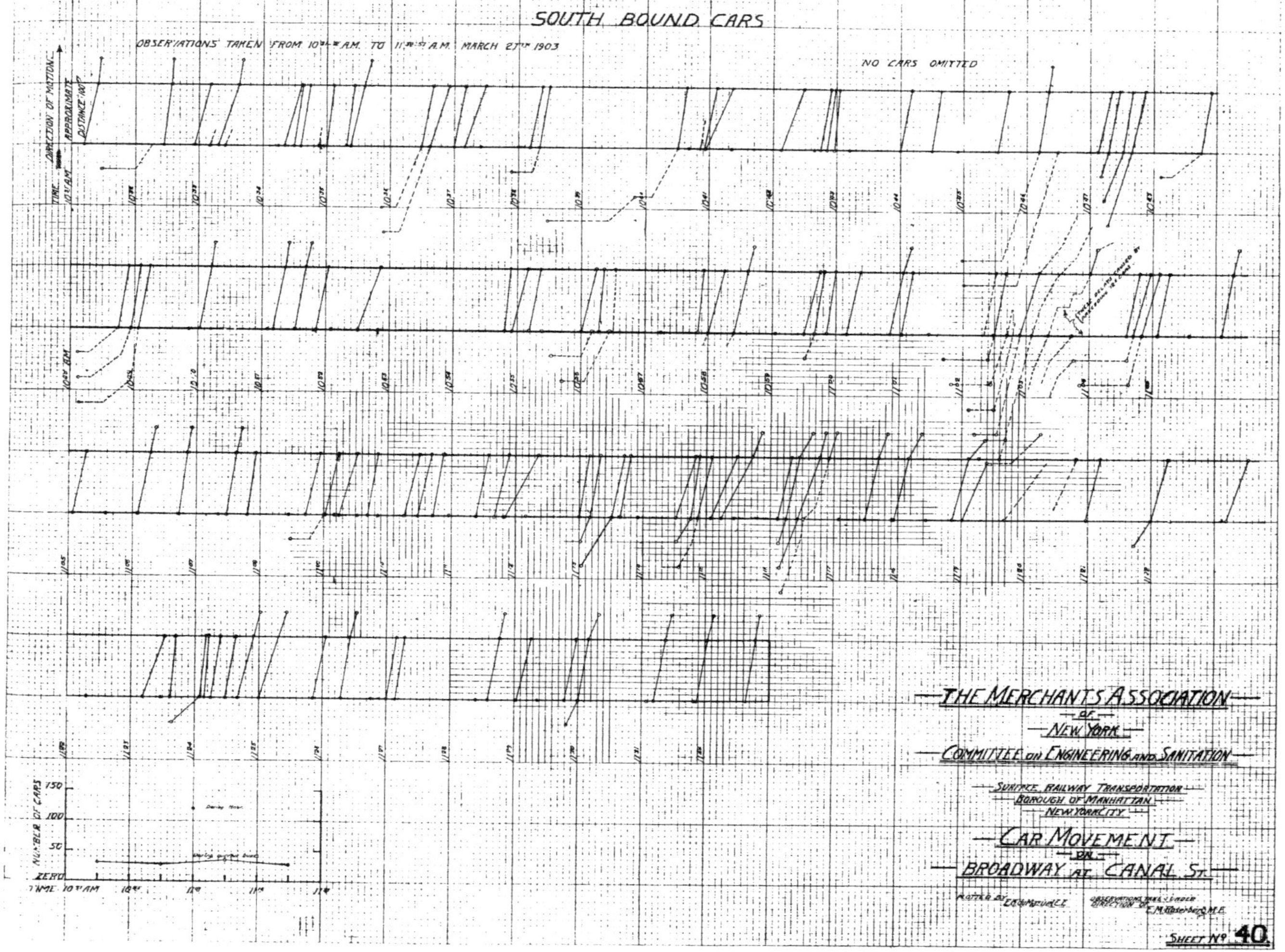

DIAGRAM 15.

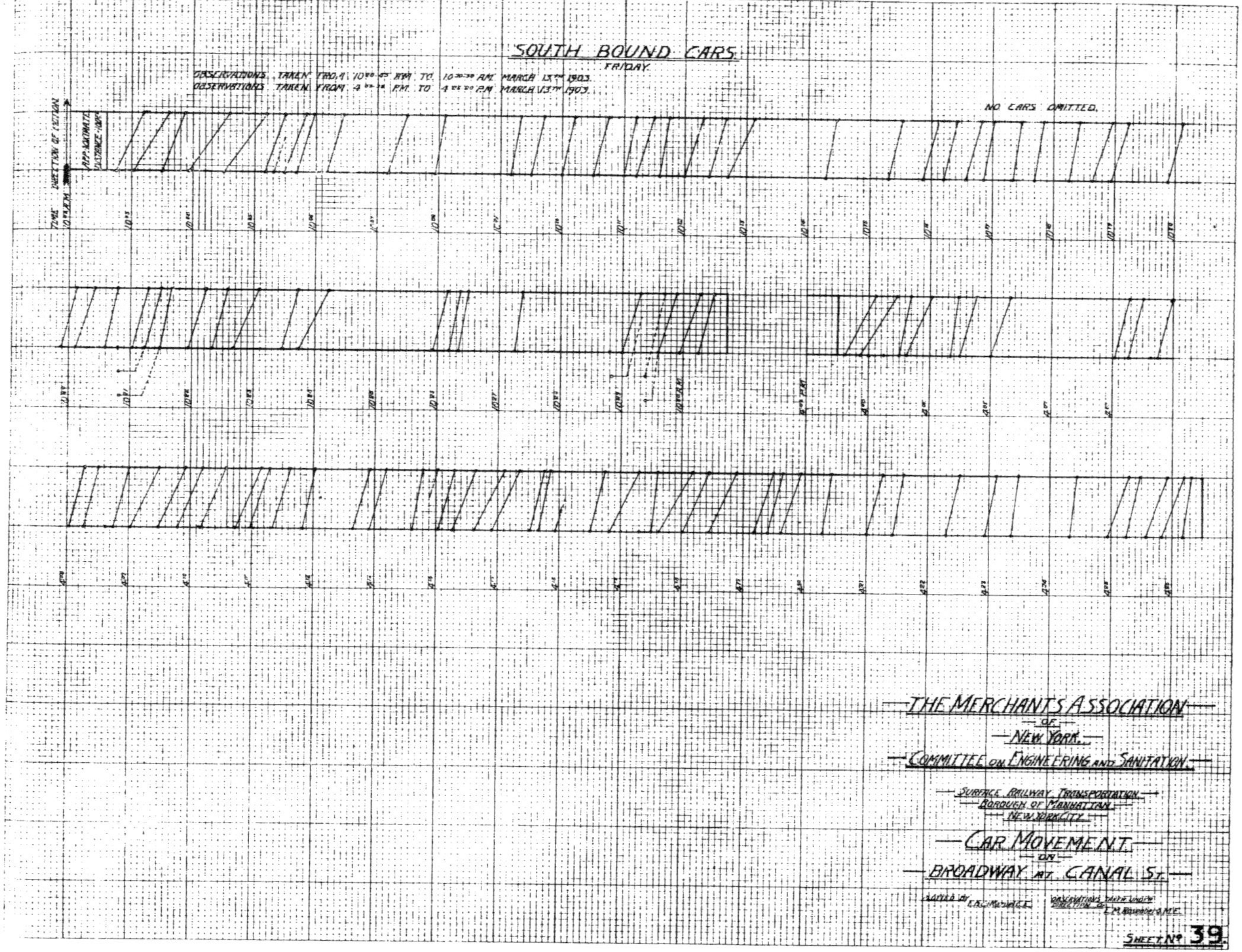

SOUTH BOUND CARS.
FRIDAY.
OBSERVATIONS TAKEN FROM 10.00 A.M. TO 10.20 A.M. MARCH 13TH 1903.
OBSERVATIONS TAKEN FROM 4.00 P.M. TO 4.20 P.M. MARCH 13TH 1903.

NO CARS OMITTED.

TIME DIRECTION OF MOTION
APPROXIMATE DISTANCE - 100 FT.

THE MERCHANTS ASSOCIATION
OF
NEW YORK.
COMMITTEE ON ENGINEERING AND SANITATION.

SURFACE RAILWAY TRANSPORTATION
BOROUGH OF MANHATTAN
NEW YORK CITY

CAR MOVEMENT
ON
BROADWAY AT CANAL ST.

SHEET NO. 39.

DIAGRAM 14.

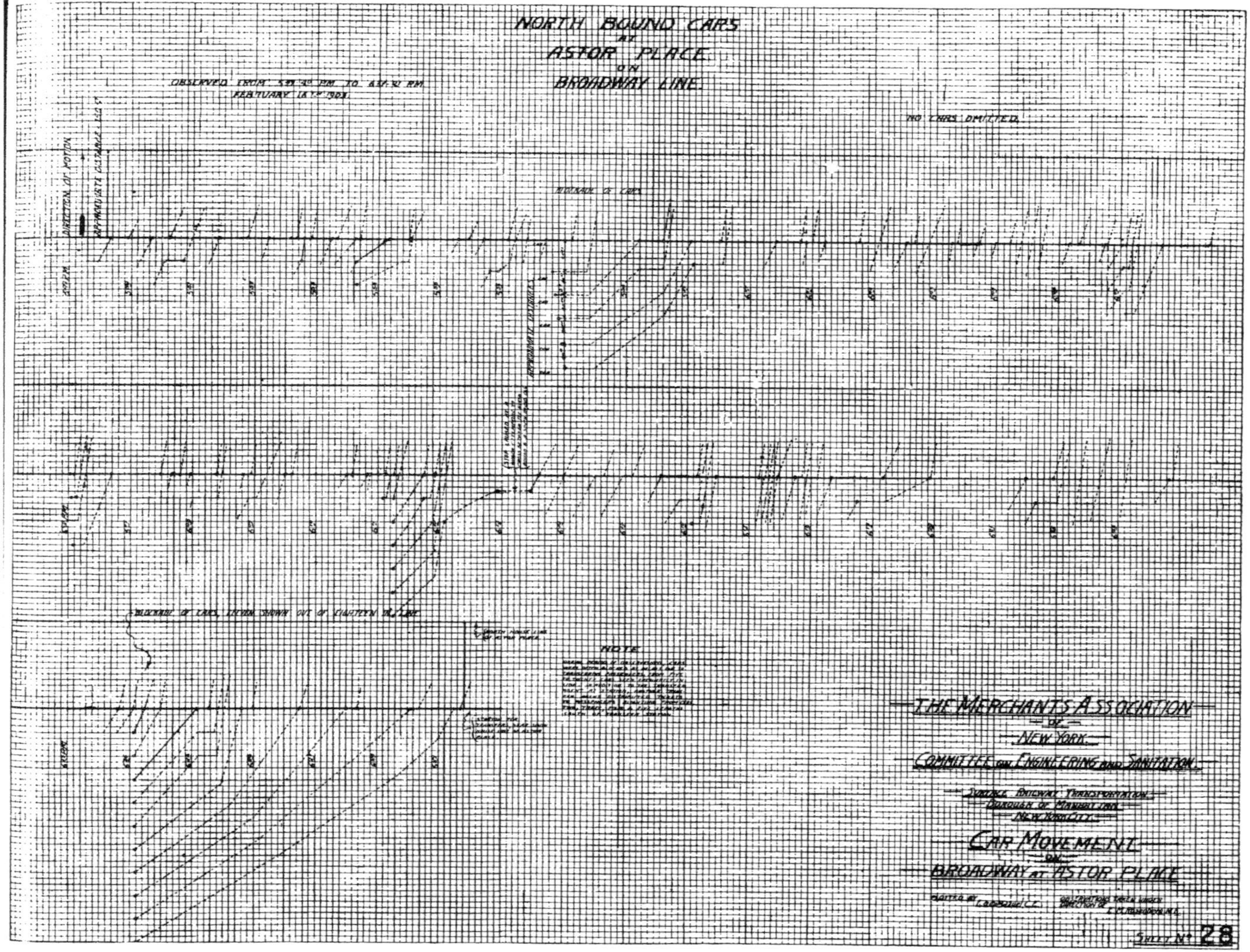

NORTH BOUND CARS
AT
ASTOR PLACE
ON
BROADWAY LINE.

OBSERVED FROM 5:31:40 P.M. TO 6:37:30 P.M.
FEBRUARY 13TH 1903.

NO CARS OMITTED.

DIRECTION OF MOTION

APPROXIMATE DISTANCE

BLOCKADE OF CARS

APPROXIMATE DISTANCES

BLOCKADE OF CARS, SEVEN SHOWN OUT OF EIGHTEEN IN LINE

NOTE

THE MERCHANTS ASSOCIATION
OF
NEW YORK.
COMMITTEE ON ENGINEERING AND SANITATION.
SURFACE RAILWAY TRANSPORTATION
BOROUGH OF MANHATTAN
NEW YORK CITY.
CAR MOVEMENT
ON
BROADWAY AT ASTOR PLACE

SHEET Nº 28

DIAGRAM 13.

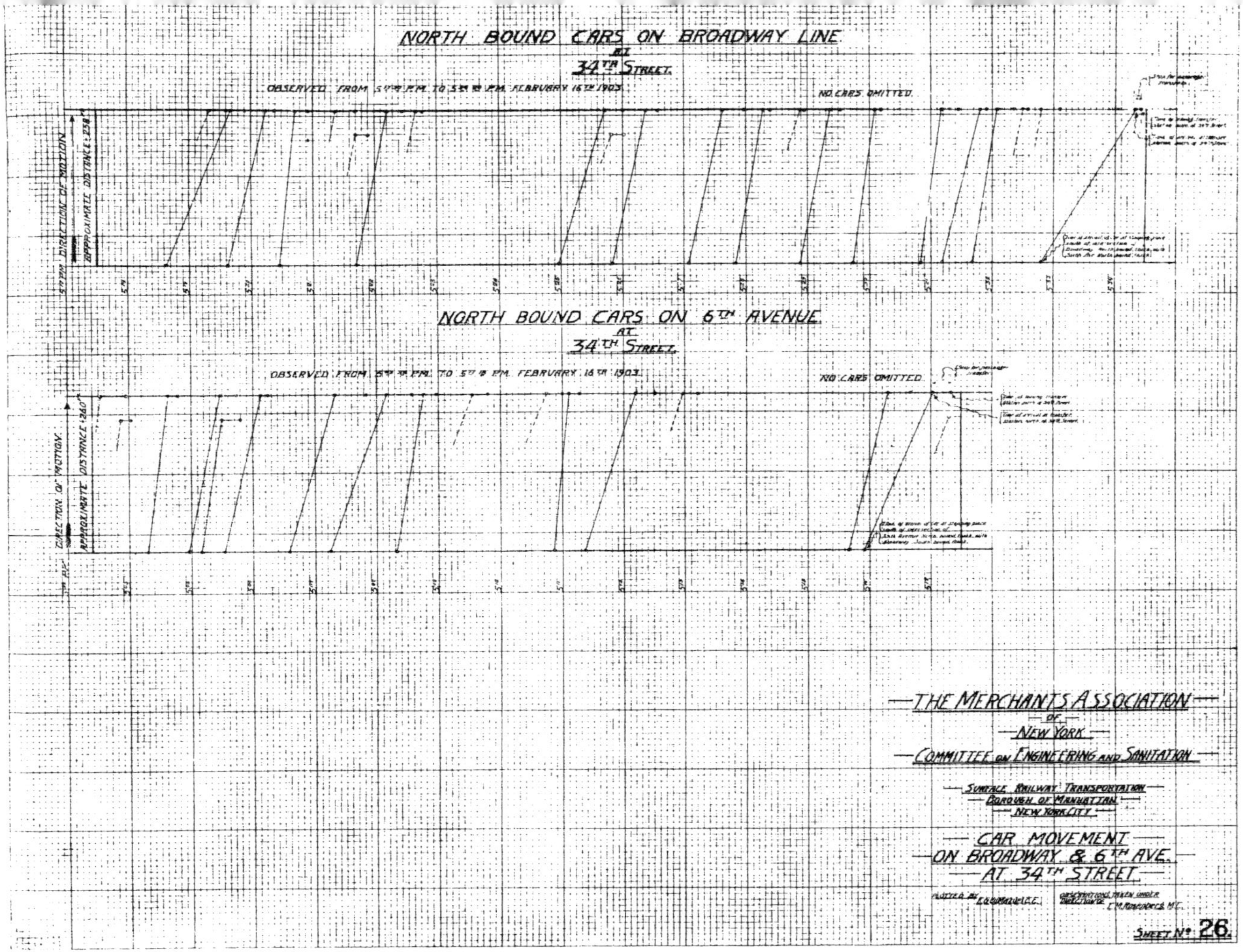

NORTH BOUND CARS ON BROADWAY LINE
AT
34TH STREET.

OBSERVED FROM 5:00 P.M. TO 5:30 P.M. FEBRUARY 16TH 1903.

NO CARS OMITTED.

DIRECTION OF MOTION

APPROXIMATE DISTANCE: 258'

NORTH BOUND CARS ON 6TH AVENUE
AT
34TH STREET.

OBSERVED FROM 5:00 P.M. TO 5:30 P.M. FEBRUARY 16TH 1903.

NO CARS OMITTED.

DIRECTION OF MOTION

APPROXIMATE DISTANCE: 260'

THE MERCHANTS ASSOCIATION
OF
NEW YORK
COMMITTEE ON ENGINEERING AND SANITATION

SURFACE RAILWAY TRANSPORTATION
BOROUGH OF MANHATTAN
NEW YORK CITY

CAR MOVEMENT
ON BROADWAY & 6TH AVE.
AT 34TH STREET.

SHEET No. 26.

DIAGRAM 12.

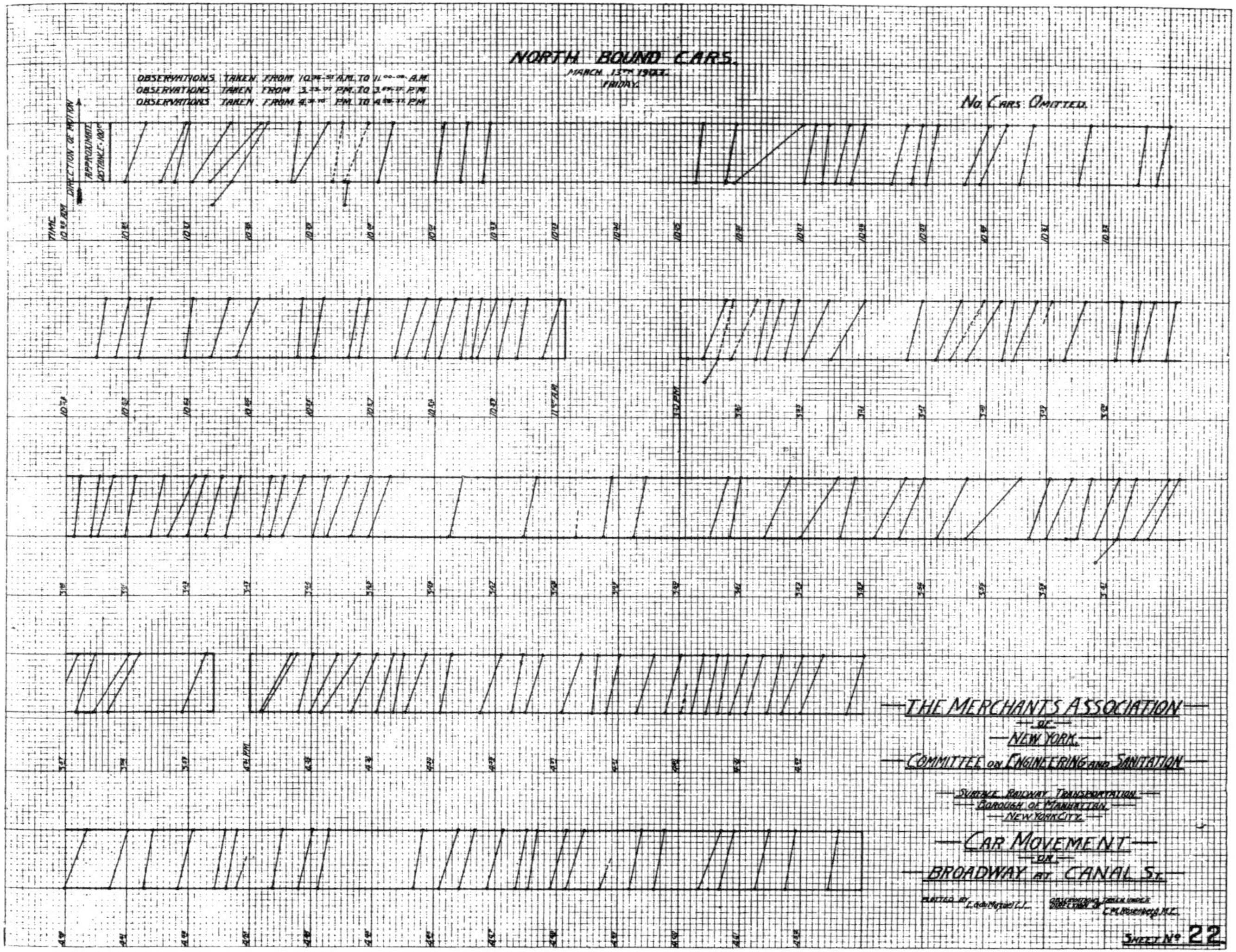

NORTH BOUND CARS.
MARCH 13TH 1903.
FRIDAY.

OBSERVATIONS TAKEN FROM 10.24 A.M. TO 11.00 A.M.
OBSERVATIONS TAKEN FROM 3.25 P.M. TO 3.56 P.M.
OBSERVATIONS TAKEN FROM 4.31 P.M. TO 4.56 P.M.

NO CARS OMITTED.

TIME

DIRECTION OF MOTION

APPROXIMATE DISTANCE - 100 FT.

THE MERCHANTS ASSOCIATION
OF
NEW YORK.
COMMITTEE ON ENGINEERING AND SANITATION

SURFACE RAILWAY TRANSPORTATION
BOROUGH OF MANHATTAN
NEW YORK CITY.

CAR MOVEMENT
ON
BROADWAY AT CANAL ST.

SHEET NO. 22

DIAGRAM 11.

ADDENDUM B.

DOUBLE-DECK CARS IN EUROPEAN CITIES.

REPORT OF MR. JOHN P. FOX.

To the Committee on Engineering and Sanitation of The Merchants' Association of New York.

Gentlemen:

WHOEVER would relieve congestion on street railways in American cities by foreign methods must expect opposition and criticism, both from the public and from street railway companies, and rightly to a certain extent, because of differing conditions. The open roofs of double-deck cars and omnibuses may double or treble the number of seats and be exceedingly popular with Americans in London; but no one would care to ride outside in a snowstorm, even though used to riding in open sleighs. And even if upper decks could be enclosed so as to be warm in winter and pleasant in summer, and all other possible objections were overcome, it would be a good deal to expect any private company to replace or reconstruct its entire rolling stock without having the prospect of increased earnings as a result.

While England and the Continent of Europe may have lagged behind the United States in the spread of electric traction in certain ways, there are things which they have developed that would be of great value in this country if practical. The double-deck car is one of those things; and it seems as though, if its enormous seating capacity could be utilized at rush hours, the discomforts and dangers to passengers and losses to companies from overcrowded street cars could be practically if not wholly done away with; for, with a seat for every passenger or a hundred seats to a car, there would be no such rushing as now, and in other ways less chance of accidents and less damages for a company to pay, fewer fares would be lost, and cars could be better operated in many ways.

But one is at once confronted with the fact that, though double-deck cars are in use in Europe, Africa, Australia, South America, and as near as Mexico, they have never gained a foothold in the United States, though have been tried in many places at different times. The experience of the past would seem to be conclusive were it not for the possibilities opened up by recent American car construction and developments in England. These made it seem worth while to review again the whole question of practicability in this country, and about a year has been spent in the inquiry, including several months' careful study in Europe. With the assistance of many street railway managers and other officials, electrical and other engineers here and abroad, it has been possible to go into the details of the matter; and the results seem to justify the opinion of one of the best tramway managers in Europe, who, after having seen the situation in American cities, and taken up with the writer the problems involved, was positive, not only that double-deck cars were now practicable in America and could be built to meet every condition and objection, but that the worst congestion could be wholly relieved by their use, with great advantage to companies as well as to the public.

The chief advantage to a company, as recognized by some of the leading American managers, is that of having a single equipment of cars, of enormous capacity compared with single-deck cars of similar weight, length, cost and current consumption. This capacity is always available on the road, after the theaters, blockades, games, processions, etc.

But there are many difficulties to be overcome; and, considering previous unsatisfactory experience with double-deck cars in the United States and the radically different conditions of climate and traffic to be found in European and other countries where such cars are in use, it is not to be wondered that American managers are sceptical about their desirability. These are some of the requirements that would have to be met in America:

1. The upper deck must be tightly enclosed in winter, and as warm and well ventilated as the lower deck; in summer it must allow for plenty of air circulation and yet afford perfect protection against the heaviest rains.

2. The car must be designed so as to load and unload as quickly and as safely as single-deck cars.

3. The stairs must be absolutely safe, so that passengers can go up and down at any time, even when rounding curves.

4. The roof must be low enough to pass under any elevated structures, wires and bridges, and yet all headroom inside must be adequate for the tallest persons.

5. The ceilings must not be nor appear too low, and the entire interior must be as light as with other cars.

6. The car must be no heavier than single-deck cars of similar capacity, and as strong, must not cost more nor wear the track more, nor take more current, and must be stable enough to run at high speeds and to stand any wind pressure.

7. Aisles and stairs must be of ample width and so arranged that the conductor can get quickly from one part of the car to another and the car started and stopped with no more delay or danger of accidents than with single-deck cars.

At this point it may be interesting to read the opinion of one of the best-known American car builders, advertising single-deck cars in an English street railway publication. He says:

"To American observers the present conditions in the United Kingdom seem to presage an early and general change in rolling stock in favor of the long double-truck car. In this rapidly progressive era of electrical locomotion the limitations of the double-deck car must gradually become more apparent. The loss of mileage, due chiefly to slowness in loading and unloading, is naturally the most important consideration with managers, and will, in the writer's opinion, compel them to seek another form of car. In the United States the double-decker has long been obsolete, because of the extent to which it curtails earning capacity.

"With the public the double-decker will diminish in popularity in proportion to the advent of faster and more comfortable types. The light, airy appearance of a modern high and wide monitor-deck car contrasts strongly with the low and dark ceiling of the double-decker. The new transverse seating arrangement obviates all the discomfort of the old longitudinal seats by preventing crowding, lurching sideways and unpleasant publicity. When it is considered that to provide seats on the roof the car must needs be made slow and uncomfortable, and that the awkwardness, if not danger, of mounting the stairway prevents all but the young and strong essaying it, one cannot fail to be impressed with the lack of compensation."

But it is important in this connection to read an editorial in the English *Tramway and Railway World,* to wit:

> "To managers who have had to select types of cars for an electric tramway, the double-deck car has often been a source of no little perplexity. Its disadvantages were manifest, even to the amateur tramway administrator, while to the responsible manager the possibility of accidents, inseparable from its use, at times proved an objection that was not overbalanced by the increased carrying capacity afforded by the outside seats. A few years ago the influence of American models was a factor to be considered, and the advocates of the single-deck car clung with conviction to the fact that on the whole twenty thousand miles of American electric tramways not a double-deck car was to be found. Speed, we were told, was the very essence of electric traction, and with a cheerful disregard of Board of Trade regulations the argument was pressed against the top-seat car on the ground that it was slow. Chiefly for these reasons the single-deck car was chosen to inaugurate the electric service on several tramways, and for a time it seemed that the American model would generally be followed. Very soon, however, the difference in the conditions under which tramways in the two countries have to be conducted began to be appreciated; and it was seen that the top-seat car was not only more popular, and consequently more remunerative, but that it was a necessity if the people were to be provided with seats at the hours of dense traffic. The British public will not consent to be crowded in the way that is usual in every American city, where a single-deck car has a carrying capacity limited only by the number of passengers who can be squeezed into it. This fact alone would have established the position of even the old-fashioned, top-deck car as the standard type for the United Kingdom, but the improvements that have since been made have now given it an advantage in every respect over the single-deck car. The reversed stairway—the practical introduction of which is due to Mr. Bellamy—has reduced the danger of accidents to passengers, and has increased the running time of the car inasmuch as passengers can safely ascend or descend the stairway while the car is in motion. The introduction of various forms of 'dry' seats has also done something to increase the serviceability of the double-deck car, and as a summer car it is certainly thoroughly well adapted to the needs of British tramways. Yet in winter

weather the cars have disadvantages that cannot be wholly removed. That they can be materially reduced is, however, shown by the account given elsewhere in this issue of Mr. Bellamy's new design for a canopy top. While this still preserves the agreeable features of the top-seat in pleasant weather, it provides adequate protection against wind and storm, and at the same time considerably increases the capacity of the car—an advantage that will appeal to any manager who feels the pressure to provide comfortable seats even at the expense of running cars with the upper decks unoccupied. That the new arrangement does not add to the appearance of the car must be admitted, but it is not a serious detriment to it, and considering its other advantages we expect to see it largely adopted."

There is an impression in America that double-deck cars are not satisfactory to foreign managers and are likely to go more and more out of use. The writer made special inquiries in Europe on this matter. According to the latest returns, of the 6,660 electric cars in Great Britain and Ireland, 90 per cent. are double deck, 10 per cent. single deck. Of the 3,517 cars in cities having 100 or more in use, 94 per cent. are double deck and 6 per cent. single deck. Of the 450 electric cars in Manchester, 425 are double deck or 94 per cent.; of the 611 electric cars in Glasgow, 590 are double deck or 97 per cent.; of the 480 electric cars in Liverpool, 468 or 98 per cent. are double deck; of the 400 electric cars in use in and about London, all are double deck. The single-deck cars are used more on country lines and routes with low bridges. One manager said that he used them solely on the latter account, preferring the double-deck cars used elsewhere on his system. Another manager, who also greatly prefers the double-deck type, still uses some single-deck cars for economical reasons, they having cost him $4,500 apiece; but he will never get any more, and wonders that any managers get them, especially for lines along which there is anything attractive to be seen. The writer found considerable wonder that double-deck cars were not used in the United States, as with one street railway editor, who thought they were just the thing needed to relieve congestion in New York. The preference of the English public is illustrated by the following about the Nottingham Corporation Tramways in the *Tramway and Railway World:*

"This country has gone to America for nearly all its precedents in tramway construction and equipment, but it

> refuses to be led by American practice in its adoption of a single-deck car. The advantage of a double-deck car in this country is easily understood; it deals with the separation of smokers and non-smokers, it provides open-air riding, which is so much preferred by a number of the British public, even in the coldest weather, and, principally, it doubles the seating capacity of the car with only a trifling increase in weight. The double-deck car is much more popular than the single-deck car, and the public must have what they prefer; if single-deck cars were adopted generally in Nottingham, it would probably result in the undertaking being carried out at a loss instead of at a profit."

Aside from the preference of the public, the leading English tramway managers believe thoroughly in the double-deck car, and constant improvements are making it more and more satisfactory. On the Continent, development has been more slow, and the double-deck cars, even in Paris, where they are in the majority, have many imperfections, as in the poor stairs and entrances, low head room under roofs, often hard riding, etc. But with the latest double-deck cars in Paris, the writer found no dissatisfaction expressed except with some structural weakness of the under frame.

Taking up now the requirements previously stated.

1. To most Americans a double-deck car means one with an open roof without any protection from the weather, and this naturally causes them at once to condemn such a car for use in rainy and cold latitudes. But top-covered upper decks, with side curtains, are very common all over the world, and also enclosed upper decks with windows, as on the Nogentais Railway and other recent cars and station omnibuses in Paris, on old steam tram cars in England and Germany, all the double-deck steam railway carriages of the Est Railway in France and the two later types of the Ouest Railway, as well as on the Danish State Railways. Even in England, where the open roof is still the rule and not the exception, there is a spreading movement to provide some sort of cover and sides, so that on cold and rainy days, when outside riding is unpleasant (less than a third of the year in Liverpool), passengers unable to get seats inside or wishing to smoke can have a protection on the roof at least equal to that of American open cars, which protection many think is sufficient

for the mild extremes of the English climate. While the Liverpool top cover, with its side curtains like our open cars, and further its curtains in the roof capable of being pushed back to allow the full effect of open-air riding on pleasant days, may be suited to southern latitudes in the United States, a tighter protection would be needed in northern latitudes, such as found in other English covers and the Continental examples named above. Many of the Paris cars, which were built in America, have permanent roofs over the upper decks, while the upper sides consist of large removable wood and steel sections containing windows that can be lowered in winter, while in summer the sections are taken out and stored. One English top cover has all the windows on each side capable of being raised and lowered together at once; another has glass in sashes and wood sections like a roller-top desk, allowing the roof to be almost entirely open or wholly closed as with the Liverpool type. But for this country, perhaps the best solution would be treating the roof like a semi-convertible car, with very large windows to be opened on pleasant summer days, but when closed forming an interior as tight as that below, capable of being warmed in coldest weather. This construction allows a more substantial and attractive appearance than others.

2. There is a strong opinion among street railway men, not only in America, but found by the writer on the Continent and even in England, an opinion already quoted above, that double-deck cars make longer stops than single-deck cars and must do so to enable passengers to go up and down the stairs safely; and that this slowness of loading and unloading is a serious objection to their use, a fatal objection in American cities, where such a continual source of delay would mean longer headway between cars at rush hours and hence fewer seats for passengers, as well as slower speed, also cutting down car mileage and so requiring more cars and more men to operate them, with other increase of operating expenses. This objection seems to have been the chief one found with Mr. Pullman's double-deck car when it was tried in Boston ten years ago, and to avoid it the Liverpool Corporation, when introducing electric traction in 1898, thought it desirable to follow the Continental and American practice of adopting single-deck cars. So, while trying some double-deck cars, the corpora-

tion imported single-deck ones from America and Germany. Of the American car it was written at the time:

> "The idea in its construction was to make a car which should take the place of the ordinary double-deck horse car used in that city. It was desired for the sake of speed to have all the passengers on one deck and at the same time it was necessary to keep the car within the length of the ordinary horse car and team. It might, therefore, be called a double-deck car run tandem; the open compartment being placed on the same level as the closed, and the entrance being between the two. . . .
>
> "The speed in English cities is so limited that the double-deck car, though much liked, cuts the average daily mileage down to a point where only a small profit remains; this car, so low that only a single step is needed, brings the mileage up as high as is possible with the limitations."

The experience of Liverpool then is of the greatest interest in this matter, and the writer spent a month there this year in order to study every detail of this question. It is important here to compare the American single-deck car used in Liverpool with the latest top-covered, double-deck car in the same city. The former seats 40 passengers, the latter 64. The former is 34 feet 4 inches long over collision fenders, weighs 25,340 pounds, and requires two 35 horse-power motors on maximum traction trucks. The double-deck car is 28 feet long over collision fenders, weighs 21,-336 pounds, has two 25 horse-power motors with a single truck, uses 65 per cent. as much power as the single-deck car, yet can climb steeper grades and run at higher speeds, costing complete, about 60 per cent. as much. Points like these told strongly in favor of the double-deck car, but the weak point was the staircase and its effect on stops. The insecurity of the common staircase is familiar to every one who has ridden on London omnibuses, the type being in universal use on the Continent as well as still on many English cars. The possibility of having passengers pitched backwards off the stairs had tended to make stops long enough to enable people to safely ascend or descend, and hence the feeling in favor and the trial of single-deck cars. But this difficulty was entirely solved in Liverpool by the introduction of the reversed staircase, in descending which a passenger faces in toward the car body and is in every way completely enclosed, a stairway so safe that the Liverpool Corporation has absolutely no case on record of a person being injured on it, and it is now adopted on almost all new cars built in England. The result is of immense importance, for stops can now be made as short as with single-deck cars, it being the rule in Liverpool that passengers on the upper deck wishing to alight must descend to the platform before the conductor gives the signal to stop. The absolute safety of the reversed staircase at all speeds and on curves makes this requirement practicable, and for the same reason there is absolutely no waiting for passengers to ascend to the upper deck before a car is started.

Not only this, the Liverpool double-deck cars actually tend to make shorter stops than single-deck cars; for, as the general manager pointed out to the writer, the upper-deck passengers are more ready to get off promptly than those inside, having, of course, to be always ready on the platform; whereas those inside are often seen to linger even till the car stops before leaving their places. Moreover, the writer accurately timed many stops in Liverpool and found the average time consumed by each passenger getting on and off to be 1.9 seconds, including persons boarding and leaving the cars when in motion. He then timed the stops in one of the largest American cities, where the cars are operated quite similarly to Liverpool, and found that, even with a twelve-bench open car and all its entrances at every seat, the time per passenger averaged 2.8 seconds. But this is not surprising when one considers the obvious disadvantages of open cars, such as the hunting for seats after a car has stopped, the effect of the high steps on old, large, or infirm passengers, and the difficulty of the conductor to determine just when all passengers are safely on and off. Whereas the double step and entrance of the latest English double-deck cars seems to be the safest and quickest feature of the kind in use. The center post adds greatly to safety; the double passage enables two seats of passengers to get on or off at once, or one set on and one off, all under the eye of the conductor, and much better than with open cars because of the easier steps and more convenient handles; and passengers again do not delay the car to find seats, doing this below or above after the car has started.

As to whether the single-deck car can be loaded and unloaded at terminal points more quickly than the double-deck car, one English manager was recently quoted as saying that they can be much more quickly, but another says that he does not find the difference in time appreciable. Both men use only double-deck cars, both have been to America, but the second studied specially the relative merits of single and double deck cars before finally choosing the latter. As entrance steps are higher than those of any staircases, they would seem to be the determining factor to a large extent of speed in loading and unloading. The writer found once that, at a very crowded terminal under the most favorable conditions for open cars, the latter were no more quickly loaded than closed cars, the average time for each passenger to board working out the same in each case within 3-1000 of a second. Judging from this, one would expect the open car to require longer stops at ordinary terminals than closed cars, especially when one has seen a full minute's stop required for one infirm woman to get on and often found ten-second stops common for other single passengers.

3. A stairway perfectly safe at all times is evidently an absolute necessity for a satisfactory double-deck car service on crowded lines. The English reversed stairway meets this requirement, and, as well as other kinds, has been most carefully studied and tested by the writer under many conditions. Its widespread adoption throughout England is a sign of its perfection. Equally safe other types can be made, careful enclosing being essential. Accidents on any car stairs have been very rare in England. A clerk in the Board of Trade office, where returns are sent in, remembered none. The writer has two cases, however, where one man was jerked off one of the old common staircases on a tramcar into the street and another off the stairs of a London omnibus. Some of the first stairs were nothing but iron ladders with bars instead of treads. Omnibus stairs have been very steep in many places till quite recently, and still without accidents. Of the 1,004 accident in 1902 of two of the largest Paris companies using double-deck cars and omnibuses less than 1½ per cent. occurred on the stairs.

4. It is generally believed in America that the headroom under bridges, elevated railway girders, subway roofs, etc., is too low to allow double-deck cars to be run. This impression was also found in Berlin. The mistake is readily made of be-

lieving that such cars must have a height above the lower floor of at least two ordinary men added together, making a total height of 15 or 16 feet. While such a height may be desirable, it is not necessary, even for the amplest headroom, as two forms of the knife-board seat car, which has been built and tried in this country, allow the total height to be cut down, say from 15 feet 9 inches to 13 feet 8 inches, still keeping the standard English headroom on each deck. In Europe it is usually thought better to give every passenger a seat, even though reducing the headroom, so that one has to stoop a little in moving about, rather than to use a single-deck car with only one-half or one-third the capacity. In order to use double-deck cars in England expensive street lowerings are often made or bridges raised to give uniform clearance throughout a system. One city has just voted the money to get rid of the last low bridge in order to make possible the abandonment of the last line of single-deck cars. In Paris there is always headroom for the tallest persons to sit down, but the aisles of the upper deck are sometimes even less than five feet from floor to ceiling. The writer has carefully studied the minimum height which a double-deck car could have, and has designed an electric motor car of the knife-board seat type with enclosed upper deck, using European precedents for every feature throughout, so as to leave no question open as to practicability, and found, without using even the lowest European headroom inside, a height possible from rail to roof of 11 feet 2 inches. Such a car in New York, if enclosed throughout, could probably seat eighty passengers. This result may seem incredible, but it does not even then take the minimum French headroom, viz.—that found on the upper decks of the double-deck steam cars of the Ouest Company, model of 1879, still largely used in suburban service about Paris, which have a maximum height under the center of the roof of 51⅞ inches, enough, however, for a man 6 feet 2 inches high to be seated, even with a tall hat on; but he would have to stoop to pass under the 45¼-inch entrance. If one applied these dimensions to the upper deck of the "minimum" car it would cut the height down about 6 inches more to 10 feet 8 inches, and still allow what is given the majority of suburban third-class passengers from the most used station in the world. Fortunately, even in American cities, such a sacrifice of headroom to seating capacity would be unnecessary, and it is possible to run double-deck cars anywhere with more clearance inside than found under any of the Paris roofs, as much as found with the English cars where the height is practically unrestricted.

A few heights of cars may be interesting. The lowest enclosed roof French street cars are probably those of the Nogentais Railway, which measure 14 feet 5¼ inches from rail to roof. The double-deck steam cars of the Ouest Railway just mentioned are 13 feet 11 inches high. A 6-foot man on the Berlin trail car roofs would come about 14 feet 9 inches above the rail. The standard Liverpool top-covered car is 16 feet 5 inches over the trolley base, having cross seats on the roof. The Cardiff Corporation cars, with cross seats, but no top covers, were designed to pass under bridges 15 feet above the rail. Double-deck motor cars are not used in Berlin, the chief reason given, and for Germany, also, being the low headroom under bridges, and except for which they would be used, but the minimum height underneath seems to be about 13 feet 6 inches, not at all too low, as the writer pointed out to the street railway engineers there. The latest double-truck motor car in Berlin, with double-truck trailer, has only sixty-five seats, requiring two conductors, taking twice the street space of the Liverpool cars with their sixty-four seats, easily looked after by one conductor, illustrating in other ways easily seen the advantages of the double-deck type.

5. Some Americans are disagreeably impressed with the lowness of ceilings in European cars, and one car builder was quoted above who spoke of how "the light, airy appearance of a modern high and wide monitor-deck car contrasts strongly with the low and dark ceiling of the double-decker." But the ceiling of the latter can no longer be called dark, consisting as it does in the latest types of millboard painted white and easily cleaned. And when one is used to the lowness he never seems to think of it, especially as it is now associated with very efficient methods of ventilation. From the stuffiness of the London omnibuses in summer to the many ventilating devices on the Liverpool cars is a long step, a step farther than one taken in this country, for some of the Liverpool transoms could be open in a driving rain

or snowstorm; others at the front end can open the way the car is going and send in a strong breeze, passing out through the rear transoms opened the opposite way. There is still further a sliding panel in the tops of the doors. Everything is arranged to allow fresh air to enter in all weathers without draughts. Those passengers who in this country would want the inside windows open or to ride in open cars, merely go up on the upper deck, where the top cover, when open, allows more air and light even than our open cars, with equal protection from rain and sun, if desired.

The total air space inside the two decks of a Liverpool top-covered car is slightly greater than that of a double truck closed New York car, thus allowing more air space per passenger when the cars are equally filled. This should tend to offset any objections to low ceilings, especially on account of the many provisions for circulating air, as found in the Liverpool cars.

Those passengers who would object to the low European ceilings and compact seating arrangement should remember that by introducing such things in America it should be possible to give every one a seat, practically, even at the rush hours. It is surely pleasanter to be seated under a low but light white ceiling, illuminated at night with softened incandescent lights, than to stand packed in with others under a high ceiling with naked lights staring one in the face at night. The utilization of every inch of room for seats is one of the ways that such congestion as is found in America has been prevented in Europe. Of course, the limited amount of standing allowed by authorities abroad forces foreign managers to provide every seat possible, for when a car is *"complet"* its earning ceases. The American manager is more fortunate, and gets his best return from standing passengers. But it seems as though standing has been overdone in this country, even from a financial standpoint. Extreme overcrowding causes loss of fares, encourages accidents and results in very serious loss of time in stops, the writer having timed stops of over a minute for two or three passengers to get off closed cars.

6. The comparative figures for the Liverpool single and double deck cars are perhaps sufficient to illustrate the economy of the latter type when the ratio is taken between seating capacity,

or even comfortable carrying capacity, and length, weight, cost and current consumption. One further comparison, however, may be of interest. Some of the Liverpool single-deck American cars had stairways and an upper deck added, being used Saturdays, Sundays, holidays, and other times when cars of large capacity would be useful. Their seating capacity was increased by 60 seats on the upper deck, from 40 to 100, the length over all being 41 feet; weight, 31,360 pounds, complete; two 35 horse-power motors still being sufficient. The largest closed cars in New York, the semi-convertible Third avenue, with cross seats, formerly seated 48 passengers, being 41 feet 10 inches over all, weighing 36,000 pounds, and having four Westinghouse No. 69 motors.

Any one who has studied the construction of the best European double-deck cars has no doubt of their strength. The weakest ones of the type seen by the writer were made in America, and he failed to notice any such creaking and movement of the windows as found on some of the best lines in this country.

As to the relative amount of track wear by single and double deck cars, the writer found it impossible in Liverpool to determine the speed of cars from the number of rails passed over, because the joints were in such good condition; but, of course, most English rails are comparatively new. The writer certainly found no track in England as bad as that in at least one American city, where an immense amount is gouged on the surface, for long distances on tangents as well as on curves, due chiefly, according to a high authority, to the running of too light cars. English managers are evidently thinking about the future of their rail joints, partly as a result of seeing American track wear, but if their cars are too heavy, they are likely to avoid the perhaps worse evil just mentioned, which often causes intolerable noise, especially when cars run at any speed.

As to the stability of double-deck cars, it was surprising to find in England how smooth-running the single-truck cars were, no oscillation being noticed even on curves. Where derailments have occurred, it would seem as though the chief blame should rest on the Board of Trade, which does not allow a large enough groove to the rails nor a high enough guard rail on curves. Speeds in England in the cities, both maximum and average, as tested by a speed indicator, seem often quite as high as in American cities. The long and extensive use of double-deck cars on steam railways in France and elsewhere is a sign of their safety. As to the ability to withstand wind pressure, all the Liverpool top-covered cars were out in the gale of February 27, 1903, with their roofs enclosed by mistake, but they were uninjured, though great damage was done by the wind everywhere, and a railway train was blown over on a viaduct.

One of the reasons given for trying single-deck electric cars in Liverpool was "that the speed would render outside traveling dangerous," and the writer has a case before him where a man standing on the roof of a Leeds car was jerked off into the street. But this is evidently a rare accident, and people are often jerked off other parts of cars; moreover, it could not occur with the enclosing found on the new Liverpool cars, much less with a semi-convertible upper deck.

7. The providing of adequate room in double-deck cars for the circulation of passengers is a matter that requires careful study to meet American conditions, but almost any arrangement would afford more space than is now found at the rush hours, both in closed and in open cars, when one has to push his way between standing passengers in closed cars, or sitting passengers in open cars. The collection of fares in a double-deck car and the proper stopping and starting by the conductor could not be more difficult than now at times, and could hardly fail to be better with all or 100 of the passengers seated instead of 36 or 55 at the most. One conductor has no trouble abroad with cars seating 70 or 80 passengers, in spite of the half-penny fares and the having to punch and give out tickets. The advantage of the English entrance has already been given out.

It seems as though the double-deck car should present an attraction at this time to American managers. The drawbacks which made it a failure in this country hitherto have all been overcome in England. England has profited greatly by American experience in electric railway developments. There seems no reason why we should not profit by hers, and catch up with the congestion which has assumed such appalling proportions in some of our cities. Once having caught up with it, as seems possible now, perhaps we can in the future avoid such dangerous overcrowding just as Europe has done, to the advantage both of the public and the street railway companies.

Enough has been said to show that the American car builder quoted above was mistaken in saying that the double-deck car "must needs be made slow." That it must needs be "uncomfortable," also, in order to have seats on the roof, probably refers to having longitudinal seats inside; but those seats in England, as a rule, are almost identical in shape and covering with those in the standard closed New York cars, and the writer never found any cross seats as comfortable as the luxuriously cushioned, spring-supported seats of the London United Tramways. One other quoted statement needs consideration, viz., that "the awkwardness, if not danger, of mounting the stairway prevents all but the young and strong essaying it." The immense popularity of the London omnibus roof, with the worst stairs in England, and the successful record of the reverse stairway, would seem to answer this sufficiently.

Still, an American car builder raised the question whether people in this country would climb any stairs, even to get a seat. But every person asked has answered this in the affirmative. It would be less than seven feet to climb, and probably not so hard for many people as getting on open cars, especially if the stairs were as easy as in an ordinary house; only it has been pointed out by an expert that accidents would be even less likely to occur on steep than on easy stairs, for passengers would tend to take more care on the former than on the latter; and that this would also be the case with any drunken man, for the same reason that one sobers up when he sees a policeman. Drunken men, however, seem to give no trouble in Europe, none that the writer could learn of.

As double-deck cars have never gained a foothold in America, it seems less important to quote the opinions in their favor of those who experimented with them than to find out why the cars were given up. The *Street Railway Gazette* of June 1, 1895, contains the following of interest:

> "The St. Louis *Globe-Democrat* recently interviewed several street railway managers in reference to the use of double-deck cars. One official, when asked why these cars were not operated, stated that his company had trouble

enough on hand without trying to find new ones. 'One St. Louis line,' he said, 'had a few of them a few years ago. They are popular in Paris, but would not be in St. Louis for the simple reason that our cars climb too many hills, turn too sharp and short corners, and, above all, run too fast. Speedy cars must not be top-heavy, which is just the case with the double-deckers. Besides being a constant source of annoyance, they also invite accidents. At least, that is my opinion from the construction of the car. Then there is too much work for one conductor and not enough for two.' "

"Winthrop Bartlett, civil and electrical engineer, and connected with the St. Louis and Suburban Railway Company, readily gave his experience with the double-deckers. 'The St. Louis Cable and Western Railway,' he said, 'tried that kind of cars and soon tired of them. In 1885 an order for fourteen cars was given, and a few weeks after their arrival the officials were convinced that they would not prove a success. On the contrary, they were a nuisance, as every drunken man or hoodlum who boarded the car wanted to go 'upstairs,' as they called it. One conductor had charge of both decks, and many threw up their jobs in consequence. I am firmly convinced that the old cable company lost many nickels each day through neglect on the part of the conductor or the shrewdness of the passengers. The cars were run two seasons, then the officials of the company decided that they were not suitable for the line and they were turned into the sheds. Later on the upper deck was removed and the car fixed up as an every-day car.' "

The difficulties mentioned in the first interview have all been overcome in England, and taken up above except the question of climbing hills. Ten-per cent. grades are quite common in England and are climbed by double-deck cars without any trouble. In regard to difficulties for conductors it must be remembered and emphasized again that double-deck cars in this country need not carry any more passengers than are carried now, crowded on a single deck, and that such passengers would be distributed so that each should have a seat and the aisles be kept free. If the foreign designs of cars do not allow an overseeing of the upper deck that would seem desirable here there is another type which has been carefully studied out to suit American conditions and approved by leading European authorities. This type, at least, would allow a separate compartment for smokers all the year round—a thing considered very necessary in England.

If there are any who would condemn double-deck cars because of their appearance, one must plead that, whenever it is a case of relieving congestion, which is both inconvenient and dangerous, our ideas of what a car ought to be in form should give way, as in other countries, to what is most practical, to what affords the largest number of seats and other considerations. If new cars were cleaned daily with oil as in England the result would go far to make up for any unattractive novelty of form.

It would seem as though the success and popularity of the modern double-deck electric car in other countries, considering all the advantages, would appeal to American companies. Granted that they do, could the companies afford to introduce them? There are several features that could be added to new cars which some authorities seem to think would make them not only pay for themselves, but be a source of greater profit to a company than cars now in use. The astonishing record of the Minneapolis gate in cutting down the damage account of the Twin City Rapid Transit Company one-half makes one wish that such a money-saving device could be used in connection with double-deck cars. An expert for one large American street railway company strongly approved a double-deck car design with such a feature, and said the car would save his company $150,000 a year. Such a saving would probably enable that company to scrap its entire rolling stock, to buy new cars with twice the present seating capacity, and, the writer has been assured, to have something still left over in the way of yearly profit. But, while the public are used to gates or doors on all elevated trains, it has been considered doubtful whether they would take kindly to any such feature added to surface cars in such a city as New York, even though it would reduce accidents to themselves enormously and really increase the schedule speed instead of diminishing it. The writer has been trying to devise a modification of the Minneapolis gate, which could be even more quickly and easily operated and satisfy both passengers and company under the severest conditions of city traffic.

But even if such a thing would not be satisfactory, there is still another effective way of cutting down damage accounts, so as to leave income available for interest on indebtedness for new equipment. Liverpool cars not only have a perfect staircase, but they have an even more astonishing feature in the plow life-guard—a device which makes it absolutely impossible for any one to get run over. The record of this fender may seem even more incredible than that of the staircase, but the writer sees no room for doubt after the fullest examination and inquiries on the spot. The guard consists of a wide board entirely surrounding the wheels, plow-shaped under the ends of the cars, fastened to the truck so as to keep at a fixed level above the track. The ends are blunt and covered with rubber; the bottom has a strip of belting close to the track; the collecting of snow in the rear is provided against. As in Berlin, also, the fronts of the Liverpool cars have very sharp corner and projecting feature done away with, so that if any one is struck the chance of injury shall be reduced to a minimum and nothing will hit a person lying on the track till the plow pushes him off. Every child, man and woman who has been under cars equipped with the Liverpool plow life-guard has been pushed off the track practically uninjured. The writer has records of every such accident up to February of this year where persons were actually under cars, and not once was even medical attendance required. Last year a bicyclist got under an old form of life-guard and was killed; this year one was knocked down, but was shoved out of the way by the plow guard, with his wheel, and rode off afterward. This guard can be applied to double trucks as well as single, and its introduction into American cities seems of the utmost importance. As street railway companies maintain the paving between rails there need be no trouble as to unevenness, and as to speed the Liverpool cars seem to have as high a maximum as is common in similar American streets. There is no patent whatever on this guard. The wheels in Berlin are somewhat similarly protected, and the damage account there is amazingly small for one of the largest systems in the world.

One could go on naming other ways in which American damage accounts could be reduced. The universal use of power or emergency brakes in European cities undoubtedly saves many accidents. There seem to be no panics there from blowing out of fuses, circuit-breakers being the rule, and even they are being put on the car roofs in Berlin, so that no flame or sparks can possibly reach or frighten a passenger. Berlin fuses are enclosed in boxes of fireproofed wood, and should one happen to blow out, its flame is carefully directed downward into the street. Dashers and bumpers there are being covered with steel ribs to reduce injury to any one struck, and switch sticks and couplings are kept out of the way of a person falling on the track.

In considering the best type of double-deck cars to meet the conditions in New York, the writer has made many studies and designs. Where overhead structures would allow it might be best to recommend the general type perfected in England, with cross seats on the upper deck, reversed staircase at each end, double entrance, with the roof capable of being tightly enclosed in winter. This type would commend itself to railway managers because of its successful record, its freedom from accidents and other advantages already mentioned. If thought best, present closed and open cars could be remodeled, as was done with the American single-deck cars in Liverpool, by replacing the roof with an upper deck, adding staircase and improving the platforms, perhaps. With liberal allowance of space for each passenger on the upper deck 48 seats could be added to the capacity of a closed car, giving a total of 84 seats instead of 36. If passengers were seated as closely as in England, a total of 104 seats or even 110 would be possible. If such a car had the English heights inside of 6 feet 6 inches from floor to ceiling of the lower deck and 6 feet 1⅛ inches under the roof of the upper deck, it would be 15 feet 9 inches high from rail to roof. Types of the knife-board seat car could be made about two feet lower from rail to roof with the same headroom inside, and, as already shown, could be run wherever single-deck cars are now, still allowing more headroom than found in Europe.

SUMMARY OF FACTS IN REGARD TO DOUBLE-DECK CARS.

TO summarize some facts in regard to double-deck cars:

1. *Extent to which used.* Of the 6,660 electric cars in Great Britain and Ireland, 90 per cent. are double deck and 10 per cent. single deck. Of the 3,517 cars in cities having 100 or more in use, 94 per cent. are double deck and 6 per cent. single deck. Of the 450 electric cars in Manchester, 425 are double deck or 94 per cent.; of the 611 electric cars in Glasgow, 590 are double deck or 97 per cent.; of the 480 electric cars in Liverpool, 468 or 98 per cent. are double deck; of the 400 electric cars in use in and about London, all are double deck. Double-deck cars are also much used in Paris, also in Lyons, some in Italy, on steam railroads in and about Paris and in Denmark, and in Egypt, Australia, Tasmania, New Zealand, South Africa, Buenos Ayres and the City of Mexico. They have been tried at different times in many places in the United States.

2. *Experience of Liverpool.* The general manager of the Liverpool Corporation Tramways states that, "When electric traction was introduced in Liverpool (in 1898), it was thought desirable to follow the Continental and American practice of adopting single-deck cars. The two main arguments in their favor were (first) that the speed would render outside traveling dangerous, and (second) that too much time would be occupied in ascending or descending the staircase. The first objection can only apply to one-half the year, and the second was entirely met by adopting a staircase which enables conductors to refuse to stop the car excepting to the order of a person actually on the lower deck, as the staircase can be safely used whilst the car is traveling at any speed." Double-deck cars are now the standard in Liverpool. They seat more passengers than the first single-deck cars, while they are shorter, lighter in weight and take less power. The upper decks are now being enclosed with a top cover, making them somewhat similar to American open cars, and furnishing protection against rainy and wintry weather. No accidents have ever occurred on the Liverpool reversed staircase,

which has been largely adopted throughout England, overcoming the chief objection made against double-deck cars, both abroad and in the United States, viz., that they must be slower than single-deck cars, and hence cost more to operate, because must make longer stops in order to allow passengers to safely ascend or descend the staircase.

3. *Enclosed upper decks.* Enclosed upper decks are being tried in various places in England, besides Liverpool, such as Sheffield, Huddersfield, Halifax, Darwen and Bradford. They have been used on steam tramcars in England and Germany, are found on steam railroad cars in France and Denmark, and on recent electric cars in Paris.

4. *Heights of double-deck cars.* Following are some heights of low cars in Europe. The steam cars of the Ouest Railway of France, model of 1879, used largely for suburban service, are 13 feet 11 inches from rail to roof. The enclosed roof, single truck, electric cars of the Nogentais Railway are 14 feet 5¼ inches high. A six-foot man standing on the open upper decks of the Berlin trail cars would come about 14 feet 9 inches above the rail; and on the Cardiff Corporation cars 15 feet. The standard Liverpool top-covered car is 16 feet 5 inches over the trolley base. While single-deck cars are used on some English tramways on account of low headroom under bridges, as in Birkenhead, in other places streets have been lowered, as in Cardiff, or overhead bridges raised to gain necessary headroom.

5. *Headroom inside cars.* The standard headroom inside the lower decks of the latest Liverpool cars is 6 feet 6 inches. Inside the top-covered upper decks it is 6 feet 2 inches. Heights under French roofs are much lower, the headroom in the aisles of the enclosed upper decks of a Nogentais Railway car measuring 5 feet 4¾ inches, heights in aisles of some of the Paris cars being 5 feet 2¼ inches, 5 feet 1 inch, and 5 feet, the lowest headroom probably being that of the 1879 models of the Ouest Railway cars, where the height under the center of the roof is 4 feet 3⅞ inches and under the entrance opening 3 feet 9¼ inches.

6. *Air space and ventilation.* The total air space inside the two decks of a Liverpool top-covered car is about 6 per cent. greater than that inside a standard double-truck closed New

York car. The Liverpool car has numerous methods for adequate ventilation without draughts.

7. *Allotment of space for seats and aisles.* In England the space allowed per passenger on inside seats is 16.7 inches with the common single-truck car. It is often as little as 16 inches, rarely 18; 17 inches is called the usual allowance. Upper-deck cross seats for two passengers are usually 32 inches long and spaced from 23 to 30 inches apart, with centre aisles as narrow as 12¼ inches. The minimum allowances mentioned are found on the Liverpool top-covered cars, which seat 64 passengers with a length over collision fenders of 28 feet, as compared with the single-deck cars 34 feet 3 inches long over fenders with only 40 seats. Some of the latter have had upper decks added, providing 60 more seats, or 100 in all, with a length of 41 feet over fenders.

8. *Conductors.* One conductor handles double-deck cars in England seating up to 70 or 80 passengers. On certain cars licensed to carry 124 passengers, with two center and two end entrances, each double, two conductors are carried. Certain Paris cars, allowed to carry 78 passengers, also have two conductors.

9. *Accidents.* No government statistics are available as to accidents on English tramways. Of the 1,004 accidents officially reported in 1902 for two of the largest Paris companies using double-deck cars and omnibuses, 14 or 1.4 per cent. occurred to passengers falling from the upper deck in going up or down.

10. *Length of stops.* From timing stops of double-deck cars in Liverpool, the average time consumed per passenger getting on and off worked out at 1.9 seconds. In a large American city, where cars are operated quite similarly to Liverpool, the length of stop per passenger averaged 2.8 seconds with an open twelve-bench car. English double-deck cars generally have a double entrance at each end on one side. On the Continent, a single entrance is common, often only at one end of a car.

JOHN P. FOX.

June 27, 1903.

ADDENDUM C.

AS TO STREET OBSTRUCTIONS.

LETTER OF MR. GEORGE H. GILMAN TO THE LEGAL COMMITTEE OF THE MERCHANTS' ASSOCIATION OF NEW YORK.

(COPY.)

LAW OFFICE OF GEORGE H. GILMAN,
67 Wall Street,
NEW YORK, Jan. 15, 1903.

THERON G. STRONG, ESQ.,
Chairman, Legal Committee,
49 Wall street, New York.

Dear Sir:

I RETURN you herewith the letter of Dr. George A. Soper, dated January 12, 1903. There are six questions which he asks. From such investigations as I have been able to make, my answers are as follows:

1. A street car has a right of way over its tracks in respect to vehicles passing either way within the space embraced between its tracks, but not on points where these car tracks cross over streets. Here the rights are the same as those of other vehicles. *Buhrens v. Dry Dock Company,* 53 *Hun.,* 571; *affirmed* 125 *N. Y.* 702.

2. Section 402 of the City Ordinances provides that carts may not be placed crosswise in the streets, except for loading and unloading, and for not more than five minutes.

> "It shall be lawful for the owner or occupant of any store, warehouse or building in any street or avenue in which the rails of any railroad company are set so close to the curbstone as to prevent the owners or occupants from keeping any such

cart or other vehicle in the carriageway in front of his place of business that interferes with the passing cars of any such railroad company, to occupy with the cart or other vehicle so much of the sidewalk as is necessary for such cart or vehicle. . . . In no case shall it be lawful to place such cart, wagon or other vehicle crosswise of the carriageway on Broadway below 34th street, nor shall any cart, wagon or vehicle be allowed to remain in front of any premises on the said part of Broadway, unless placed in close proximity to the curbstone with the side parallel thereto, and only remain during the process of loading and unloading."

Since the city has authority to make the above ordinance, it might also adopt similar ordinances relative to carriages on other thoroughfares than Broadway.

3. Subdivision 6 of Section 222 of the City Ordinances provides:

"In placing building materials in the street, the said materials shall be so placed as to occupy not more than one-third of the width of the carriageway of the street or avenue. On any street or avenue where railroads occur, such materials shall not be placed nearer the track than two feet."

Comparing this section with 402 above referred to, it is evident that the ordinances intend that street car traffic shall not be interfered with by trucks, loading or unloading, at all.

Not only are the trucks forbidden to deposit anything within two feet of the car track, but if the rails are so close to the sidewalk as to interfere with the truck, it is given the extraordinary right of standing on the sidewalk.

4. In addition to the usual rule of the road which directs that the carriages shall pass each other by turning to the right, and that an overtaking vehicle pass to the left of the other, section 371 of the Corporation Ordinances prescribes that all carts, trucks or carriages driven on Broadway below 34th street, must be driven on the west side of the carriageway when going in a southerly direction, and on the east side of said carriageway when going in a northerly direction, and that a space of ten feet shall be maintained between vehicles following each other at the intersection of streets.

Since there is a corporation ordinance affecting the lower part of Broadway, there is no reason why a similar ordinance could not be passed affecting other parts of the city.

5. The only legal provision already existing, of which I am aware, are those under section 371, which further provides that in crossing streets the vehicles should go one abreast.

6. There is a provision in regard to trucks and heavy vehicles being driven on Fifth avenue, the legality of which I have never seen questioned. I think it would be a constitutional ordinance if certain streets were specifically designated for loaded vehicles, but I am unable to formulate any plan as to the extent to which this should be done.

Yours respectfully,

GEORGE H. GILMAN.

ADDENDUM D.

REPORT OF MR. EMMETT R. OLCOTT

FOR THE LEGAL COMMITTEE OF THE MERCHANTS' ASSOCIATION OF NEW YORK AS TO THE LAWS GOVERNING USE OF STREETS.

(COPY)

THE Committee on Engineering and Sanitation have propounded the interrogatories hereinafter set forth to the Legal Committee of The Merchants' Association for answer:

1st. What are the respective rights of pedestrians and of vehicles upon the roadway, as distinguished from the sidewalk; discriminating, if necessary, between the rights of the pedestrian upon crosswalks, and upon other parts of the roadway?

2d. What, if any, are the limitations upon the use of the roadway by vehicles? For example: Can vehicles stop and stand for an indefinite time upon the roadway for any purpose, and particularly for loading and unloading merchandise, etc.?

3d. How far may city ordinances assume to regulate or limit travel upon, or the use of city streets, without encroaching upon the constitutional or Common Law rights of persons entitled to use the streets?

ANSWERS.

1st. The answer to the first question is succinctly given in the following language used by the Court of Appeals of this State:

"Neither footmen nor teams have any right of way superior to the other. They each have the right in common, and equally with the other."

Barker vs. Savage, 45 *N. Y.* 196,
54 *N. Y.* 245.

"A person on foot has a right to cross the street where he pleases."

***Moebus** vs. Herrman,* 108, *N. Y.* 349.

2d. To the second interrogatory:

The law as to the use of streets is tersely stated by the language of the Court of Appeals in the case of *Callahan vs. Gilman,* 107 *N. Y.* 365:

The primary purpose of streets is use by the public for travel and transportation, and the rule is that any obstruction of a street or encroachment thereon which interferes with such use is a nuisance. All interruption must be reasonable with reference to the rights of the public, which may not be sacrificed or disregarded."

The rule appears to be that all interruptions to traffic must be reasonable. It is a matter for the Courts to decide as to what is reasonable. The obstruction of a street by the carts of a private individual in business has been adjudged a nuisance, against the plea that the business could not be as advantageously carried on elsewhere.

Rex vs. Cross, 3 *Camp.* 224.
Matthews vs. Kelsey, 58 *Me.* 56.

In addition to the general rule as laid down in the decisions cited, there is a special ordinance as to the matter, among the General Ordinances of the City of New York under the Greater New York Charter, that is set forth in Chapter 1, Sec. 402 and reads as follows:

> "It shall not be lawful for any public cartman, or for any person driving or having charge of any public cart, or any other cart, wagon, or other vehicle, to drive or back any such public cart or any other vehicle onto the sidewalk of any of the streets of said city, or to stop any such cart or any other vehicle on any of the crosswalks or intersections of streets so as to obstruct or hinder the travel along such crosswalks or intersections of streets, or to place any such carts or any other vehicles crosswise of any streets of said city, except to load thereon or unload therefrom; but in no case shall it be lawful for any person to permit such cart or other vehicle to remain so crosswise of any street for a longer period than may be actually necessary for such purpose and not to exceed five minutes; but it shall be lawful for the owner or occupant of any store, warehouse, or building in any street or avenue in which the rails of any railroad company are laid so close to the curbstone as to prevent the owner or occupant from keeping such carts or other vehicles in the carriageway in front of his place of business without interference with the passing cars of any such railroad company, to occupy with such cart or other vehicle during business hours so much of sidewalk as may be necessary for such cart or other vehicle; provided that sufficient space be retained for the passage of pedestrians between the cart or other vehicle so permitted to occupy such part of the sidewalk and the stoop or front of every such store, warehouse or other building. In no case shall it be lawful to place any such carts, wagons or other vehicles crosswise of the carriageway on Broadway below 34th street, nor shall any such cart, wagon or other vehicle be permitted to remain in front of any premises on said part of Broadway unless placed in close proximity to the curbstone, with the side of such cart, wagon or other vehicle parallel therewith; but carts, wagons and trucks shall only be allowed to remain during the process of loading and unloading the same."

3d. To the third interrogatory:

The Legislature of the State represents the public at large, and has, in the absence of special and constitutional restraint and subject to the property rights and easements of the abutting owner, full and paramount authority over all public ways and public places. (*Dillon on Municipal Corporations, Fourth Edition, Chap.* 18, *Sec.* 656.) This authority is delegated to the Legislature to the municipal corporation.

The powers of the municipal authorities of Greater New York, under its charter from the Legislature, and the duties of such as are to enforce the same will be found in the excerpts now quoted:

The Board of Aldermen has power "to regulate the use of the streets and sidewalks by foot passengers, animals or vehicles; to regulate the speed at which horses shall be driven or ridden, or at which vehicles shall be propelled in the streets."

The Greater New York charter, Chap. 1, *Sec.* 50.

To prevent encroachments upon and obstructions to the streets and to authorize and require their removal by the proper officers. *Id.*

To make all such regulations in reference to the running of stages, omnibuses, trucks and cars as may be necessary for the convenient use of the streets, piers, wharves and stations. *Id.*

The word vehicle or the plural thereof shall be deemed to include wagons, trucks, carts, cabs, carriages, stages, omnibuses, motors, automobiles, locomobiles, locomotives, bicycles, tricycles, sleighs or other conveyances for persons or property. *Id.*

The Board of Aldermen has likewise power to provide for the licensing and otherwise regulating the business of dirt-carts, public cartmen, truckmen, hackmen, cabmen, expressmen, cab drivers and boatmen. *Id., Sec.* 51.

It is the duty of the Police Department and force * * * "to regulate the movement of teams and vehicles in streets, bridges, squares, parks and public places; * * * to enforce and prevent the violation of all laws and ordinances in force." *Id., Chap. VIII, Sec.* 315, *Police Department.*

The care, supervision and control of the streets, squares and commons within its limits is vested in the city.

The power to make ordinances respecting the streets, wagons, cars, drays, etc., as shall be necessary for the security, welfare and convenience of the city has been passed upon by the Court of Appeals.

The broad proposition is well established that all municipal corporations have the right to make ordinances to regulate and limit travel upon, and use of, the city streets, without encroaching on the constitutional or Common Law rights of persons entitled to use the streets, the only limitation being that the ordinance must be reasonable.

The test of reasonableness would seem to be largely in favor of the restriction of travel according to the uses and purposes of the street, as, for instance, certain vehicles are not allowed on the Speedway or upon Riverside Drive.

All of which is respectfully submitted.

FOR THE LEGAL COMMITTEE,

(Signed) EMMET R. OLCOTT.

Dated, New York, March 16, 1903.

ADDENDUM E.

RULES FOR THE REGULATION OF VEHICULAR AND SURFACE CAR TRAVEL UPON THE STREETS OF NEW YORK AND TO PREVENT OBSTRUCTIONS TO SUCH TRAVEL.

PROPOSED BY THE COMMITTEE ON ENGINEERING AND SANITATION OF THE MERCHANTS' ASSOCIATION OF NEW YORK.

1. The word vehicle as used herein shall include everything on wheels or runners, except street cars and baby carriages. Horses or other animals led or driven through the streets must, so far as possible, conform to the rules prescribed for vehicles.

2. Vehicles shall keep to the right and as near to the right-hand curb as possible. Vehicles meeting shall pass each other to the right. Vehicles overtaking others shall, in passing them, keep to the left. A vehicle turning to the right into another street shall keep to the curb in making the turn. A vehicle turning to the left into another street shall pass to the right of the center of the street intersection and thence to the right-hand curb of the street turned into. No vehicle shall stop with its left side to the curb at which the stop is made. If necessary to cross a street in order to stop at a point on the opposite or left-hand curb, a vehicle shall continue beyond such point to a sufficient distance, shall cross the street as nearly as possible at right angles and return to the desired point in the same direction as the travel on that side of the street.

Vehicles shall not be driven or propelled at a speed exceeding eight miles per hour, and they must be restricted to lower speeds wherever necessary to prevent accident or injury to persons or property.

Vehicles must approach all street crossings with speed under such control that accidents may be avoided. No turn shall be made in a street at a speed exceeding four miles per hour.

3. No vehicle shall stand on any street between the hours of 8 A. M. and 7 P. M. upon which electric cars are operated at regular intervals of three minutes or less each way, except while actually engaged in taking on or discharging passengers or while actually engaged in loading or unloading merchandise, unless the street at the point of stopping is of such width as to leave a clear space of at least ten feet between the standing vehicle and the nearest rail of a car track.

4. For taking on or letting off passengers and for loading and unloading merchandise between the hours of 7 A. M. and 8 P. M. upon streets having car tracks, over which cars are regularly operated at intervals of three minutes or less in each direction, the following periods of time, and no more, during which vehicles may stand on such streets shall be allowed, viz.:

For loading and unloading passengers.. 2 minutes

For loading and unloading merchandise,
such time only as may be necessary
not to exceed...................... 5 minutes

No vehicle shall stop to load or unload merchandise or freight on any such street in front of any business house or residence which has a side or rear entrance on another street upon which electrical cars are not operated, without a permit from the Police Department to do so.

5. When stopping for any purpose on any street between the hours of 8 A. M. to 7 P. M. vehicles shall stand parallel

with and as near to the right-hand curb as possible, with the front of the vehicle in the direction of the movement of travel on that side of the street, provided that vehicles may stand against and at right angles to the curb, where at least ten feet will thereby be left clear between such standing vehicle and the nearest car tracks, or, where there be no car tracks, two vehicles may meet or pass abreast on the unobstructed part of the street.

No vehicle shall stand upon any street for any purpose in such a position as to obstruct the car tracks and prevent the free operation of cars thereon.

The words "stop" and "stand" as used herein shall not apply to stops caused by accident, or by unavoidable unobstruction or by other causes over which the owner or driver of the vehicle has no control.

Upon streets having more than one railroad track no vehicle shall be driven upon any track regularly used for cars going in an opposite parallel direction, except for the purpose of crossing such track.

6. Except when forced to do so by standing vehicles or by other obstructions, no vehicle shall travel upon or so near to any car track as to obstruct cars moving in the same direction. And vehicles shall leave the track at the first opportunity, so that cars may pass them. The intent of this article is that no vehicle shall obstruct the regular movement of any car moving in the same direction as the vehicle, except where it is absolutely necessary to do so in order that the vehicle may proceed along the street.

7. The officers and men of the Fire Department and Fire Patrol, with their fire apparatus of all kinds, when going to, on duty at, or returning from, a fire, and all ambulances and the officers and men and vehicles of the Police Department and all physicians having permits from the Police Department shall have the right of way in any street and through any procession except over vehicles carrying the United States mail.

8. At street crossings cars or vehicles moving north or south shall have the right of way over all others, except as above mentioned, whenever the front end of the north or south bound car or vehicle shall reach the house line at the same time or before any part of an east or west bound car or vehicle, or the horses of the latter, shall reach the house line, unless otherwise directed by a police officer.

ADDENDUM F.

LIST OF UNUSED SURFACE TRACKS IN MANHATTAN.

BLEECKER STREET AND FULTON FERRY RAILROAD COMPANY.

	Miles.
On Beekman street, from Park Row to South street, single track	
On William street, from Fulton street to Ann street, single track	.624
On Ann street, from Fulton street to Park Row, single track	
On Bleecker street, from Wooster street to Crosby street, double track	
On Crosby street, from Bleecker street to Howard street, double track	
On Howard street, from Crosby street to Elm street, double track	1.648
On Elm street, from Howard street to Canal street, double track	
On Canal street, from Mulberry street to Elm street, single track	.139
On Pearl street, from Park Row to New Bowery, single track	.170
On Eleventh avenue, from 23d street to 14th street,, double track	.766
	3.347

SIXTH AVENUE RAILROAD COMPANY.

	Miles.
On Lenox avenue, from 110th street to 116th street, double track	.570

On Vesey street, from Broadway to Church street, double track	
On Vesey street, from Church street to West Broadway, single track	.259
On Varick street, from Watt street to Canal street, double track	.155
On Church street, from Barclay street to Chambers street, single track	.174
	1.158

BROADWAY AND SEVENTH AVENUE RAILROAD COMPANY.

	Miles.
On Thompson street, from Canal street to Fourth street, single track	.673
On Sullivan street, from Grand street to West Third street, single track	.567
On Wooster street, from Bleecker street to University place, single track	.102
On University place, from Eighth street to Fourteenth street, double track	.327
On Greene street, from Bleecker street to Eighth street, single track	.593
On Barclay street, from Broadway to Church street, double track	.327
On Barclay street, from Church street to West Broadway, single track	
On Park place, from Broadway to Church street, double track	.251
On Park place, from Church street to West Broadway, single track	
On Broome street, from Broadway to West Broadway, double track	.372
On Church street, from Chambers street to Walker street, single track	.360
On McDougal street, from Eighth street to Fourth street, double track	.312
On Fourth street, from McDougal street to Thompson street, single track	.095
	3.979

METROPOLITAN CROSSTOWN RAILROAD COMPANY.

	Miles.
On Fourth street, from West Broadway to Thompson street, single track	.043
On West Broadway, from Third street to Fourth street, single track	.052
On Waverly place, from McDougal street to Bank street, single track	
On Bank street, from Waverly place to Greenwich avenue, single track	
On Greenwich avenue, from Waverly place to Thirteenth street, double track	
On Thirteenth street, from Greenwich avenue to Thirteenth avenue, double track (including short piece of single track on south side of Jackson square)	
On Thirteenth avenue, from Thirteenth street to Fourteenth street, double track	2.190
	2.285

DRY DOCK, EAST BROADWAY AND BATTERY RAILROAD COMPANY.

	Miles.
On Lispenard street, from Broadway to Church street, single track	.050
On Vestry street, from West street to Greenwich street, double track	.094
	.144

CENTRAL PARK, NORTH AND EAST RIVER RAILROAD COMPANY.

	Miles.
On Grand street, from Mangin street to Monroe street, single track	.061

NEW YORK AND HARLEM RAILROAD COMPANY.

	Miles.
On 33d street, from Lexington avenue to Fourth avenue, single track	
On 32d street, from Lexington avenue to Fourth avenue, single track	.291

28TH AND 29TH STREET CROSSTOWN RAILROAD COMPANY.

	Miles.
On 33d street, from First avenue to East River, double track	.083
On Eleventh avenue, from 34th street to 42d street, double track	.795
	.878

HOUSTON, WEST STREET AND PAVONIA FERRY RAILROAD COMPANY.

	Miles.
On Pitt street, from Houston street to Madison street, single track	1.097
On Ridge street, from Madison street to Houston street, single track	
On 35th street, from First avenue to Lexington avenue, single track	.373
On 36th street, from First avenue to Lexington avenue, single track	.373
	1.843

SECOND AVENUE RAILROAD COMPANY.

	Miles.
On First avenue, from Fourteenth street to Allen street, single track	.670
On Oliver street, from South street to Chatham square, single track	.316
On Peck slip, from Water street to South street, single track	
On New Bowery, from Chatham square to Pearl street (one track not in use).	
On Worth street, from New Bowery to Broadway, single track	.702
On 96th street, from First avenue to Second avenue, double track	.284
On Allen street, from First avenue to Grand street, single track	.400
	2.372

42*D STREET, MANHATTANVILLE AND ST. NICHOLAS AVENUE RAILROAD COMPANY.*

	Miles.
On 109th street, from First avenue to Pleasant avenue, single track	.135
On Pleasant avenue, from 109th street to 110th street, single track	.050
On Amsterdam avenue, from 72d street to Manhattan street, double track	2.740
On Twelfth avenue, from 34th street to 35th street, double track	.106
	3.031

METROPOLITAN STREET RAILWAY COMPANY.

	Miles.
On 130th street, from Broadway to Twelfth avenue, double track	.181
On Broadway, from Manhattan street to 130th street, double track	.100
	.281

ADDENDUM G.

URBAN RAILWAY TRANSPORTATION IN NEW YORK CITY.

Passengers carried on the Elevated and Surface Lines in all the Boroughs during periods stated. Compiled for the Committee on Engineering and Sanitation of the Merchants' Association of New York, from statistics given in the "Report of the Board of Railroad Commissioners of the State of New York, in the Matter of the Transportation Problem in Greater New York," dated June 30, 1903.

	Passengers Carried in Feb., Mar., April and May (Not Including Transfers).			Per Cent. of Increase.	Transfers in Feb., Mar., April and May.			Per Cent of Increase.
	1902	1903	Increase.		1902	1903	Increase.	
Interborough, Manhattan Division	78,611,734	88,666,725	10,054 991	12.75	Not stated.	Not stated.	....	....
Interurban, Metropolitan Street Railway	126,767,510	131,085 617	4 318,107	3.41	46,321 834	51,788,180	5,466,346	11.80
Total, Borough of Manhattan	205,379,244	219 752,342	14,373,098	7.00	46,321,834	51,788,180	5,466,346	11.80
Brooklyn Heights, all lines B. R. T.	82 069,869	89 396,634	7,326,765	8.93	15,703,648	17,137,914	1,434,266	9.13
Coney Island and Brooklyn	9 059,996	9,985,780	925,784	10.20	2,001,218	2,024,105	22,887	1.14
Total, Borough of Brooklyn	91,129,865	99,382,414	8,252,549	9.05	17,704,866	19,162,019	1,457,153	8.23
New York and North Shore	560,628	681,125	120,497	21.49	None.	None.	....	....
New York and Queens County	3,340 428	3 909,018	568,590	17.00	517,176	629,642	112,466	21.75
Total, Borough of Queens	3,901 056	4,590,143	689,087	17.66	517,176	629,642	112,466	21.75
Union Railway, total, Borough of the Bronx	5,858,471	6,649,402	790,931	13.50	5,772,551	6,241,936	469,385	8.00
Staten Island, Midland	593,051	758,411	165 360	27.88	88,745	91,556	2,811	3.17
Richmond Light and Railroad Co.	1,112,112	1,257,574	165,360	10.90	115,967	110 445	*Dec.* 5,522	....
Total, Borough of Richmond	1,735,163	2,015,895	280,822	16.19	204,712	202,001	*Dec.* 2,711	....
Grand total, city of New York (not including transfers), for four months	308,003,799	332,390,286	24 386 487	7.91	70,521,139	78 023,778	7,502,639	10.62
Grand total, city of New York, passengers (including transfers), for four months	378,524,838	410,414,064	31,889,126	8.42	....	....	....	....

Daily average number of passengers (not including transfers) .... **2,770,000.**
Total number per year, estimated on above basis of four months .... **997,170,858.**

www.ingramcontent.com/pod-product-compliance
Lightning Source LLC
LaVergne TN
LVHW050519100826
845148LV00002B/385
* 9 7 8 1 4 2 5 5 2 1 4 6 2 *